CAMBRIDGE URBAN AND ARCHITECTURAL STUDIES

GENERAL EDITORS

LESLIE MARTIN
Emeritus Professor of Architecture, University of Cambridge

LIONEL MARCH
Professor, Department of Systems Design, University of Waterloo, Ontario, and University Lecturer, Department of Architecture, University of Cambridge

ASSISTANT EDITOR: STEPHEN ZOLL

VOLUMES IN THIS SERIES

1. *Urban Space and Structures*, edited by Leslie Martin and Lionel March

2. *Energy, Environment and Building*, by Philip Steadman (forthcoming)

3. *Urban Modelling*, by Michael Batty (forthcoming)

4. *The Architecture of Form*, edited by Lionel March (forthcoming)

Urban space and structures

EDITED BY
LESLIE MARTIN
AND
LIONEL MARCH

CAMBRIDGE UNIVERSITY PRESS

Published by the Syndics of the Cambridge University Press
Bentley House, 200 Euston Road, London NW1 2DB
American Branch: 32 East 57th Street, New York, N.Y.10022

© Cambridge University Press 1972

Library of Congress Catalogue Card Number: 79-176254

ISBNs:
0 521 08414 8 hard covers
0 521 09934 X paperback

First published 1972
First paperback edition 1975

Printed in Great Britain by
Alden & Mowbray Ltd
at the Alden Press, Oxford

Foreword

More and more the environment of our world is manmade; in its own right it deserves serious study. The Syndics of the Cambridge University Press have agreed to publish a series of books or monographs under the general title *Cambridge Urban and Architectural Studies*. The books are, in the main, to be written from an architectural point of view. But since their range extends outside the usual boundaries of the world of architecture – to the measurement of that environment and its history and to the methods that a greater self-consciousness can bring to the process by which the environment is created – we have chosen to call them urban and architectural studies.

The papers collected and presented in this first volume were written by their various authors from the Cambridge School of Architecture and its Centre for Land Use and Built Form Studies over the last four years. Many of the ideas and much of the research work they contain have since been extended and developed.

However, taken together, the early papers are especially well suited to describe and illustrate the growth of a particular attitude of thought that has been building up around architectural studies in Cambridge in the last few years. And in relation to each other, these studies tend to remove the distinctions between architecture and planning, between design of individual buildings and the collective choice of the shape of the environment.

Since they are early and sometimes tentative expositions, they are in a true sense explorations. In this volume, we have tried to relate the developing threads of thought by means of an introduction to each section and an afterword. Held together in this way, the collection seems to present the best kind of introduction that we can make to the more detailed and extended studies that have emerged and are being developed at a research level and which form the substance of the later volumes in the series.

LESLIE MARTIN

LIONEL MARCH

1972

Acknowledgments

The editors wish to acknowledge their gratitude for the generosity of several previous publishers of material in this volume, both for their cooperation and for their interest in the work in its earliest stages of development. Footnotes to each chapter heading record prior publication. However, especial thanks ought to be extended to the University of Hull for the republication of 'The Grid as Generator' and to the Royal Institute of British Architects for extracts from two lectures by Leslie Martin published in the *R.I.B.A. Journal* which have been used in Chapter 2. For the diagrams on pp. 34 and 39, permission for reproduction was granted by the Controller of Her Majesty's Stationery Office. In Chapter 4, the two diagrams from Christopher Alexander's book, *Notes Towards a Synthesis of Form*, are reproduced with the permission of Harvard University Press. *Universities Quarterly* originally published 'A Theoretical Basis for University Planning' which is reprinted here with their permission. Chapter 6 consists of an amalgamation of two previously printed articles, 'Activities, Space and Location' which was originally in the *Architectural Review*, and 'The Modelling of Day to Day Activity Patterns' in *Architectural Design*. 'Models: A Discussion' was first published as Working Paper Number 6 of the Land Use and Built Form Studies, and later reprinted in *Architectural Research and Teaching*; it is published here as Chapter 7. Both Chapters 8 and 9 started off as Land Use and Built Form Studies (L.U.B.F.S.) Working Papers: numbers 26 and 25, respectively.

Much of the research work represented in this volume was supported at the Centre for Land Use and Built Form Studies by grants from a number of sources: the Centre for Environmental Studies, the Calouste Gulbenkian Foundation, the Department of Education and Science, the University Grants Committee and Wates Limited.

Lastly the editors wish to thank Miss Anne Boyd of the Cambridge University Press for her patience and capability in dealing with the organisation of an unruly manuscript.

Contents

Foreword   *page* v

Acknowledgments   vi

PART 1: EXPLORATIONS

Introduction   1

1 The grid as generator: *Leslie Martin*   6

2 Speculations: *Leslie Martin, Lionel March and others*   28

3 Elementary models of built forms: *Lionel March*   55

4 The use of models in planning and the architectural design
   process: *Nicholas Bullock, Peter Dickens and Philip
   Steadman*   97

PART 2: ACTIVITIES, SPACE AND LOCATION

Introduction   109

5 A theoretical model for university planning:
   Nicholas Bullock, Peter Dickens and Philip Steadman   113

6 The modelling of day to day activities:
   Nicholas Bullock, Peter Dickens and Philip Steadman   129

PART 3: URBAN SYSTEMS

Introduction   159

7 Models: A discussion: *Marcial Echenique*   164

8 Development of a model of urban spatial structure:
   David Crowther and Marcial Echenique   175

9 A structural comparison of three generations of New Towns:
   Marcial Echenique, David Crowther and Walton Lindsay   219

Afterword   260

Bibliography   265

PART 1
EXPLORATIONS

Introduction

In 1963 some preliminary studies of science buildings were made in Cambridge. The limitations of certain predetermined building forms like the slab or the tower were recognised and an attempt was made to investigate the potentialities of other geometries, for instance various types of spreading forms within which individual faculties could more easily intercommunicate and changes of size could be more readily accommodated (Martin and March 1964). It eventually appeared from these studies that the form of a building had a considerable effect on the efficiency of land use. One form of building with precisely the same light angles, with the same number of floors and on exactly the same area of land, could provide 50% more floor space than another.

Further and more detailed studies of land use in central urban areas again raised a question. How was it that one form of building with a floor area to ground space ratio of 3:1 could be accommodated in 8-storey buildings, whereas elsewhere, in some situations, the same plot ratio apparently required tall towers? As the geometrical and mathematical explanation became clearer an opportunity arose to test the principles at the scale of an environmental area. The existing chequerboard of buildings and streets is one pattern. But if the geometry of the pattern is changed then precisely the same amount of floor space can be accommodated in the same general height of building but with a considerable increase in open space. It seemed that in most towns which appear to be overcrowded all the land that is needed is there if the right principles are used to find it. It was from such primitive observations, which have been summarised elsewhere (Martin 1967), that the study of the use of land by buildings gradually grew in Cambridge from 1963 and has been rapidly and extensively developed during the last three years since the Centre for Land Use and Built Form Studies has been established as the research centre of the School of Architecture.

The bulk of the work presented in the following section dates from 1967. In relation to the work that has been done since, these papers can now be recognised as preliminary formulations of certain attitudes towards architecture and planning. The first paper is an effort to stress that there are in any urban situation certain simple interrelations of street pattern, plot size and building form and the patterns of living which elaborate these: that there is in fact a framework which itself offers choice and within which a plurality of choices can operate.

It would now be possible to define more precisely what it is that operates and what factors are at work within this framework. It would be possible to say far more about the pressures that build up nodal points within a development and about the restrictive effect of regulations on the building form (Hawkes 1968), and any such argument to be more complete would need the evidence of the urban sociologists and the geographers. (Robson 1969. See Chapter 1 for a summary.)

But this paper by its insistence on the relatedness of things; by its emphasis of the effect of the initial framework of a city on the future elaboration and development of this by patterns of living; by the stress that it lays on neutral measurement and finally by its suggestion of the possibility of mathematical analysis and comparative assessments of various built forms, begins to outline, at least, one way of looking at the physical structure of a city.

It is, in a sense, a kind of conceptual model expressed in words, which is perhaps a counterpart, however inadequate, to those mathematical models which are now regarded as the most effective way of describing the mass of relationships that exist in the urban system. And in a sense too, it links back to one of the more neglected aspects of Unwin's work: for instance his use of comparative measurement in 'Nothing to be Gained by Over-crowding' (1912) or his geometrical application of the Fresnel diagram in his illustration of town expansion (Unwin 1912, p. 122). But the firmest link is earlier than this, with such pioneers of the study of urbanisation as Ildefonso de Cerda, to whom plot size, building form and movement were fundamental and by whom the city and the country were regarded as aspects of the self-same problem (de Cerda 1867).

Although the argument is not developed with any finality, the attitude implicit in this essay and in this volume is that planning is not concerned with visual images. Neither should it be an attempt to predict future uses or to outline desirable goals. The object indicated here is the more modest one of attempting to understand the relationships that exist in the physical structure of the city. Once this is done it may be possible to indicate a wider range of choice and a greater opportunity for a variety of patterns of living to develop. The objective is the discovery of those neutral guide lines that set out the least restrictive framework and allow the maximum elaboration by use.

The worked examples that are given are an attempt to support the argument by preliminary formulation of theory. Perhaps the most important aspect of this from the point of view of the general line of thought is the demonstration of the way in which one network of streets and building forms which has congealed, can be released by a larger pattern and by changing the arrangement and geometry of the building form.

The second paper is built up from a series of extracts from work in progress about 1967. The introductory note from a paper by Martin (Martin 1967) sets the general argument. Rational and speculative thought are not opposite modes stemming from opposing attitudes of mind. Nor are they to be associated with particular activities, for example science and art. They are in fact essentially complementary and interrelated forms of thought. Through one we understand the factual nature of a problem more accurately and through the other we extend the range of our thought about it.

Once this is recognised, measurement and geometry become a valuable means of testing existing assumptions. The new evidence that arises from this in turn gives rise to new ideas about application. The examples that are studied in this section were all generated from a consideration of practical problems and from a method of work. Since they are not at this stage supported by any developed theory, they are essentially speculations. They pose a number of questions that need examination: What are the factors that have to be related in considering the efficiency of buildings? What form of building makes the most effective use of land? How reliable are the measures that we are accustomed to use in planning?

Some preliminary attempts are made to raise these issues in measurable or mathematical terms. A step towards theoretical formulation is taken when it is recognised that the question of tall or low buildings is not simply an argument about two alternative building forms. These are in fact points of recognition in a more generalised spectrum in which, as the envelope constantly changes from high to low, and from a tower to its inverse, the hollow square, this in turn gives rise to a series of constantly changing internal relationships and to constantly changing space around the building itself.

How can such a complex problem be studied? The answer is given in the last two essays of this section. These describe some of the tools with which complex and dependently shifting geometries may be analysed: by mathematical modelling and by mechanical computation.

The paper by Lionel March is an introduction to the extension of analytical geometry into the mathematical modelling of architectural subjects. The paper outlines the procedure of modelling in general, and then illustrates this with four examples concerned with the overall form of buildings. Although it describes thermal performance in one of the examples, the intention is not to sharpen the capabilities of heating engineering, but to demonstrate the incisive nature of mathematical argument. Even in these elementary techniques, a difference is revealed between an apparent and a real value connected with the well-intentioned intuitive or wrongly-conceived conventional perception of architectural design. Or, conversely, the demonstration shows that mathematical modelling is extremely supple and precise in making formulations by which earlier speculations are proven and given rational expression.

In more difficult geometries, especially in the representation of the highly complex sets of relationships that can exist within groups of buildings, the last essay adds the capacity of the computer to handle the working of large amounts of simultaneous mathematical computations. The essay comes from the early work of a group of research workers dealing with the study of universities (Bullock, Dickens and Steadman 1968) and is paralleled by the almost contemporary paper by Echenique (1968a) at the outset of his studies of urban systems. Both papers illustrate the need for some better means than are habitually used for describing, first of all, the complexity of the relationships in any urban system or sub-system, and then possibly observing the effect on the whole of any changes in the individual parts.

This last paper suggests for the universities study the formulation of a mathematical model similar to those already used in planning, and Lowry is quoted (1965). In its original publication, the paper hoped that by modelling existing universities a highly complex real world situation could be represented in abstract form.

The purpose of this would be to examine the utilisation of existing capacity, the problems of putting new buildings on the campus and the possibilities of expansion onto adjacent sites. We shall hope to emphasize the importance in making an assessment of future needs, or making proper measurement of the potential capacity of existing facilities: and to show how the organisation of the academic timetable is dependent on the physical layout of the University site – or how different configurations of residential and teaching accommodations may have serious implications on the amount of space requiring to be provided, some involving extensive duplication of facilities.

Such a model formulation carries with it the extensive use of computers, it goes without saying, as these alone can deal with the mass of data that is involved. The essay goes on to develop the argument about the use of mechanical aids in the design cycle, and it formulates an attitude which still remains central to the Cambridge work. It is an attitude which contrasts with the pioneering work of Alexander (1966) by maintaining, first, that a complex physical situation can be described in an abstract way and, second, that automatic aids can never fulfil every aspect of the design cycle but have their proper and indeed highly important place within it. The formulation is clear:

Whilst it is impossible with architectural problems to generate a range of feasible *complete* and *finished* solutions by a similar single and uninterrupted predetermined procedure of a mechanical nature, there is no objection to a stepwise process in which the first hypothesis is evaluated, the terms of the problem revised and the second series modified and tested again.

This preliminary formulation of the use of mechanical aids in the design cycle has since been effectively supported by Tabor (1970a) who, in following through several methods of automatically producing plans, has demonstrated their inadequacy. But he has shown, as have contributors to this volume, the central and powerful place that a mathematical formulation can take when it is used for its proper function of descriptive analysis and evaluation within the total design process.

1. *The grid as generator*[†]

LESLIE MARTIN

1

The activity called city planning, or urban design, or just planning, is being sharply questioned. It is not simply that these questions come from those who are opposed to any kind of planning. Nor is it because so many of the physical effects of planning seem to be piecemeal. For example roads can be proposed without any real consideration of their effect on environment; the answer to such proposals could be that they are just not planning at all. But it is *not* just this type of criticism that is raised. The attack is more fundamental: what is being questioned is the adequacy of the assumptions on which planning doctrine is based.

What are those assumptions? To put this in the most general terms, they resolve themselves into two powerful lines of thought. The first, which stems from the work of the Viennese writer Camillo Sitte, whose book *City Planning according to Artistic Principles* was published in 1889, can be called the doctrine of the visually ordered city. To Sitte the total city plan is the inspired and the all encompassing work of art. But Sitte went further: civic art must be an expression of the life of the community, and finally 'works of art cannot be created by committee but only by a single individual' (Collins 1965).[‡] The planner then is the inspired artist expressing in the total city plan the ambitions of a society. There are indeed many who, though not prepared to accept this total – it would not be inaccurate to say this totalitarian – role of the planner, have nevertheless been profoundly influenced by Sitte's doctrine of the visually ordered city. The doctrine has left its mark on the images that are used to illustrate high density develop-

[†] Some parts of 'The grid as generator' were used in the Gropius Lecture at Harvard University in June 1966. The argument was developed later into the theme delivered at the University of Hull under the title, 'The Framework of Planning', as the inaugural lecture by Leslie Martin as Visiting Ferens Professor of Fine Art. It is presented here in essentially that form.

[‡] See also a review of both Sitte 1889 and Collins 1965 in L. March (1966).

ment of cities. It is to be seen equally in the layout and arrangement of Garden City development. The predominance of the visual image is evident in some proposals that work for the preservation of the past: it is again evident in the work of those that would carry us on, by an imagery of mechanisms, into the future. It remains central in the proposals of others who feel that, although the city as a total work of art is unlikely to be achieved, the changing aspect of its streets and squares may be ordered visually into a succession of pictures. The second line of doctrine is severely practical. It can be called the doctrine of the statistically ordered city. We know it well. It is the basis of those planning surveys in which uses are quantified, sorted out and zoned into particular areas; population densities are assessed and growth and change predicted. It is the raw material of the outline analyses and the town maps of the 1947 Act.

Now it is precisely these two aspects of planning (the first concerned with visual images and the second with procedure, and sometimes of course used in combination by planners), that were so sharply attacked by Mrs Jane Jacobs in her book *The Death and Life of Great American Cities* (1961). For Mrs Jacobs, both 'the art of city planning and its companion, the pseudo-science of city planning, have not yet embarked on the effort to probe the real world of living'. For her a city can never be the total work of art, nor can there ever be the statistically organised city. Indeed, to Mrs Jacobs, the planning of any kind of order seems to be inconsistent with the organic development of cities which she sees as a direct outcome of the activities of living. Planning is a restrictive imposition: the areas of cities 'in which people have lived are a natural growth...as natural as the beds of oysters'. Planning, she says, is essentially artificial.

It is of course just this opposition between 'organic' growth and the artificial nature of plans, between living and the preconceived system within which it might operate, that has been stressed so much in recent criticism. Christopher Alexander in a distinguished essay 'A city is not a tree' puts the point directly when he says:

I want to call those cities that have arisen spontaneously over many many years 'natural cities'. And I shall call those cities or parts of cities that have been deliberately created by planners 'artificial cities'. Siena, Liverpool, Kyoto, Manhattan, are examples of *natural cities*. Levittown, Chandigarh and the British New Towns are examples of *artificial cities*. It is more and more widely recognised today that there is some essential ingredient missing in the artificial cities (Alexander 1966).

Let us consider this. First of all would it be true to say that all old towns are a kind of spontaneous growth and that there have never been 'artificial' or consciously planned towns in history? Leaving on one side ancient history, what about the four hundred extremely well documented cases of new towns (deliberately planted towns) that Professor Beresford

has collected for the Middle Ages in England, Wales and Gascony alone?
(Beresford 1967.) What about the mediaeval towns such as those built in
Gascony between 1250 and 1318 on a systematic gridiron plan? All these
towns were highly artificial in Alexander's sense. The planted town, as
Professor Beresford observes, 'is not a prisoner of an architectural past: it
has no past'. In it the best use of land meant an orderly use, hence the grid
plan. In siting it and building it estimates had to be made about its future,
about its trade, its population, and the size and number of its building
plots. This contributes a highly artificial procedure.

But it is of course by no means uncommon. Indeed it is the method by
which towns have been created in any rapidly developing or colonial
situation. A recent book by John Reps, *The Making of Urban America*
(1965) is a massive compendium of the planting of new towns throughout
America, practically all of them based on highly artificial gridiron plans.
He points out that there is a sense in which not merely cities but the whole
of Western America is developed within an artificial frame: 'the giant
gridiron imposed upon the natural landscape by...the land ordinance of
1785'.

The coloniser knows that the natural wilderness has to be transformed:
areas must be reserved for agriculture as well as plots for building. The
man-made landscape is a single entity: cities and their dependant agricultural areas are not separate elements. All these things are matters of
measure and quantity. They are interrelated between themselves and
numbers of people. The process demands a quality of abstract thought:
a geometry and a relationship of numbers worked out in advance and
irrespective of site. The 20-mile square plan for the proposed colony of
Azilia, the plans of Savannah and Georgetown, are typical examples of
this kind of thought. William Penn's plan for Philadelphia, the plans of
such towns as Louisville, Cincinnati, Cleveland, New York City itself,
Chicago and San Francisco, are all built on the basis of a preconceived
frame.

In the case of the mediaeval towns described by Beresford, whilst some
failed, a high proportion succeeded in their time. In a large number of
American cities, the artificial grid originally laid down remains the working frame within which vigorous modern cities have developed. It is quite
clear then that an artificial frame of some kind does not exclude the
possibility of an organic development. The artificial grid of streets that was
laid down throughout Manhattan in 1811 has not prevented the growth of
those overlapping patterns of human activity which caused Alexander to
describe New York as an organic city. Life and living have filled it out but
the grid is there.

And this brings us closer to the centre of Alexander's main argument

What he is criticising in the extended content of his essay, is the notion that the activities of living can be parcelled out into separate entities and can be fixed for ever by a plan. The assumption is common in much post-war planning. Consider an example. Housing is thought of in terms of density: 75, 100, 150 people per acre. That will occupy an area of land. Housing requires schools and they need open space: that will occupy another specific area. These areas in turn may be thought to justify another need: an area for recreation. That is one kind of thought about planning. But alternatively an effort may be made to see the needs of a community as a whole. It may be discovered that the way housing is arranged on the ground may provide so much free space that the needs of schools or recreation will overlap and may even be contained within it (Martin 1968).

In the first instance the uses are regarded as self-contained entities: Alexander equates this kind of thinking with an organisation like that demonstrated by a mathematical tree. In the second instance the patterns of use overlap: the organisation in this case is much closer to a far more complex mathematical structure: the semi-lattice. The illustration of the separate consideration of housing, schools and open space is elementary. But it is Alexander's argument that whole towns may be planned on this basis. And it is this attempt to deal with highly complex and overlapping patterns of use, of contacts and of communications in a way which prevents this overlap from happening that Alexander deplores. Hence the title of his paper: 'A city is not a tree'. In this sense of course he is correct. But the argument can be put in a different way. It can be argued that the notion (implied by Mrs Jacobs) that elaborate patterns of living can never develop within a preconceived and artificial framework is entirely false. This can be developed by saying that an 'organic' growth, without the structuring element of some kind of framework, is chaos. And finally that it is only through the understanding of that structuring framework that we can open up the range of choices and opportunities for future development.

The argument is this. Many towns of course grew up organically by accretion. Others, and they are numerous and just as flourishing, were established with a preconceived framework as a basis. Both are built up ultimately from a range of fairly simple formal situations: the grid of streets, the plots which this pattern creates and the building arrangements that are placed on these. The whole pattern of social behaviour has been elaborated within a limited number of arrangements of this kind and this is true of the organic as well as the constructed town. Willmott and Young, studying kinship in the East End of London (1957), were able to show that everywhere elaborate patterns of living had been built up. All these elaborations, and a great variety of needs, were met within a general building pattern of terraces and streets. Change that pattern and you may prevent these relationships from developing or you may open up new choices that were not available in the original building form.

The grid of streets and plots from which a city is composed, is like a net placed or thrown upon the ground. This might be called the framework of urbanisation. That framework remains the controlling factor of the way we build whether it is artificial, regular and preconceived, or organic and distorted by historical accident or accretion. And the way we build may either limit or open up new possibilities in the way in which we choose to live.

The understanding of the way the scale and pattern of this framework, net or grid affects the possible building arrangements on the land within it, is fundamental to any reconsideration of the structure of existing towns. It is equally important in relation to any consideration of the developing metropolitan regions outside existing towns. The pattern of the grid of roads in a town or region is a kind of playboard that sets out the rules of the game. The rules outline the kind of game; but the players should have the opportunity to use to the full their individual skills whilst playing it.

2

How does the framework of a city work? In what way does the grid act as a generator and controlling influence on city form? How can it tolerate growth and change?

The answer to these questions is best given by historical examples, and in order to give the argument some point we can deliberately choose the most artificial framework for a city that exists: the grid as it has been used in the United States, and so well illustrated by Reps (1965).

We can start with the notion that to the coloniser the uncultivated wilderness must be tamed into a single urban–rural relationship. In the plan for the proposed Margravate of Azilia (the forerunner of the colony of Georgia) the ground to be controlled is 20 miles square, or 256,000 acres. Implicit in the subdivisions of this general square is a mile square grid; and out of the basic grid the areas for farmland, the great parks for the propagation of cattle and the individual estates are built up. At the centre is the city proper.

The Margravate was never built, but the concept of the single urban–rural unit and the principle of a grid controlled land sub-division within this remains. In the County map of Savannah, Georgia, made in 1735, a grid of (slightly less than) one mile square sub-divides a rectangle nearly 10 miles long and 6 miles deep. Thirty nine of these squares remain wooded areas: within this primary sub-division, further sub-divisions create farms of 44 acres and 5-acre garden plots. These are the related grid systems of the city region. On the river front within this main system is the city itself.

Now it is this city grid of Savannah that can be used as a first example of a city grid. A view of Savannah in 1734 illustrated in John Reps' book describes the principle: the plots and streets of the embryo city are being laid out: some buildings are complete. The unit of the Savannah grid is square: it is called a ward and is separated from its neighbours by wide streets. Within each square (or ward) building plots for houses are arranged along two sides, the centre itself is open, and on each side of this open square are sites for shops and public buildings. Savannah grew by the addition of these ward units. In 1733 there were four units: in 1856 no less than twenty-four. The city became a chequer board of square ward units, marked out by the street pattern. But within this again, the plaid is further elaborated. The central open spaces of each ward are connected in one direction by intermediate roads, in the other direction the central areas become a continuous band of open spaces and public buildings. Here is a unit grid with direction and orientation.

The second example of a grid is absolutely neutral. It lays down an extensive and uniform pattern of streets and plots. The whole process can be illustrated in one single large scale example. In 1811 the largest city grid ever to be created was imposed upon a landscape. The unlikely site for this enterprise was an area of land between two geophysical provinces in which a succession of tilts, uplifts and erosions had brought through the younger strata two layers of crystalline rock. These appeared as rocky outcrops under a thin layer of soil and vegetation. Into their depressions sands and gravels had been deposited by glacial action to create swampy areas through which wandered brooks and creeks. Some of these still wander into the basements of the older areas of what is now Manhattan.

In 1613 the original Dutch settlement was limited to the tip of the island. In 1760 there was little expansion beyond this and contemporary illustrations depict to the north a rolling landscape. Taylor's plan of 1796 shows the first modest growth of a city laid out on a gridiron pattern. Surveys in 1785 and 1796 extending up the centre of Manhattan set out the basis for a grid, and in 1811 the special State Commissioners confirmed this in an 8 ft long plan which plotted the numbered street system of Manhattan as far north as 155th Street. The plan showed 12 north–south avenues each 100 ft wide and 155 cross streets each 66 ft wide. The size of the rectangular building plots set out by this grid are generally 600 ft by 200 ft. There were some public open spaces. (Central Park was of course carved out later.) And it is this framework that has served the successive developments of the built form from 1811 to the present day.

The third example of a city grid is of interest because of its dimensional

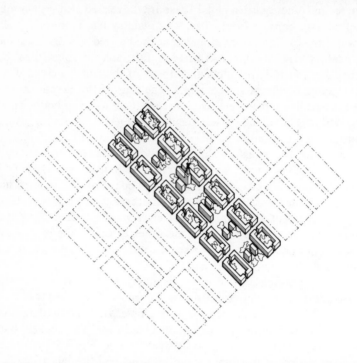

Fig. 1.1. The basic plot layout of Manhattan is shown in the dotted lines. On this, four wards of the Savannah type of development have been superimposed. The example shows the effective way in which this layout opens up broad bands of green space and public buildings running across the developed areas.

links with the land ordinance, suggested by Thomas Jefferson and passed by Congress in 1785. Under that ordinance a huge network of survey lines was thrown across all the land north and west of the Ohio river (Robinson 1916). The base lines and principal meridians of the survey divided the landscape into squares 36 miles each side. These in turn were subdivided into 6-mile squares or townships and further divided into 36 sections each one mile square. The mile squares are then subdivided by acreage: the quarter section 160 acres with further possible subdivisions of 80, 40, 20, 10 or 5 acres. The 5-acre sites lend themselves to further division into rectangular city blocks (not unlike those of Manhattan) and subdivision again into lots or building plots.

In 1832, according to Reps (1965), Chicago was not much more than a few log cabins on a swamp. The railway came in the mid-century and by the seventies and eighties a mile square grid had been extended over a considerable area of the prairie and the city framework had developed

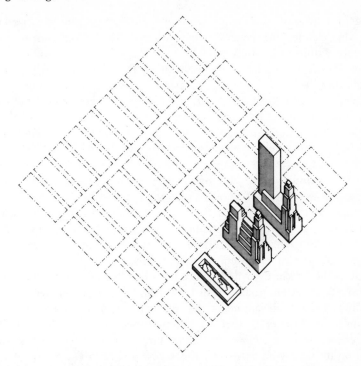

Fig. 1.2. The basic plot layout of Manhattan is shown again in the dotted lines. The building forms show three stages of development including the original 4–6-storey perimeter form with a garden at the centre which was characteristic of the city in the 1850s, and two examples of the more intensive development during the present century.

within this through a plaiting and weaving of the subdivisions that have been described.

Here then are three types of grid, that of Savannah, the gridiron of Manhattan and that of Chicago. Each one is rectangular. Each one has admitted change in the form and style of its building. Each one has admitted growth, by intensification of land use or by extension. Savannah, as it grew, tended to produce a green and dispersed city of open squares (Fig. 1.1). In Manhattan, the small scale subdivision of the grid and the exceptional pressure to increase floor space within this, forced buildings upwards. Chicago spread, continually opening out the pattern of its grid. In each case the influence of the original grid remains: each one offers different possibilities and choices of building and of living.

In order to trace the influence of the grid, we can examine the building arrangement that developed within it in New York. We can identify at once what might be called the streets and the system that is established by the grid. If we now use the language of the urban geographers, we know that this defines the general plot pattern. The building arrangement develops within this (Conzen 1962).

The stages of this latter process can be traced in the early plans of Manhattan produced in 1850. The grid of roads is already built. Within this general plot pattern the separate building plots are being established. To the north, on the building frontier, there is a line of huts and shacks. Further south more permanent but separate buildings are being built. And in the most developed area further towards the tip of Manhattan the full building arrangement has solidified into connected terraces of four to six-storey houses arranged around the perimeter of the site and enclosing private gardens. Views of Manhattan in the 1850s show a city developed in this way: and this pattern of building arrangement can still be seen in many areas. At this point the building land is replete. A balance is maintained between the plot, the amount of building that it can reasonably support and the street system that serves this.

But as the pressure for floor space increases, the building form changes intensively at certain nodal points (Fig. 1.2). Deeper and higher perimeter buildings first of all submerge the internal garden space. A process of colonisation of the individual building plots begins, so that larger areas of the general plot are covered by higher buildings. In 1916 the first single building to occupy an entire city block rose a sheer 600 ft; its roof space almost exactly equalled the area of its ground plan. It was this building that most clearly illustrated the need for the comprehensive zoning ordinances adopted that year, after arduous study and political compromise, to safeguard daylight in streets and adjoining buildings. But the grid now exerts a powerful influence: the limited size of the grid suggests the notion that increased floor space in an area can only be gained by tall buildings on each separate plot. The notion suggests the form; the regulations shape it into ziggurats and towers. Under the regulations that prevailed until recent years, if all the general building plots in central Manhattan had been fully developed, there would have been one single and universal tall building shape. And, to use an old argument by Raymond Unwin (1912), if the population of those buildings had been let out at a given moment, there would have been no room for them in the streets. The balance between area of plot, area of floor space and area of street has disappeared.

Now these descriptions of the grid, which have been used as a basis for the argument, have exposed the points at which it can be, and has been, extensively attacked for more than a century. A grid of any kind appears to be a rigid imposition on the natural landscape. It is this reaction against the grid that is voiced by Olmstead and Vaux writing in support of their design for Central Park in 1863: 'The time will come when New York will be built up, when all the grading and the filling will be done and the picturesquely varied rocky formation of the island will have been converted into formations for rows of monotonous straight streets and piles of erect buildings' (Reps 1965).

In their opposition to the grid, the relief from its monotony became a specific aim. Central Park itself is an attempt to imitate nature and to recreate wild scenery within the grid.† The garden suburb with its curving streets is one form of attack on the grid system, and an attempt to replace it. And at the end of the century, the Chicago Fair (1893), Cass Gilbert's schemes in Washington (1900), and the plans for San Francisco (1905) and Chicago (1909) by Burnham are another attempt to transform the urban desert by means of vistas and focal points, into the 'city beautiful'. However, we recognise at once a contrast. The various types of grid that have been described opened up some possible patterns for the structure of a city but left the building form free to develop and change within this. The plans of the garden city designers or those concerned with making the 'city beautiful' are an attempt to impose a form: and that form cannot change.

It is not possible to deny the force behind the criticisms of the grid. It can result in monotony: so can a curvilinear suburbia. It can fail to work: so can the organic city. What has been described is a process. It is now possible to extract some principles. Artificial grids of various kinds have been laid down. The choice of the grid allows different patterns of living to develop and different choices to be elaborated. The grid, unlike the fixed visual image, can accept and respond to growth and change. It can be developed unimaginatively and monotonously or with great freedom. There can be a point at which the original grid fails to respond to new demands (Fig. 1.3). As in Manhattan, it congeals. And it is at this point that we must try to discover from the old framework a new ordering principle that will open up new opportunities for elaboration by use.

It is precisely this that Le Corbusier underlined when he paid his first visit to New York in 1935 and made the comment: 'What about the road?' (Le Corbusier 1939, 1947.) The diagrams by which he illustrates this

† This movement which began with gardens, was less appropriately applied to city layout. In Olmstead's words, 'lines of roads were not to press forwards'. Their curving forms suggest leisure and tranquility. Compare this with the almost contemporary (1859) statements by Cerda in his plan for Barcelona in which there is 'a reciprocal arrangement between that which is contained' (building plot and arrangement) and 'that which contains' (grid and street system). 'Urbanisation is an appendix to universal movement: streets are for movement but they serve areas permanently reserved and isolated from that movement which agitates life' (the environmental area).

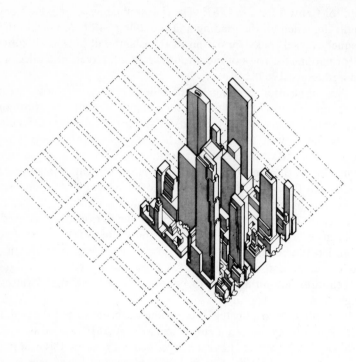

Fig. 1.3. The illustration shows building plot development in its most intensive form.

remark show the regenerative process that is necessary (Fig. 1.4). By increasing the size of the street net in Manhattan, Le Corbusier shows that the grid ceases to restrict. New building arrangements become possible and the balance between plot, building and street can be restored.

In the larger and more open mile square network of Chicago Frank Lloyd Wright had given a similar and vivid illustration of the capacity of the grid to respond to diversity and freedom. In 1913 a competition was held in order to 'awaken interest in methods of dividing land in the interests of a community' (Yeomans 1916). The site was the standard section of the mile square grid. The standard subdivision of the grid, if rigidly applied, could divide it into 32 rectangles each 600 ft long by 250 ft deep. Mr Wright accepts the established gridiron of the city 'as a basis' for subdivision. He accepts the 'characteristic aggregation of buildings... common to every semi-urban area of Chicago'. The same number of people are housed. The business buildings, the factories, the heating plant, the utilities of the area are all there. But to use his words 'they cling naturally to the main arteries of traffic. By thus drawing...all buildings of

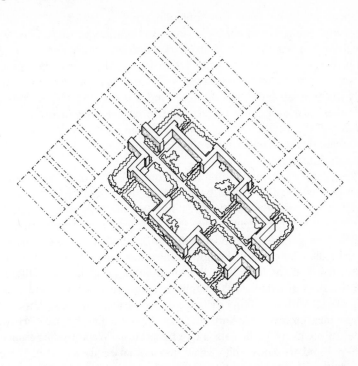

Fig. 1.4. Change in the scale of the grid. Le Corbusier's proposals for dwellings with set-backs (from his proposals for a city for 3 million people) are superimposed on the Manhattan grid and open up new possibilities in the building form.

this nature into the location that they would prefer the great mass of the subdivision is left clear for residence purposes'. Within this area parks (with their exhibition galleries and theatres), tree-lined avenues and stretches of water diversify the layout. The range and choice of housing is wide. It is all natural, relaxed, capable of infinite variation and change as it develops within the framework of the grid. Mr Wright's descriptive text includes these words: 'in skilled hands the various treatments could rise to great beauty'. It is prefaced by a quotation from Carlyle: 'Fool! the ideal is within thyself. Thy condition is the stuff thou shalt shape that same ideal out of.'

3

In the case of these American cities the grid or framework can be regarded as an ordering principle. It sets out the rules of the environmental game. It allows the player the freedom to play with individual skill. The argument can now be extended by saying that the grid, which is so apparent in the

American examples, is no less controlling and no less important in cities nearer home that would normally be called organic: London, Liverpool or Manchester. They too have a network of streets and however much the grid is distorted, it is there. At a certain scale and under certain pressures the grid combined with floor space limits and daylight controls is just as likely to force tall building solutions. And it is just as likely to congeal. It lends itself just as readily to regenerative action. The theoretical understanding of the interaction between the grid and the built form is therefore fundamental in considering either existing towns or the developing metropolitan regions.

The process of understanding this theoretical basis rests in measurement and relationships and it goes back certainly to Ebenezer Howard. Lionel March has recently pointed out a number of interesting things about Howard's book *Tomorrow: a peaceful path to real reform* first published in 1898. It is a book about how people might live in towns and how these might be distributed. But the important thing is that there is no image of what a town might look like. We know the type of housing, the size of plot, the sizes of avenues. We know that shopping, schools and places of work are all within walking distance of the residential areas. On the basis of these measurements we know the size of a town and the size of Howard's cluster of towns which he calls a city Federation. We know the choice that is offered and we know the measurements that relate to these. If we disagree with the choice we can change the measurements. Lionel March (1967) took Howard's open centred city pattern linked by railways and showed that it could be reversed into a linear pattern linked by roads and that such patterns could be tested against the land occupied by our present stock of building and our future needs.

Now that is theory. It contains a body of ideas which are set down in measurable terms. It is open to rational argument. And as we challenge it successfully we develop its power. The results are frequently surprising and sometimes astonishingly simple. Ebenezer Howard's direct successor in this field was Raymond Unwin. The strength of his argument always rests in a simple demonstration of a mathematical fact. In an essay 'Nothing gained by overcrowding' (Unwin 1912), he presents two diagrams of development on ten acres of land. One is typical development of parallel rows of dwellings: the other places dwellings round the perimeter. The second places fewer houses on the land but when all the variables are taken into account (including the savings on road costs) total development costs can be cut. From the point of view of theory, the important aspect of this study is the recognition of related factors: the land available, the built from placed on this, and the roads necessary to serve these. He demonstrated this in a simple diagram.

Unwin began a lecture on tall building by a reference to a controversy that had profoundly moved the theological world of its day, namely, how many angels could stand on a needle point. His method of confounding the urban theologians by whom he was surrounded was to measure out the space required in the streets and sidewalks by the people and cars generated by 5-, 10- and 20-storey buildings on an identical site. The interrelationship of measurable factors is again clearly demonstrated. But one of Unwin's most forceful contributions to theory is his recognition of the fact that 'the area of a circle is increased not in the direct proportion to the distance to be travelled from the centre to the circumference, but in proportion to the square of that distance'. Unwin used this geometrical principle to make a neat point about commuting time: as the population increases round the perimeter of a town, the commuting time is not increased in direct proportion to this.

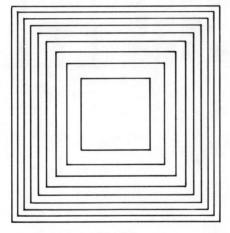

Fig. 1.5

The importance of this geometrical principle is profound. Unwin did not pursue its implications. He was too concerned to make his limited point about low density. But suppose this proposition is subjected to close examination. The principle is demonstrated again in Fresnel's diagram (Fig. 1.5) in which each successive annular ring diminishes in width but has exactly the same area as its predecessor. The outer band in the square form of this diagram has exactly the same area as the central square. And this lies at the root of our understanding of an important principle in relation to the way in which buildings are placed on the land.

Suppose now that the central square and the outer annulus of the Fresnel diagram are considered as two possible ways of placing the same amount of floor space on the same site area: at once it is clear that the two buildings so arranged would pose totally different questions of access, of how the free space is distributed around them and what natural lighting and view the rooms within them might have. By this process a number of parameters have been defined which need to be considered in any theoretical attempt to understand land use by buildings.

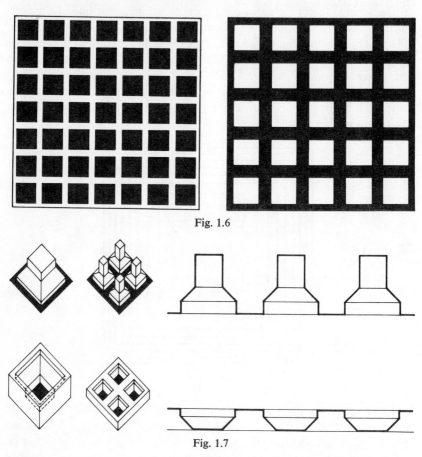

Fig. 1.6

Fig. 1.7

This central square (which can be called the pavilion) and the outer annulus (which can be called the court) are two ways of placing building on the land. Let us now extend this. On any large site a development covering 50% of the site could be plotted as forty-nine pavilions, as shown in Fig. 1.6, and exactly the same site cover can be plotted in court form. A contrast in the ground space available and the use that can be made of it is at once apparent. But this contrast can be extended further: the forty-nine pavilions can be plotted in a form which is closer to that which they would assume as buildings (that is low slab with a tower form over this). This can now be compared with its antiform: the same floor space planned as courts (Fig. 1.7). The comparison must be exact; the same site area, the same volume of building, the same internal depth of room. And when this is done we find that the antiform places the same amount of floor space into buildings which are exactly one third the total height of those in pavilion form (Martin and March 1966).

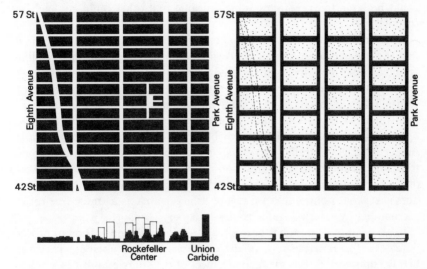

Fig. 1.8

This brings the argument directly back to the question of the grid and its influence on the building form. Let us think of New York. The grid is developing a certain form: the tall building. The land may appear to be thoroughly used. Consider an area of the city. Seen on plan there is an absolutely even pattern of rectangular sites. Now assume that every one of those sites is completely occupied by a building: and that all these buildings have the same tower form and are twenty-one storeys in height. That would undoubtedly look like a pretty full occupation of the land. But if the size of the road net were to be enlarged by omitting some of the cross streets, a new building form is possible. Exactly the same amount of floor space that was contained in the towers can be arranged in another form. If this floor space is placed in buildings around the edges of our enlarged grid then the same quantity of floor space that was contained in the 21-storey towers now needs only 7-storey buildings. And large open spaces are left at the centre.

Let us be more specific. If the area bounded by Park Avenue and Eighth Avenue, and between 42nd and 57th Street is used as a base and the whole area were developed in the form of Seagram buildings 36 storeys high, this would certainly open up some ground space along the streets. If, however, the Seagram buildings were replaced by court forms (Fig. 1.8) then this type of development while using the same built volume would produce buildings only 8 storeys high. But the courts thus provided would be roughly equivalent in area to Washington Square: and there could be 28 Washington Squares in this total area. Within squares of this size there could be large trees, perhaps some housing, and other buildings such as schools.

Of course no one may want this alternative.† But it is important to know that the possibility exists, and that, when high buildings and their skyline are being described, the talk is precisely about this and not about the best way of putting built space on to ground space. The alternative form of courts, taken in this test, is not a universal panacea. It suggests an alternative which would at once raise far-reaching questions. For instance, the open space provided in the present block-by-block (or pavilion) form is simply a series of traffic corridors. In the court form, it could become traffic-free courts. In this situation the question which needs answering is: at what point do we cease to define a built area by streets and corridors? At what point could we regard a larger area as a traffic-free room surrounded by external traffic routes?

In all this the attempt has been simply to give a demonstration of procedure. The full repercussions of the questions are not obvious. They are highly complicated. But the factual aspect of the study establishes a better position from which to understand the nature of the complication and the limits of historical assumptions. What is left is something that can be built upon and needed decisions are brought back to the problem of the built form of an urban area not merely of a building. Here, the choice of the built form is critical in a number of ways, not least as a means of securing a new unity of conception.

Take for instance the question of the size of the road net. Professor Buchanan has looked at this from another angle (Ministry of Transport, 1963). Looking at cities in relation to traffic, he saw that most of them are built up from a collection of localities. He called these 'environmental areas'. These areas are recognisable working units. They are areas in which

† It is simply a demonstration of a possible choice within a general strategy, such as that for instance proposed by the Goodmans (1960) in *Communitas* Appendix A. The Goodmans also suggest a change in the scale of the grid by street closure (1961) and note (1960 p. 230) that with better layout on the residential acreage of Manhattan every room could face onto a Madison or Washington Square.

a pattern of related uses holds together: local housing, shopping, schools, etc., would be one obvious example. These areas are recognisable in Manhattan just as clearly as they are in London. They form, in Professor Buchanan's terms, 'the rooms of a town'. They need to be served by roads but they are destroyed when roads penetrate and subdivide them. His solution was to try to recognise and define these working areas and to place the net of roads in the cracks between them. By estimating the amount of traffic that might be generated by the buildings in such areas, Professor Buchanan was able to suggest some possible sizes for the networks. He had in fact by this procedure redefined the grid of a town in terms of modern traffic.

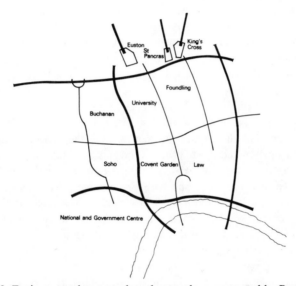

Fig. 1.9. Environmental areas and road networks as suggested by Buchanan.

Here then is a proposition for a framework within which we can test out some possible arrangements of the built form. Professor Buchanan selected St Marylebone as one of his test areas. This happens to adjoin the main London University site (already defined as a precinct in the London Plan) and this in turn is contiguous with the area around the Foundling Estate which has been used in some Cambridge studies of the built form (Fig. 1.9). All three areas are approximately equal in size. The Foundling area (bounded on the north and south by Euston Road and Theobalds Road, and on the west and east by Woburn Place and Grays Inn Road), is about 3700 ft from north to south and 2000 ft wide. It developed a cohesion of its own. How did this happen?

This in turn can be related back to the main line of argument. In 1787 the whole of this area consisted of open fields: there were no controlling features. A plan of 1790 divides the land into building plots by its network of streets and squares. The subsequent history, so well traced by Olsen (1964), shows the development and elaboration within this pattern. By 1900 the area could have been described by the language that Mrs Jacobs applies to Greenwich Village. The intellectuals were there: so were the working Londoners: so were the Italians around their hospital in Queen Square. There were handsome houses; tenements and mews; hotels and boarding houses. The area had its own Underground station and its own shopping area along Marchmont Street. It served a complex community.

By 1960 the balance within the original pattern had radically altered. Fast moving traffic using the small scale grid of streets had subdivided the area. Site by site residential development at a zoned density of 136 people to the acre produces only one answer: tall blocks of flats. Redevelopment of sites for offices created taller and thicker buildings. The hospitals, which needed to expand, were hemmed in by surrounding development. The pattern congealed.

In this situation only a new framework can open up a free development. And if Professor Buchanan's surrounding road net is accepted as a basis for the development of the environmental area, the problem can be seen within a new unifying context. What sort of advantages could a rearrangement of the built form now create? Professor Buchanan in his study area outlined three possible solutions with progressive standards of improvement. The merit of this is that it sets out a comparative basis of assessment. But even his partial solution leads to an extensive road and parking system at ground level. From the point of view of the pedestrian the position is made tolerable by the use of a deck system to create a second level. Above this again, some comparatively tall buildings are required to rehouse the built space that is at present on the ground. This kind of image of the architecture of cities has a considerable history in modern architecture and has been much used as an illustration of central area reconstruction. But, as Professor Buchanan himself asks, what building complications does it produce and what sort of an environment does it create? Is it in fact worth building?

Professor Buchanan's range of choices could in fact be extended by applying some of the theoretical work which has been described. And when this is done the results are significantly different. The boundaries of the total area that are being considered have been defined by this new scale of the road network: the grid. Within this, the existing floor space can be assessed (Fig. 1.10): 34% of the site is occupied by housing: 25% by roads: 15% by office and commercial use: 12% is open space. In addition there is an important shopping street, a major hospital and several schools and educational buildings. With this information available it can be considered at a theoretical level how this might be disposed in a new building arrangement.

First, the shopping street, Marchmont Street, could be established as a north/south pedestrian route associated with the Underground and some housing. If all the office space which is at present scattered throughout the area could be placed in a single line of buildings around the perimeter of

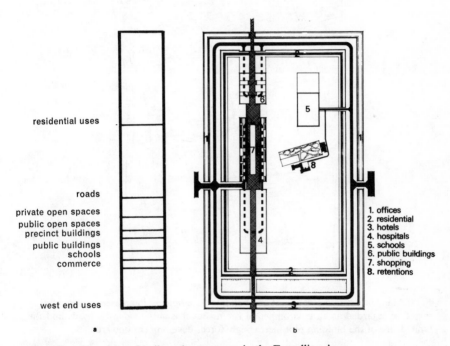

residential uses

roads

private open spaces
public open spaces
precinct buildings
public buildings
schools
commerce

west end uses

1. offices
2. residential
3. hotels
4. hospitals
5. schools
6. public buildings
7. shopping
8. retentions

a   b

Fig. 1.10a. Quantities of built and open space in the Foundling Area.
Fig. 1.10b. Possible geometric layout of the same quantities of built space in perimeter form.

the area (where some of it already is), it need be no higher than eight storeys. All the housing at present in the area could be placed within another band of buildings sited inside this and no higher than five storeys. Of course it could be arranged on the ground to include other forms and types of housing, But in theory, the bulk of the building at present covering the area could be placed in two single bands of building running around its edge, leaving the centre open, which would be a park-like area about the same size as St James's Park (Fig. 1.11). Precisely the same

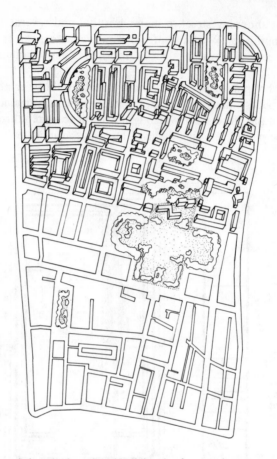

Fig. 1.11a. The existing plot layout and building development in an area of London that might be regarded as an environmental room. But it is sub-divided by roads and the limited size of the building plot increasingly forces development upward.

amount of floor space would have been accommodated. There need be no tall buildings, unless they are specifically wanted. All the housing could look onto a park. Buildings such as schools could stand freely within this. There would be a free site and a park-like setting for new hospital buildings.

All that may sound theoretical and abstract. But to know what is theoretically possible is to allow wider scope for decisions and objectives. We can choose. We can accept the grid of streets as it is. In that case we can never avoid the constant pressure on the land. Housing will be increasingly in tall flats. Hospitals will have no adequate space for expansion. Historic areas will be eaten into by new building. A total area once

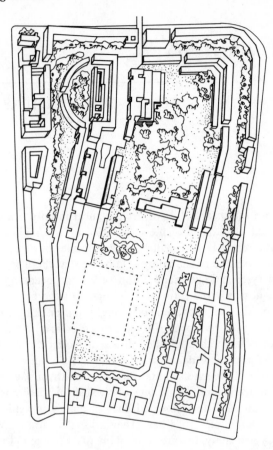

Fig. 1.11b. The same area as that in 1.11a. The road network is now enlarged and runs around the boundary of the area. Theoretically an entirely new disposition of buildings is possible and the illustration shows exactly the same amount of floor space in a new form. Tall buildings are no longer necessary: the buildings themselves have a new freedom for development and a considerable area of open space is discovered.

unified by use will be increasingly subdivided by traffic. We can leave things as they are and call development organic growth, or we can accept a new theoretical framework as an outline of the general rules of the game and work towards this. We shall know that the land we need is there if we use it effectively. We can modify the theoretical frame to respect historic areas and elaborate it as we build. And we shall also know that the overlapping needs of living in an area have been seen as a whole and that there will be new possibilities and choices for the future.

2. *Speculations*†

LESLIE MARTIN, LIONEL MARCH & OTHERS

In the 1920s an important shift of architectural intention and process – a shift of social attitude – became clear. However complicated the historical situation may have been, three powerful lines of thought appeared. The first came from the passionately held belief that there had to be some complete and systematic re-examination of human needs and that, as a result of this, not only the form of buildings, but the total environment would be changed. The second line of thought, interlocking with this, was simply that change in the form of buildings, or environment, would only be achieved completely through the full use of modern technology. These two ideas produced a third, which was that each architectural problem should be constantly re-assessed and thought out afresh (Wurster 1965).

Now it is clear that no single one of these principles was ever completely demonstrated. They remained lines of action sometimes followed up separately, sometimes together. The rational examination of needs went some way, certainly, towards a fundamental change in the plan form of buildings. But of technical innovation, there was not a great deal. There was a lot of talk about the machine but its end products were not very evident in buildings. What the designers saw, often in a confused way, were the possibilities that arose from their beliefs and attitudes, and it is around these anticipations that they built up their formal systems. In this sense their buildings were symbols of what a new architecture might be. And for their day they had an immensely powerful meaning.

All this is something very different from an attempt to produce new forms as a primary objective: i.e. as a kind of rootless formalism. What

---

† This essay is a compilation from many sources. The introductory pages are from an article by Sir Leslie Martin entitled, 'Architect's Approach to Architecture', published in the *R.I.B.A. Journal*, May 1967. It introduces paraphrased excerpts from other papers and articles which are here presented as 'Speculations'. The word is fitting as the attempt was to raise questions which could only be answered by subsequent formulations.

seems to be important about it are the intentions that caused these forms. The difference between a chair produced by the arts and crafts movement and a chair designed by Rietveld is not just a difference of form. The form comes from a different emphasis on who makes it, on how it is made and how many people can have it. Now to stress this distinction is to make a declaration of attitude. The design of an object becomes a statement of conviction about what a society may need, the way it might consider its surroundings, the kind of products that it might have and how it might manufacture and use them. It is indeed an intellectual commitment; and this attitude of mind will apply equally to any aspect of design. The work resulting from the 1920s and 1930s is of interest and value today because of the ideas that it embodies (Wilson and Rowe 1965).

The change from art and craft intuition towards rational analysis, measurement, technical innovations and speculative thought about these things, is one manifestation of this. The change is there at an early date in the opposition to the intuitive craft approach, and in buildings that are 'built to a purpose' and thought out, rather than drawn. It is this matter-of-factness in which the act of design cannot be separated out as a form-making process that remains central. It is re-echoed in the various catch-phrases around which theory (and particularly German theory) was discussed.

But history is never clear cut. Against this attempt to reintroduce rationalism as a basis for architecture, there is, all along the line, the opposition of a powerful wing of 'individualist' creators. The situation is confused. Rational thought about needs and processes by one school was in some way considered by another to be dangerous and inhibiting. Practical reason and intuition were seen as opposites. And it is also true, as C. B. Wurster (1965) and J. M. Fitch (1965) have noted, that just as the products of practical reason were being demonstrated on an impressive scale in the housing projects of Holland and Germany, the developing theory became dogma. The principle that rational thought about use and construction must produce (as an integral part of this process) its own formal systems required a continuous reassessment of every aspect of a problem. Knowledge would be established by analysis, advanced by experiment and confirmed or corrected by test. A ruthless reassessment of each achievement was an essential part of this process. But, in that important and major housing achievement of the 1930s, the process stopped. The speculative thought that could have extended the range of built forms into totally new environments dried up. In Germany and elsewhere the set housing solution solidified into parallel rows of slab blocks.

The fact that this happened was of enormous consequence. The rational approach was at once suspect. The end result of practical reason appeared to be sterility: and it was assumed that this could be countered only by intuitive processes – by feeling. Thus the old nineteenth-century oppositions were continued.

What was wrong with parallel slab layout was not the rational thought that it contained, but the failure to extend this by further speculative, formal invention. As A. N. Whitehead (1929) once pointed out, it is speculation that makes rational thought live: and it is rational thought that gives speculative invention its basis and its roots. To analyse, to measure and to rationalise the problem is an essential part of the process of scientific thought. And, in the scientific process, intuition (or what Alfred North Whitehead (1929) prefers to call conjecture or speculative reason) is itself entirely arbitrary unless it is guided by thought or system. Practical reason is the means by which methods are developed for dealing with different kinds of facts. Speculative reason is an extension of this into theoretical activity. Progress depends on a lively interest in speculative reason. Through the interaction of these two forms of thought, factual assessment can take its place within an overall scheme of things: speculative reason is 'robbed of its anarchic character without destroying its function of reaching out beyond set bounds' (Whitehead 1929, p. 66). Whitehead goes on to add that the massive advance of modern technology is due to the fact that these two forms of thought (rational and speculative) have again made contact. That, translated into architectural terms, is equivalent to saying that the rational understanding of a problem and the extension of this into speculative (intuitive) thought is one single process: that is, that thought and intuition are not opposed but complementary. We may recognise at once an older (pre-nineteenth century) concept of architecture in which the design process cannot be isolated from the thought processes by which the problem is analysed and solved.

The decisions that are taken about the planning of buildings, their form and the grouping in relation to the land available may be based on assumptions which appear to be eminently sensible and rational. However, rigorous reassessment – despite the initial form of refutation that it might assume – will always prove productive. The argument presented here is that things are not always what they seem to be. Refutation can begin as an intuition of imposture; but to prove that, speculation and rational formulations must be able to demonstrate first the fallacy and then alternative and more useful deployment. The fallacy may exist at any scale: of site resources assumed to be needed, of the relationship of rooms within the building to the corridor space connecting them, of grouped buildings to each other and to each other's uses, of buildings within the city and the streets by which they are connected.

It is particularly fortunate when out of speculation, research has its beginnings. The points here raised were formulated out of a series of separate studies as they arose from practical problems. Since they were not contained within a formulated body of theory they can best be described as speculations.

Speculation 1 (Martin & March 1965)

How can we study the efficiency of the planning of buildings? There is a common assumption that the most economic building is that in which the circulation space is reduced to a minimum when set against the total floor area: that is to say that maximum efficiency of planning is measured by the relationship of circulation to gross area. This measure is frequently used in assessing costs and awarding grants. At the same time other standards, possibly conflicting, may be introduced, for example room sizes based on increments, or constructional sizes resulting in modular dimensions. These are all interrelated factors and the interaction can be studied in a few simple diagrams.

In the example selected, 12 rooms have to be accommodated. These vary in size and their areas are based on graded increments of 25–50 sq ft. The planning and structural module is based on a 4-ft grid. In the first layout (Fig. 2.1a), the rooms are arranged along each side of a minimum 6-ft corridor, in what may be considered to be an efficient plan. The rooms are made 18 ft deep and arranged in length to form the most convenient fit between the incremental sizes and the planning unit. There is a clear over-allocation of floor space per room: the area increment being 72 sq ft instead of the required increment of 25–50 ft.

In the second diagram (Fig. 2.1b), the variation in room size has a two-way freedom, the depth of the room being controlled by the 4-ft module. The room over-allocation is reduced. The corridor is increased in space in what might appear to be a wasteful manner, but the total floor area remains the same as in the first example.

If the module for room depth is now reduced to 2 ft (Fig. 2.1c) then room allocation has a tighter fit. The corridor width is 8 ft over 80% of its length and may be more pleasant and at the same time more useful by accommodating waiting areas or filing space.

In the previous examples the building block is 29 units in length and $10\frac{1}{2}$ in width. The effect of an increase in the width of the block can now be considered. In the next diagram (Fig. 2.1d), with the block now only 21 modules long and $14\frac{1}{2}$ modules deep, a 6-ft corridor is again introduced. The over-allocation is now the highest in the series. The circulation area is the least and the external face is 16 modules less than in the previous examples.

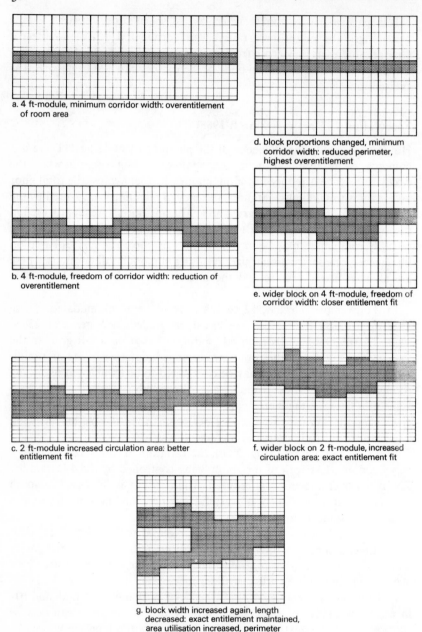

a. 4 ft-module, minimum corridor width: overentitlement
   of room area

b. 4 ft-module, freedom of corridor width: reduction of
   overentitlement

c. 2 ft-module increased circulation area: better
   entitlement fit

d. block proportions changed, minimum
   corridor width: reduced perimeter,
   highest overentitlement

e. wider block on 4 ft-module, freedom of
   corridor width: closer entitlement fit

f. wider block on 2 ft-module, increased
   circulation area: exact entitlement fit

g. block width increased again, length
   decreased: exact entitlement maintained,
   area utilisation increased, perimeter
   decreased, worst ratio of circulation area
   to gross area

Fig. 2.1. A comparative study of office layout with varying planning modules, room depths, and perimeter lengths.

If the rooms are now given freedom in depth and the depth is controlled by the 4-ft module (Fig. 2.1e), the room entitlement has a closer fit and the corridor is nowhere less than 8 ft wide. With a further reduction of module depth to 2 ft (Fig. 2.1f), there is no over entitlement and nowhere is the corridor less than 10 ft. When the block is widened again to 16 modules (Fig. 2.1g) the increased depth allows a conference room to be inserted in the central area. The external perimeter face is reduced from 42 modules to 38. By some criteria this layout is the best, though it has the least favourable circulation to gross area ratio (26.6%) in the series. It gives a perfect fit of entitlement to allocated space, has the least external wall surface (perimeter length) and the least gross area. The ratio of circulation to gross area as a measure of efficiency can certainly be questioned.

Speculation 2 (Martin & March 1965)

Many measures of the 'efficiency' of buildings may be developed but these can only be of use when they can be seen in relationship and when values can be defined in measurable terms. It may be asked, for example, what building forms make the best use of land? The question necessarily involves a value judgement of what is meant by 'best use' and this can only be answered objectively insofar as the values can be defined in measurable terms. It might be assumed that current planning controls, where they use measures, will supply an answer and that the question is asked wherever a development is proposed for a given site.

Current planning techniques, in fact, offer two measures which have dominated planning and architectural action for many years. The first is a measure of floor space index (or its alternative plot ratio) and the second is concerned with daylight considerations.† These two measures are assumed to provide a rational relationship of floor space to site and an assurance that buildings will be adequately lit. The use of the first measure has sometimes been extended to give an indication of the population accommodated in the buildings.

Martin, March and Taylor (1965) examined this last point by producing a set of graphs to show the relationship of three of the factors which may be considered in determining the population capacity of a given site. (These graphs are illustrated in Fig. 2.2.) In relation to a typical site area of 100,000 sq ft the plot ratio may be 2:1, 3:1 or 4:1. This generates floor areas of 200,000, 300,000 and 400,000 sq ft (Fig. 2.2a). The gross

† Floor space index is the gross floor area measurement of the building including the thickness of the external walls; this total is divided by the site area including half the width of the surrounding roads. Plot ratio is the same gross measurement of floor area divided by the net site area. These measures are expressed as 2:1, 5:1 etc. Daylight considerations are measured by special protractors and nomograms.

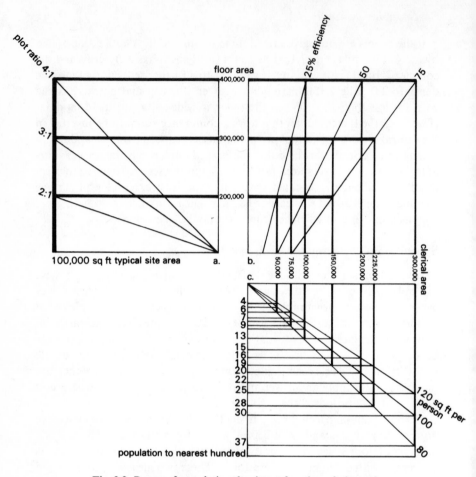

Fig. 2.2. Range of population density as function of plot ratio.

floor area may then be used with varying degrees of efficiency, for example 25%, 50% or 75%. The clerical areas generated from these (Fig. 2.2b) yield nine possible results ranging from 50–100,000 sq ft at 25%, 150–200,000 sq ft at 50% to 150–300,000 sq ft at 75%. If these possible clerical areas are now related to an allocation of square feet per person (Fig. 2.2c) this too may fall within allowances of 80, 100 or 120 sq ft per person. In this example seventeen different populations ranging from 400 to 3700 could arise from the same site area as a result of these relationships of plot ratio, general plan efficiency and floor space allocation per person.†

† Other factors will clearly limit this range, for instance, building codes. Similarly, land and development costs, particularly in central business districts, will tend to secure intensive use. But coordinated relationships between bulk and density and use and density are not usually even formulated.

It is clear that plot ratio in itself is no satisfactory measure of population, though it is useful as an assessment of the total floor space provided by buildings on any given site in any area of a town.

Speculation 3 (Martin & March 1966)

But continued scrutiny can go on to reveal whether this plot ratio measure will insure in any way that the site area will be effectively used. In order to demonstrate this we might place on any given site parallel rows of 4-storey buildings spaced apart by a conventional light angle of 45°: in this case the plot ratio will be 2:1. If however the building remains at 4 storeys but is arranged as a solid block lit by courts, in which the prescribed light angle is still used, the plot ratio will increase from 2:1 to 3:1, that is by a factor of 50%. Assuming for a moment that both forms of building lend themselves equally to internal planning, it becomes clear that the building form can have a pronounced effect on the total floor space possible on any given site. If urban land is to be developed economically and if reliable measures of this are necessary, it is desirable to know which forms of building appear to make the most effective use of ground area.

In approaching this question we are at once confronted with some deeply embedded ideas. One of these, for example, is the prevalent notion that high tower buildings are necessary in order to use land efficiently. Tower buildings have been used indiscriminately in London on sites which differ considerably in both size and surroundings. Any form of building is permissible within the measure of floor space index. If certain limits are set, such as size of site, the amount of floor space required, the acceptable depth of building, the amount of floor space with outlook, the amount without and so on, it is possible to demonstrate that a development might assume many building forms including tall towers and that a very considerable number of variables exist and a wide range of choice requires examination. In one case studied with six co-ordinates, this reached a total of 60,000 possible solutions.

Speculation 4 (Martin & March 1966)

How can such a problem be studied in a systematic manner? The site utilisation of various layouts can be studied by classifying the built forms under three headings: the pavilion or tower, the street and the court. These can be considered within a rectilinear universe. The pavilion is finite in its plan form. The street extends, potentially, infinitely along one axis. The court extends infinitely along two. From these built forms rectangular lattices can be derived. In fact the pavilion, the street and the court consti-

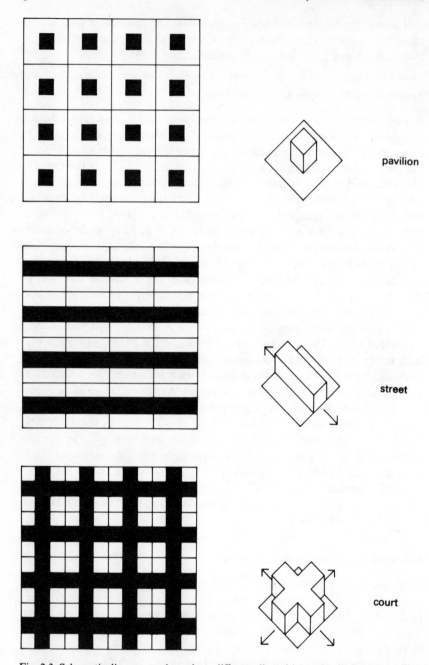

Fig. 2.3. Schematic diagram to show three different dispositions of built forms: pavilion or tower, street or slab, and the generating cruciform in a continuous pattern of courts.

tute points of recognition in what may more properly be seen as a continuous transformation from one extreme to the other (Fig. 2.3); from an array of isolated blocks elongated into continuous parallel rows, and these joined in the perpendicular direction to form a net of courts.

This can now be examined. The co-ordinates used must be constant for each case: the same site area, the same block depth, the same width of interspace, the same floor height, etc. Two factors reveal certain aspects of the problem: one is the site utilisation factor, that is the ratio of the site covered to the area not covered. The other is the built potential, that is the ratio of the floor area of the built form to the site area.

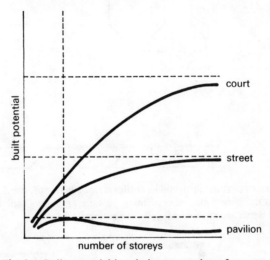

Fig. 2.4. Built potential in relation to number of storeys.

When the built potential is plotted against the number of storeys for each one of the three built forms described, assuming all other factors are constant, then it is seen that after a certain height the tower form ceases to use land with increasing efficiency and lower towers more closely packed together, but with no change in the angle between contiguous towers, will give the same degree of built potential. (Fig. 2.4) This could be one reason that the 'City of Towers', free standing towers in a park-like setting, has never been built. It is inherently inefficient in terms of land use. In comparison to the pavilion or tower form at its maximum, the built potential of the street form has twice its value, and the built potential of the court form is no less than three times as great.

The form of a typical high density development, a low podium surmounted by a tower, corresponds closely to the building envelope obtained by using daylight protractors. Day lighting controls have determined to a large extent the massing of building seen in the central city of today (Watts, 1963). The type of study described can be developed by considering pyramidal forms which approximate more closely to the actual building form (Fig. 2.5). This generalised pavilion form may again be compared with its antiform, the court. When this is done, the court form is seen to place the same amount of floor space on the same site area with the same condition of building depth and in approximately one-third the height required by the pavilion form.

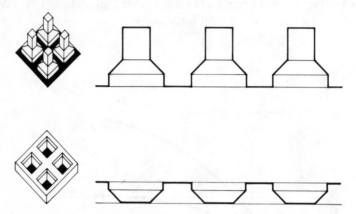

Fig. 2.5. Generalised pavilion form and its antiform; modified antiform of the generalised pavilion form at the same scale and containing the same amount of built volume on the same site; the heights are approximately in the ratio of 3:1.

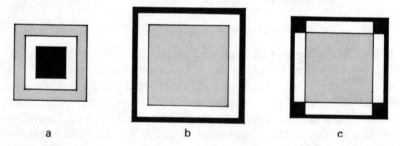

a   b   c

Fig. 2.6. The illustration shows (a) a pavilion development and (b) and (c) court developments, in which several proportions of site utilisation: coverage, built potential (bulk) and percentage of floor area without outlook, are the same. For the same number of storeys, the built potential will be the same for all three buildings. The different size site area needed to equalise these proportions suggests that each form has an optimum site size. (Fig. 2.6c takes into account the internal angle condition required to maintain the proportion of floor space with outlook, while building the court form on a smaller site.) Black areas represent floorspace without outlook; white areas represent floorspace with outlook; tinted area represents that part of site uncovered by development.

Speculation 5 (Martin & March 1966)

What is to be observed, however, is that if the built potential is held constant for the pavilion and the court, and if the proportion of the built form having outlook and that with no outlook is again constant, then the size of the site for these two developments will differ (Fig. 2.6). This seems to suggest that each form of development probably has its own optimum size. If the highest densities were to be allowed only on the larger sites, then it appears to be the case that high and deep buildings would be unnecessary in terms of land use, though they may be required on other functional grounds. This kind of consideration could lead to the general loosening up of the texture of building on ground space. In that case a new relationship

Fig. 2.7a. A 50-acre site developed with typical bye-law streets at a density of 100 persons per acre.

of building to road must be sought. The development of larger areas of land and the possibility of buildings occupying less ground space offers the possibility of a new scale of road network in which the interrelationship of land, building content and the traffic which it generates is made more balanced.

Speculation 6 (Martin & March 1968)

This question of the relatedness of things is central to the consideration of any single issue like the provision of housing, schools, open space or the roads by which they are served. All these things are aspects of the main problem of relationships: and by looking at a question in this way the old barriers created by zoning are immediately removed.

Professor Vaizey (1968) once stated that the older areas of towns may continue to have the oldest schools. The problem, he said, was that even if the housing priorities did not eliminate them, the larger sites which they tend to demand displaces the stock of housing.

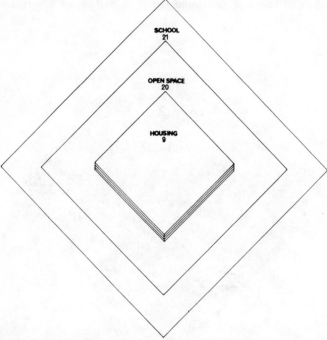

Fig. 2.7b. The land-use requirement of the 5000 people housed on the 50-acre site. The area allocated to schools includes 7 acres for buildings and 14 acres for playing fields. When an allowance is also made for open space, only 9 acres remain for housing. The housing floor area is 3 times that of the land available.

It could be argued that educational need and housing need cannot be separated: both are part of the larger theoretical problem of how we use land by buildings. When the issue is considered in this light the results are sometimes surprising. Consider an area of land in a nineteenth-century industrial city: suppose that there are 50 acres of by-law street housing inside a frame of busy commercial and shopping streets. (Fig. 2.7a). The residential density is 100 persons per acre. Assume that there is one obsolete primary school embedded in the housing; most of the children attend schools elsewhere. Now consider the rebuilding of this area. Can houses be provided for the present population at the same time that schools are made available for its children? There appear to be competing land uses, and in any rebuilding there may be the added requirement of public open space.

Let us look at this from the point of view of schools. Fifty acres generate 5000 people, and these in turn might demand an infants' school for some 300, a junior school for something over 400, and for the sake of argument

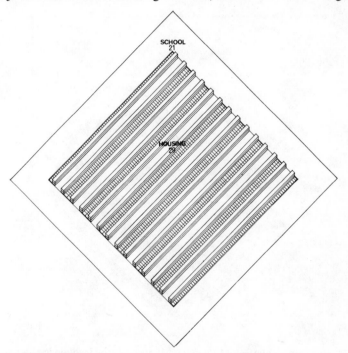

Fig. 2.7c. If the schools are accommodated, and this open space omitted, there remain 29 acres of land for housing. 3600 people could be accommodated in 2-storey housing arranged in the simplest possible way. 5000 people would require most of the site.

we may assume also a secondary school of around 600. The school buildings alone would occupy 7 acres of land. Playing fields will require an extra 14 acres. Altogether 21 acres, or 42 % of the land, would be required for educational purposes. If another 4 acres per thousand were to be claimed within the area for recreational needs, then 41 of the 50 acres or 82 % of the land would have been pre-empted, and the housing would have to take place on the remaining 18 %, on which again there would be some demand from access roads. In terms of sheer space the housing would occupy a solid block of building three storeys high (Fig. 2.7b).

It certainly looks as though Professor Vaizey is right. It appears to be a matter of *either* housing *or* schools, but not both. But the quantification immediately draws attention to an important issue. Why is so much land needed? What is it that demands an area large enough to allow the simultaneous use by over 100 pupils playing five different soccer matches at the same time? What about overlapping uses of recreational land by a far wider range of activities – in farming terms, a double or triple cropping of the land? And if the school land were available to the locality or, as recom-

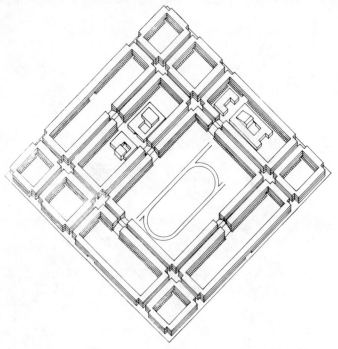

Fig. 2.7d. Three-storey housing would require 25 acres of land including roads and small 'outdoor' room space. This housing is only possible if the 21 acres of school land and the open space allocation are used to form 'urban rooms' of varying size.

mended by the U.S. Sub-Committee for Environmental Standards (American Public Health Association), if the schools used the recreational facilities provided for the neighbourhood, what saving of land would then be possible? It is clear that we have a choice: if we were to consider these relationships, Professor Vaizey's problem might still be soluble.

But this can be looked at too from another angle, that of housing. A 50-acre site redeveloped at 100 persons per acre could be completely covered with houses and their attendant roads (Fig. 2.7c). In this case there would now be no sites for schools. But we now know that this type of layout is only one point of recognition in a spectrum of dispositions of built form on the land. This primitive layout shows housing for 3600 people in two-storey houses and 21 acres for school sites. But if some sharing of the school land and open space were acceptable, this combined-use land (Fig. 2.7d), could provide 'urban rooms' within the layout and the new distribution of built form could accommodate the total population of 5000 in three-storey houses. This corresponds approximately to the layout of some of the squares in Bloomsbury. (Fig. 2.7e).

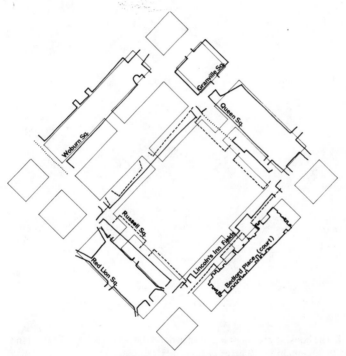

Fig. 2.7e. The 'urban rooms' compared with open spaces in the Bloomsbury area of London. Note that most of the buildings around the London squares exceed 3 storeys in height.

Accept another point in the spectrum and place the housing round the edge of the site (Fig. 2.7f and g): the total population of 5000 could be housed in narrow-fronted houses or flats, four or five storeys high around the perimeter of the site. They could all overlook and have available for use, a band of open space 180 ft wide and at the centre of this the 21 acres of land required by the schools. In this case both the housing and the schools could be provided.

Is it now preferable to accept a housing solution of this kind in order to find land for the schools? Is it really unacceptable to have a condition rather like that of overlooking Parker's Piece in Cambridge from some four or five-storey terraces around it?† (Fig. 2.7h.)

The proposition set by Professor Vaizey is clearly not insoluble. Both the housing and the schools can be sited, but not without adjustments within a total framework.

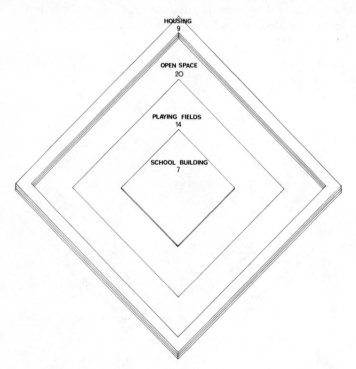

Fig. 2.7f. The housing area is now placed around the perimeter. If all other land uses are satisfied there remain just 9 acres of housing land.

Speculation 7 (Bullock, Dickens & Steadman 1968)

The lattices that can be built up around the 'pavilion', the 'street' and the 'court' forms (Bullock, Dickens and Steadman 1968, p. 104) are not arbitrarily chosen, but within the context of rectangular geometry, and treating prismatic forms only, they constitute the entire range of possible

† The results appear to be very simple. But it is curious that the forms of the layout described do not seem to have been built: at least not recently. Architects tend to think of housing in terms of building types: point blocks, slabs, maisonettes rather than land use built form relationships which may generate new types.

regular space-filling arrays. Despite their abstract geometry they indicate universal characteristics of the ways in which buildings use land and the forms are ones to which many actual buildings in the real world approximate.

In the development of this work March and Trace (1968) have formulated a mathematical description of built forms making it possible to give a standard notation to the geometry and other significant factors of these rectangular prismatic forms. This work has also been extended by the differentiation between perimeter space, that is unobstructed space around the building's edge, and core space which has refined the basic study.

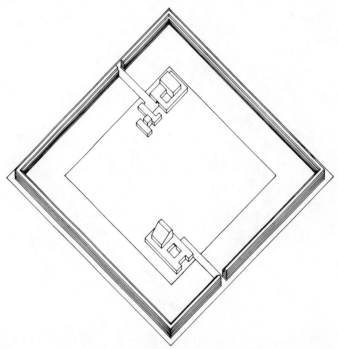

Fig. 2.7g. A 4½-storey narrow-fronted housing band could accommodate 5000 people at a density of 500 persons per acre. But they would all look out onto a vast open space: the perimeter open space is 180 ft wide and at the centre is the 21 acres of school land.

Nevertheless, evaluation of these basic forms is possible only in the simplest terms. The performance of forms may be compared, for example, in terms of the amount of land that they require to provide the same floor area: or the ratio of perimeter space to core space may be measured for different forms. Very general cost comparisons can be made by treating the cost of each building as a simple factor of the total floor area or by attempting to weight the costs to take account of the ratio of floor area to roof area, and of floor area to perimeter walling in order to give a limited understanding of the changes in cost with the change in form.

Such measures of performance are crude, however, and may provide the designer with information too coarse to use in modifying his preliminary hypothesis or even to allow him to detect the effect of many decisions. What is needed is a library of factors considered in such a relationship that a change in any one of the parts is immediately seen in its effect on all the others. This is something that the designer is usually unable to do and

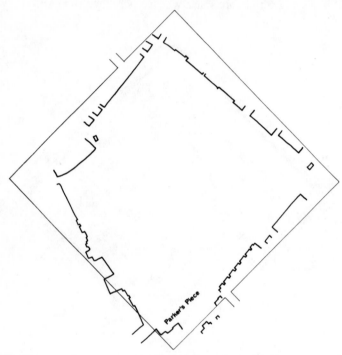

Fig. 2.7h. The central open space in Fig. 2.7g compared with Parker's Piece in Cambridge.

adjustments to design are made on the assumption that the change is largely independent of all but the most obviously related factors. The interdependence of the parts of the design problem and the validity of breaking the problem down into manageable but relatively independent parts has been studied by Christopher Alexander (1964). His work on the 'pattern of the content' seems essential as a first step to a consideration of the pattern of the form which is the problem that we are dealing with here. The total work of architecture is essentially concerned with the 'fit' between these two considerations in themselves and the technical methods through which their requirements are met.

In order to monitor back to the designer information of sufficiently 'fine grain' to illustrate the real effect of the design decisions on the building, or to compare the 'fit' between activities and alternative building solutions, it must be possible to make a systematic transformation, not only of the overall form of the building, but also of the different elements of the building. It must be possible to compare not only different building forms but alternative room layouts, alternative structural and servicing systems and alternative circulation systems in sufficient detail to trace the consequences of these choices on the performance of the building in relation to the activities which it serves. That is the problem that needs systematic formulation if we are to increase our understanding.

Speculation 8 (March 1967)

The systematic study of the pattern of the form is relevant to the building, to the group of buildings and to the city or the urban region. And it is equally revealing in each case.

Figure 2.8 is a version of Howard's cluster of towns forming a city federation of 250,000 persons. By the year 2000 we would need 250 of these clusters to accommodate the whole expected population of England and Wales. Suppose for a moment we built these clusters and demolished everything else. 250,000 people would live in easy reach of one another and all social facilities. Schools would be within walking distance of all homes. Shopping would take place indoors. Everyone who wanted to would have a house and garden. The minimum plot size is 20 ft by 100 ft. The roads would easily accommodate the motor car. The towns have hollow centres and the road system is more like a simple grid wrapped round upon itself than a radial and circumferential system. The minimum road width is 60 ft whilst the six principal boulevards are 120 ft as are the two principal avenues. The nation would then be living in towns, which could accommodate the motor car yet be small enough to permit easy pedestrian access to many different functions. Everyone would be able to own a house and garden. Yet the really remarkable thing about the proposition is this: 4,000,000 acres of land that is expected to be built on by the year 2000 would not be required. In fact, although the population would be twice the size of that of Howard's day it would have been accommodated on the same land as was urbanised in 1898. Since then the urban land stock has doubled, and it is expected to have trebled by the year 2000. Howard cannot be charged with any waste of land.

A simple question that can be asked is this: if every household in the

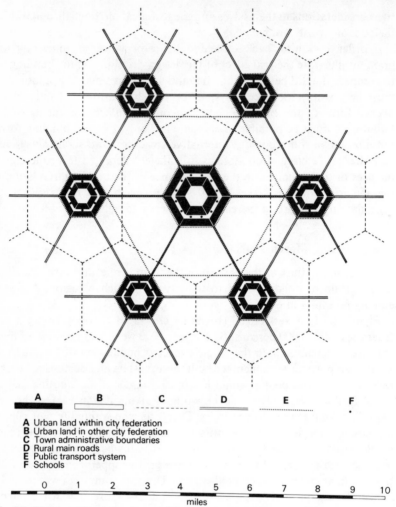

0   1   2   3   4   5   6   7   8   9   10
miles

Fig. 2.8. Ebenezer Howard's cluster of garden cities forming a city federation of 250,000 persons.

year 2000 could have a house, a garden and a car on 2,000,000 acres of urban land, why will they not have a house, a garden and a car on three times as much? A more equitable distribution of land would ensure a house and a garden for all who want one. Yet, even if land were not distributed evenly, this simple desire could be answered to some extent by more rational land use planning in relation to the built forms required for the house and garden.

First let us look at how 10% of a land area might be covered by urban

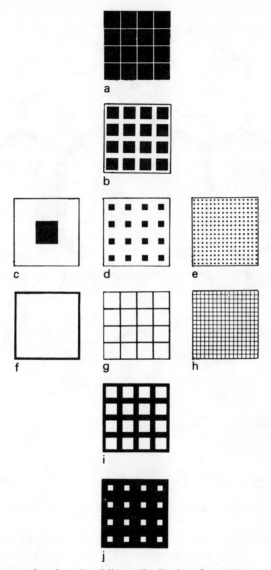

Fig. 2.9. Range of nucleated and linear distributions from 10% to 90% coverage.

uses. This 10% is the present proportion of urban land to all land in England and Wales and it includes urban open spaces like parks, but not agricultural land within urban administrative boundaries. Fig. 2.9c shows the 10% coverage distributed in a concentrated nuclear form (one single blob) and Fig. 2.9e in a dispersed nuclear pattern (in this case 256 blobs).

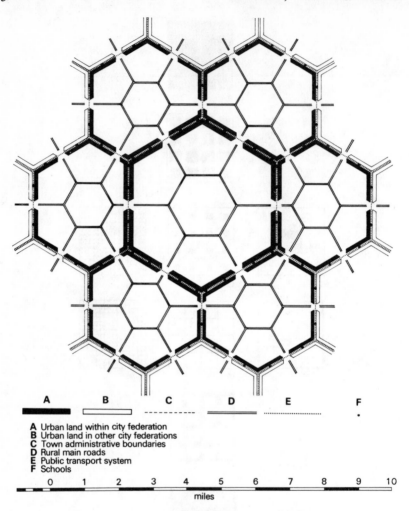

A   Urban land within city federation
B   Urban land in other city federations
C   Town administrative boundaries
D   Rural main roads
E   Public transport system
F   Schools

Fig. 2.10. Linear antiform of Howard's city federation.

Figs. 2.9f–h, however, show the same amount of urban land distributed in a linear manner. The pattern illustrated in Fig. 2.9f may be described as concentrated linear (a coarse mesh) and Fig. 2.9h as dispersed linear (a fine mesh). Fig. 2.9a shows 90% coverage, while Figs. 2.9i and 2.9j show the inverted scheme of linear coverage.

There are three properties of the distribution. The topological property of being nuclear or linear corresponds to thinking blobs, *or* thinking of the spaces between. The second property is concerned with scale. The property of being concentrated or dispersed is dependent on the scale chosen to observe the pattern. If, for instance, 1/256 of the dispersed blob pattern (9e) were to be seen at close range, it would look exactly like the concentrated blob pattern (9c). The only difference is one of scale. The third property is the amount of coverage. This can be high (90%) or low (10%). So far no set population has been given. Assume that it is fixed and is independent of land coverage. It will be clear, with a fixed population, that if the land coverage is high (90%) the gross residential density will be relatively low and proportional to 100/90 = 1.1. If, on the other hand, the land coverage is low (10%) the gross residential density will be high and proportional to 100/10 = 10. This low coverage is associated with high density. But the important point is that the notions of concentrated or dispersed developments have no relationship to population density. It is as possible to have a high-density dispersed pattern as a low-density concentrated pattern.

Next, if the pattern is assumed to be continuous and isotropic there are just three geometric arrangements – triangular, rectangular or rhombic, and hexagonal. For the sake of simplicity the rectangular pattern is used here with the sole exception of the next example. This shows (Fig. 2.10) the think-line version of Howard's city federation. Exactly the same proportion of land is urban here as in the think-blob arrangement, and approximately one-quarter of this urban land is open space. It is not solidly built-up.

It can be shown mathematically that the schools are likely to be more accessible in the linear form. The same is true of any other social function that is distributed evenly with the population. But perhaps the most significant difference between the two arrangements is that in the nuclear pattern driving across country requires movement across the town (or alternatively the construction of a special ring road), whilst the linear pattern is interrupted only briefly by urban development and, if the urban parks are placed at these points, cross-country routes need not pass through built-up areas at all.

Speculation 9 (March 1968)

Next consider the correlation of residential building forms and density. The present housing yardstick, for example, implicitly assumes that as densities increase houses decrease in favour of flats, and low buildings give way to high. This is only true because of the professional separation of land use planning from its architectural implications. With favourable land use planning, semi-detached houses can be built at 200 persons to the acre. Three-storey terraces under more normal circumstances can be built up to 265 persons per acre. These are facts. Thus, instead of permitting the highest densities in the countryside where they can make the greatest sense, we insist on putting the highest density towards the centres of our cities.

This tendency may be represented by considering a city marked out from its centre in equal width bands (Fig. 2.11a). Each of these bands accommodates an equal amount of built space. Close to the centre, the built space will have to be achieved in the sky whilst on the perimeter this same quantity of space will be found on the ground. In conventional terms, if the plot ratio is 4:1 in the centre it will be, at the 9th and outermost ring, only 0.055:1, or if a building on the outskirts is one storey high, at the centre 72 storeys will be required. Abandoning the density cone concept, the whole built form could be disposed at an average plot ratio of

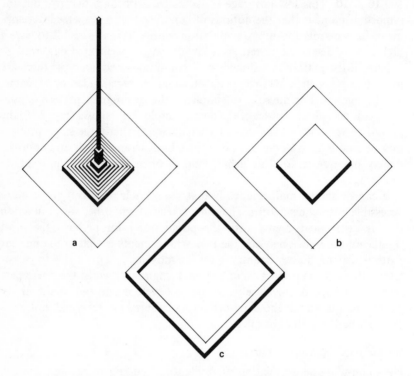

Fig. 2.11. Housing density in relation to its distribution.

0.11:1 (Fig. 2.11b), or just twice that of the 9th ring. This plot ratio of 0.11:1 is only marginally higher than the mean of the four outermost rings, but a great deal lower than the mean of the five inner rings. Fig. 2.11c shows the same built space distributed in a linear form. Closeness and accessibility of similar functions are likely to be improved in a linear route development and since skyscrapers do not use central land very efficiently, the only sense that high buildings make in nucleated centres is in terms of real estate speculation. In terms of accommodating built space on urban land they are extravagant and irrational gestures. To return to housing densities, there is not much point in thinking of densities as great as 200 persons per acre (when the mean density is likely to be not more than 25 persons per acre in the year 2000), if it were not that by taking extreme situations it is often possible to see principles more clearly.

Speculation 10 (March 1967)

In the study of Hook New Town, 16 acres of open space (including recreational areas) were allowed for every 1000 persons. At this rate 1280 persons would require about 20 acres, or a space 900 ft square (Fig. 2.12a). These persons could be housed in a ribbon of 3-storey housing with a small garden at 200 persons to the acre around their own public open space. The spatial effect would be like Parker's Piece in Cambridge. The access road would be like any simple terrace development. When one considers just how complex housing at this kind of density has become, it is timely to ask whether more might be achieved by a return to relaxed simplicity. A further modification is shown in Fig. 2.12b where all the houses might have a view of the countryside.

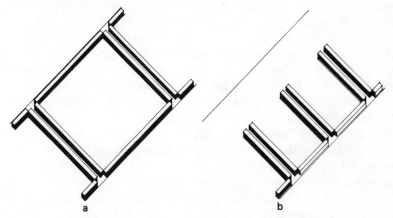

a   b

Fig. 2.12. Simple high density housing forms.

In all this the rural districts have a tremendous part to play. Already they are developing more rapidly than the urban areas, excepting the new towns. It is there that the new city is emerging. What pattern will it take? There are many excellent geometrical reasons, especially of a probabilistic nature, to suppose that a free, loose development along a network of routes has advantages of capacity, accessibility, density and use distribution not possible in nuclear development and that, with a positive policy towards open spaces, it is likely to prove the most reasonable form for the emergent city.

But planners will never know until the capacity has been developed to understand and measure the forces that are at work and to compare alternatives.

Speculation 11 (Martin 1968)

In order to find the full implications in the measurement and invention of built forms it will be necessary to use the techniques that have been developed in other disciplines and which are capable of describing highly complicated situations with greater certainty and clarity. Beyond this it is necessary for such techniques to demonstrate the relationships between different factors and the way that they affect each other. And finally it is necessary to be able to assess more accurately the effect of change. By means of such techniques it becomes possible to represent aspects of the world around us in highly complex models within which the relationships of all the measurable elements can be seen.

Econometrics, the 'mathematical movement' in economics, is only one of a number of developments in many spheres of thought in which an effort is being made to find a structuring theory of organization around which growth and change can develop, and to make this precise by mathematical expression. It has happened within the last half century and mainly since the war. The change has been profound. The description of this change by Stone (1966) with its emerging possibility of integration between studies which are now specialised and separate, has its parallel in urban geography (Robson 1969) and its various extensions.

The use of a mathematical formulation in the attempt to describe the ordering structure that lies behind a building or a city can be seen as another aspect of that texture of relationships through which we try to understand the complexity of an urban area. In developing such a study, the specialised division between architecture and planning has no particular significance and the developing language would take a form which others, notably the geographers and economists, are already using.

3. *Elementary models of built forms*

LIONEL MARCH

Much of our knowledge in architectural design is vaguely and qualitatively stated. Statements prevail such as 'high tower blocks make good use of land', or 'cube-like buildings are cheaper to build and run'. Design lore abounds in rules of this kind. Their authority rests more on intuitive conviction than on theoretical demonstration. Yet, as Edward Kasner and James Newman emphasise throughout their classic *Mathematics and the Imagination*, 'our *intuitive* notions about space almost invariably lead us astray'.

One problem which graphically reveals this point is quoted by Kasner and Newman (1949):

In a room 30 feet long, 12 feet wide, and 12 feet high, there is a spider in the centre of one of the smaller walls, 1 foot from the ceiling; and there is a fly in the middle of the opposite wall, 1 foot from the floor. The spider has designs on the fly. What is the shortest possible route along which the spider may crawl to reach his prey? If he crawls straight down the wall, then in a straight line along the floor, and then straight up the other wall, or follows a similar route along the ceiling, the distance is 42 feet. Surely it is impossible to imagine a shorter route! However, by cutting a sheet of paper, which when properly folded, will make a model of the room [see Fig. 3.1], and then by joining the points representing the spider and the fly by a straight line, a geodesic is obtained. The length of the geodesic is only 40 feet, in other words, 2 feet shorter than the 'obvious' route of following straight lines.

There are several ways of cutting the sheet of paper, and accordingly, there are several possible routes, but that of 40 feet is the shortest; and remarkably enough, as may be seen from cut *d* [in Fig. 3.1], this route requires the spider to pass over five of the six sides of the room.

This illustration is an adaptation of one of Sam Lloyd's famous teasers. It is solved by firstly sifting out the elements and relationships essential to the problem (there is no need to be concerned, for example, that the spider is hungry, or that the thing on the far wall is a fly, or that the wall is in fact wall) and then by secondly setting up a model of the structural facts (in this case a material analogue model (see below Chapter 7), which, thirdly, is

55

sufficiently representative yet manipulable to allow the problem to be simplified in order to proceed to a solution (our paper box may be easily thought of as a room, but unlike a real room it can be unfolded and spread out flat in such a way that the original three-dimensional problem is reduced to a somewhat trivial two-dimensional one).

Buildings are complex artifacts. Most are unique. Generalisations about buildings are not easy to make. It may help to look instead at *built forms* which are not buildings. Built forms are mathematical or quasi-mathematical models (Chapter 7) which are used to represent buildings to

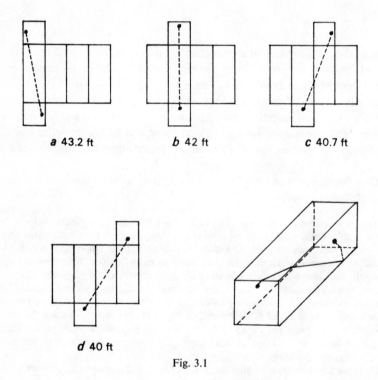

a 43.2 ft   *b* 42 ft   *c* 40.7 ft

d 40 ft

Fig. 3.1

any required degree of complexity in theoretical studies. Built forms, then, are designed and defined specifically for each study. Usually a study starts with somewhat hazy notions. To proceed, it is necessary to make some assumptions both to simplify the problem and to make it amenable to mathematical treatment. Appropriate variables must be selected and relationships established between them. And after some fact or other has been demonstrated, it is necessary to reconsider the original assumptions with a view to developing the model further to give a truer picture.

Many problems in theoretical architectural studies will find suitable expression in terms of the 'new' mathematics. Some indications of the relevance of group theory, set theory, graph theory, of transformation geometries and so on are to be found in a recent book, *The Geometry of Environment* (March and Steadman 1971). Here, however, in this skirmish into mathematical modelling of the built form the mathematics are confined to more traditional methods. In this way it is hoped that older readers who have little background in the new mathematics will be able to follow the mathematical arguments and abstractions in the examples. Basically, the kind of advanced level mathematics covered in The School Mathematics Project: *Calculus and Elementary Functions* (Montgomery and Jones 1970) will be used.

In this latter book, the authors specify a general drill to be used when faced with a problem rather vaguely stated:

(i) Make initial assumptions to simplify the problem, and make it mathematically manageable.

(ii) Choose a dependent variable which will give an answer to the problem. (Often this is clearly implied in the problem itself.)

(iii) Make a list of the variables on which it depends.

(iv) Investigate the connections between these variables. (Often – almost always at this stage – we will find that having chosen one of them, we can express all others in terms of it. If this is not so, it may be because our original assumptions were not sweeping enough; or because we have failed to make use of some of the conditions of the problem. Such a condition might state, for instance, that the volume of a variable solid is constant. In this case, give a name to the constant, and express the condition as a mathematical formula.)

(v) Choose an independent variable, express all other variables in terms of it, so that the original dependent variable (see (ii)) can be expressed as a function of it. (Make sure that the expression defining this function contains none but the independent variable and constants.)

(vi) Note the domain of the function, from the conditions of the problem.

(vii) Analyse the function, sketching its graph, and noting conclusions.

(viii) Return to the original assumptions and see whether they can be improved to give a more realistic picture of the problem.

All this may be described as giving a problem only vaguely stated a decent mathematical clothing. It has become common to describe it all – or the outcome of the initial stages – as a 'mathematical model'.

This procedure is best illustrated by a number of examples.

Example one

What shape should a building be to reduce heat losses?

Like many problems coming from outside into the mathematician's province, it is not all that obvious what is being asked for. As Montgomery and Jones (1970) point out, our immediate instinct will be to reply with a number of facile 'it depends-ons': 'It depends on the use of the building; on the method of construction used; on orientation or the local climatic conditions.' And there will always be someone who will insist that this is the wrong question to ask anyway: shouldn't we be finding out what kinds of buildings people think they feel comfortable in.

But these instincts should not immediately be succumbed to if the more modest goal of formulating a theory about a vaguely stated problem is adhered to – otherwise it becomes progressively necessary to take on the whole world without having achieved even one small but sure step forward in our understanding. The essential nature of the problem is clear enough and so is the context. It could be argued that since the sphere is a volume with a minimal surface area, spherical buildings would be a good idea, or if that is not practical why not a hemispherical building, or a cylindrical one? But most buildings, for many practical reasons, are rectangular in shape and therefore it can be assumed that the building chosen will be a simple rectangular block, that its volume will be constant (which is to say that if the floor to ceiling height is constant within the range of buildings considered, then all will have the same floor area), and that those proportions of length, width and height are being sought which minimise heat losses.

These assumptions define the nature of the problem. Buildings, however, even simple rectangular ones, have complicated fenestration patterns, upstands and tank houses on the roof, and all kinds of unique design features. Agreed it is these particular features that make each building interesting and which call our attention as we pass by in the street, but these curious irregularities must not confuse the search. For the purposes of this exercise a model is constructed of a building – a built form – which is a perfect rectangular parallelepiped each surface of which is considered to be made of a homogeneous material with a given thermal transmittance value. It is assumed for the time being that all other factors are negligible compared to the heat losses through these idealised surfaces. These initial assumptions at least have the merit that the mathematics they give rise to are manageable. Thus,

(i) The building is assumed to be a simple rectangular parallelepiped with homogeneous surfaces and constant volume.

(ii) The dependent variable chosen is some measure of heat loss which may be called q units.

(iii) Heat loss is dependent on the surface area and thermal transmittance of each face of the built form. The surface areas of the faces are dependent on the dimensions x, y, z of the block and the thermal transmittance of each face (which for the moment can be assumed to be equal) for the walls and roof, but zero (no heat loss) for the ground floor. Let the transmittance be U units (Fig. 3.2).

(iv) An equation connecting these variables can now be written:

$$q = \{2(x+y)z+xy\}U \tag{1}$$

since there are two faces of area xz, two of area yz, and just the roof area xy all with thermal conductance of U. Further, however, it is known that xyz, the volume of the built form, is constant. Let V be the volume, and then

$$V = xyz. \tag{2}$$

(v) In this example the choice cannot be limited to just *one* independent variable. There are two equations with three unknowns and no more

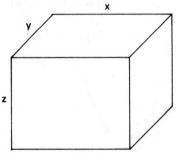

Fig. 3.2

can be done than to eliminate one of them. Let z be expressed in terms of x and y. Then

$$q = \left\{2\left(\frac{1}{x}+\frac{1}{y}\right)V+xy\right\}U. \tag{3}$$

This is as much as can be done.

(vi) It is clear that x and y are positive quantities; but there are no other restrictions on their size. If x is very large, y will be correspondingly small for any given value of z and so on.

(vii) In the usual way, to find the minimum values of q the previous equation is differentiated in (v) with respect to both x and y, setting the results equal to zero. Thus,

$$\frac{\partial q}{\partial x} = \left(-\frac{2V}{x^2}+y\right)U = 0 \tag{4a}$$

$$\frac{\partial q}{\partial y} = \left(-\frac{2V}{y^2}+x\right)U = 0, \tag{4b}$$

whence $x = y$ at the stationary value. If the curve is plotted (Fig. 3.3)

$$q = \left(\frac{4V}{x} + x^2\right)U, \tag{5}$$

by substituting x for y in Equation 3 above, the stationary value is indeed a minimum value. And so a minimum has been obtained in which

$$x^3 = y^3 = 2V \tag{6}$$

as well as where the constraint $V = xyz$ holds. Hence, for minimum heat losses

$$x = y = 2z = (2V)^{1/3}. \tag{7}$$

From this it is seen that, to reduce heat losses, in a building whose exposed surfaces have equal thermal transmittance and whose floor conducts no heat, the best shape is square in plan ($x = y$) with a height just half ($z = x/2 = y/2$) the length of its sides: that is to say, a half-cube.

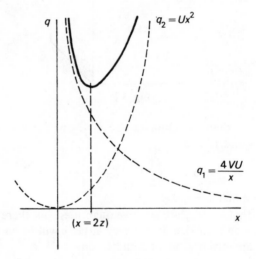

Fig. 3.3

(viii) Returning to our original assumptions. One assumption seems particularly arbitrary. It concerns the transmittance values. For one thing, ground floors do lose heat. For another, different walls will have different average transmittance values, not only because they may be constructed differently with varying proportions of fenestration, but also because of their exposure and orientation which gives rise to particular external surface transmittance values (Fairweather and Sliwa 1969). The roof, of course, can be expected to be different from the walls.

The model can be generalised and the notation can be modified for more concise expression. Call x, x_1, and y, x_2, and z, x_3. In this way a *typical* dimension may be referred to as x_i, where i may be either 1, or 2, or 3. Now let (i, j, k) be a permutation of $(1, 2, 3)$, so that when specific mention of the jth and kth dimensions is made, it is clear that the ith is omitted: for example, 2 and 3, not 1; or 1 and 3, not 2. Let the transmittances of the two walls defined by the jth and kth dimensions be U_{i1} and U_{i2} respectively, and let U_i be the mean value of these two transmittance values so that

$$U_i = \tfrac{1}{2}(U_{i1} + U_{i2}). \tag{8}$$

The relationship expressed by Equation 1 above may now be generalised to read

$$\begin{aligned} q &= (U_{11} + U_{12})x_2x_3 + x_1(U_{21} + U_{22})x_3 + x_1x_2(U_{31} + U_{32}) \\ &= 2(U_1x_2x_3 + x_1U_2x_3 + x_1x_2U_3) \\ &= 2V\left(\frac{U_1}{x_1} + \frac{U_2}{x_2} + \frac{U_3}{x_3}\right), \quad \text{since } V = x_1x_2x_3. \end{aligned}$$

This may be written more compactly

$$q = 2V\Sigma_i\frac{U_i}{x_i}, \quad \text{for } i = 1,2,3. \tag{9}$$

The most obvious thing to notice about this equation is that, unlike its predecessor (Equation 1), it is symmetrical with respect to all the x_is (that is, x, y and z in the former notation).

For the mathematician this is always a satisfying state of affairs: a kind of democracy of variables. Previously (Equation 3) z was picked out as the variable to be expressed in terms of x and y, and this could be done again, but for the sake of symmetry use will be made instead of an elegant way of finding the minimum value of q first proposed by Lagrange.† To find

† Count Joseph Louis Lagrange (1736–1813) the eminent French mathematician, was, in Napoleon's words, 'la haute pyramide des sciences mathématiques'. According to Miss A. M. Clerke his 'treatises are not only storehouses of ingenious methods, but models of symmetrical form. The clearness, elegance, and originality of his mode of presentation give lucidity to what is obscure, novelty to what is familiar, and simplicity to what is abstruse. His genius was one of generalisation and abstraction; and the aspirations of the time towards unity and perfection received, by his serene labours, an embodiment denied to them in the troubled world of politics'. *Encyclopaedia Britannica*, 9th ed. (1889) Edinburgh.

the stationary values of a function like $q(x_1, x_2, x_3)$, subject to a constraint of the form $p(x_1, x_2, x_3) = 0$, a new function is constructed

$$\Phi = q + \lambda p, \tag{10}$$

where λ is called a Lagrangian multiplier. The necessary condition for a maximum or minimum is then that

$$\frac{\partial \Phi}{\partial x_1} = \frac{\partial \Phi}{\partial x_2} = \frac{\partial \Phi}{\partial x_3} = 0,$$

or again more compactly the *three* equations (one for each value of i)

$$\frac{\partial \Phi}{\partial x_i} = 0. \tag{11}$$

In the case of our example

$$q(x_1, x_2, x_3) = 2V \, \Sigma_i \frac{U_i}{x_i}$$

subject to the volume constraint given by the function

$$p(x_1, x_2, x_3) = V - x_1 x_2 x_3 = 0,$$

or to preserve generality,

$$p = V - x_i x_j x_k, \quad (i, j, k) = (1, 2, 3). \tag{12}$$

Following Lagrange's method a new function is constructed

$$\Phi = 2V \, \Sigma_i \frac{U_i}{x_i} + \lambda (V - x_i x_j x_k). \tag{13}$$

The necessary condition for a maximum or minimum is then given by the *three* equations

$$\frac{\partial \Phi}{\partial x_i} = -2V \frac{U_i}{x_i^2} - \lambda x_j x_k$$

$$= \frac{-V}{x_i^2} (2U_i - \lambda x_i), \quad \text{since } x_j x_k = \frac{V}{x_i},$$

$$= 0. \tag{14}$$

From this the general statement is derived that the *minimum* heat loss occurs when the dimensions of the block are proportional to the mean transmittance values:

$$x_1 : x_2 : x_3 :: U_1 : U_2 : U_3 \tag{15}$$

In this form, the condition is seen to be analogous to Lamy's Theorem, first stated in the seventeenth century, concerning the equilibrium of three forces acting at a point:

If three forces acting at a point are in equilibrium, each force is proportional to the sine of the angle contained between the directions of the other two.

That is to say (Fig. 3.4)

$$X_1 : X_2 : X_3 :: \sin \theta_1 : \sin \theta_2 : \sin \theta_3.$$

This means that three forces in equilibrium may be represented by the sides of a triangle (or that the diagonal of a parallelogram represents the resolution of two forces proportional to its sides). Such a simple theorem continues to guide engineering practice despite the fact that the 'model' point may be a rivetted joint, the forces may act not in two 'model' lines

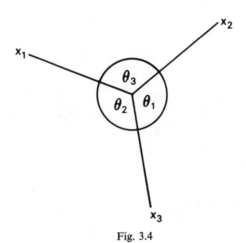

Fig. 3.4

but through two rolled steel joists, and the resultant force may act through a concrete abutment. Furthermore, whatever complicated allowances have to be made to adjust theory to practice, Lamy's Theorem has the overriding merit of being memorable and providing a conceptual context within which forces in engineering structures can be thought about sensibly. No one goes about thinking that three forces at a point will be in equilibrium if they can be represented by the sides of an *equilateral* triangle. Yet in building studies authoritative statements are continually found to the effect that a *cube* is the best form of building to reduce heat losses! If the forces are equal, yes an equilateral triangle: if the transmittance values of all six faces are equal, yes a cube. But how often is that the case?

A general and simple theorem may now be stated:

THEOREM 1. *A simple rectangular block of given volume loses the least amount of heat if the dimension of each edge is proportional to the mean thermal transmittance value of the faces defined by the other two edges.*

The fact that no general quantitative statements of this kind about built forms exist suggests how far away is a science of architectural form (artificial morphology?).

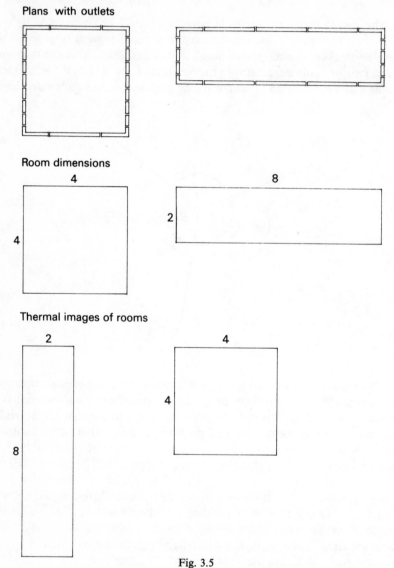

Fig. 3.5

Returning once again to our example, the original assumptions need to be re-examined to see whether they can be improved to give a more realistic picture of the problem. But there is something else that can be done which may increase an appreciation of the intrinsic structure of the problem lost in the analytical approach adopted in solving it. The solution is simple and – as often happens – once its form is seen a very direct way of arriving at it becomes apparent without all the paraphernalia of analytical calculus.

The rectangular parallelepiped with the minimum surface area is a cube. However, if opposite pairs of faces have different mean transmittance values the form which will minimise heat losses – not surface area – is the built form whose *thermal image is a cube* such that heat losses through all three pairs of opposite faces are equal. In our notation above this requires that

$$U_1 x_2 x_3 = x_1 U_2 x_3 = x_1 x_2 U_3, \tag{16}$$

whence the rule (Equation 15):

$$x_1 : x_2 : x_3 :: U_1 : U_2 : U_3.$$

A 'two-dimensional' example will make this argument clear (Fig. 3.5). Consider a rectangular room with a floor and a ceiling which transmit no heat, and walls which transmit heat only through specific outlets, the number of outlets per unit length of wall is thus proportional to the thermal transmittance value of the wall. One room is square, 4×4, and has the minimum overall wall length, 16, for its area, 16. The other room is four times as long as it is wide, 8×2, and has a wall length of 20 for the same area, 16. However, the square room has 20 outlets, 4 placed on one pair of opposite walls (low thermal transmission), and 16 on the adjacent pair of opposite walls (high thermal transmission). The heat loss from this room – proportional to the number of outlets – is 20 units. The long rectangular room has the same number of outlets per unit length as the square room along its corresponding walls. Thus the long walls have $8 \times (2/4) = 4$ outlets each, the short walls $2 \times (8/4) = 4$ outlets each. Altogether the heat loss is 16 which is less than that of the square room. Now if the thermal images are drawn of these rooms, using the number of outlets per wall as the measure (the total flow of heat through each surface) and not the length of the wall (not the surface area of each face), the pictures are exactly reversed. The 4×4 room has an 8×2 thermal image, and the 8×2 room has a 4×4 square, thermal image.† In three dimensions, the thermal image is cubic if heat losses are minimised.

It is thus misleading to suggest that cubic forms, because they minimise surface area with respect to volume, have any particular merits in terms of

† This, of course, is an example of mapping. See March and Steadman (1971), ch. 1.

heat losses and hence running costs,† or that measures of compactness which compare ratios of surface areas to volumes have any significant relation to thermal performance.‡ If they have, it is pure chance and probably the fortuitous outcome of a combination of factors including the somewhat conflicting tendencies of construction costs and maintenance.

A. C. Hardy and P. E. O'Sullivan (1967) have argued for deeper office buildings which rely on artificial lighting and air-conditioning. As F. D. Holister (1967) has pointed out there are many good reasons to support this view. But what shape of block, according to our model, and on thermal considerations alone, might deep-planning lead to? It can be shown, if one of the dimensions in the general example above is fixed, $x_1 = X_1$ say, that

$$\frac{x_2}{U_2} = \frac{x_3}{U_3} = \left(\frac{V}{X_1 U_2 U_3}\right)^{\frac{1}{3}} \qquad (17)$$

for minimum heat loss. Hardy (1966) gives the following values of X_1: for daylighting, a building width of 14 m; for permanent supplementary artificial lighting of interiors (PSALI), a width of 22.5 m; and for permanent artificial lighting (PAL), a width of 27 m. For simplicity the first can be called, 4 units wide; the second, 6; and the third, 8. Consider now a building whose volume is 288 cubic units, with $U_2 = 2$ and $U_3 = 1$ in the appropriate units. Especially note that the mean thermal transmittance of the faces of the building at right-angles to the depth X_1, that is to say the principal window walls in an office block, has no effect on the optimum shape of the built form.

(a) With daylighting:

$$X_1 = 4; x_2 = 2\left(\frac{288}{4.1.2}\right)^{\frac{1}{3}} = 12; x_3 = \frac{x_2}{2} = 6.$$

(b) With PSALI:

$$X_1 = 6; x_2 = 2\left(\frac{288}{6.1.2}\right)^{\frac{1}{3}} \doteq 10; \S\ x_3 = \frac{x_2}{2} = 5.$$

(c) With PAL:

$$X_1 = 8; x_2 = 2\left(\frac{288}{8.1.2}\right)^{\frac{1}{3}} \doteq 8; \S\ x_3 = \frac{x_2}{2} = 4.$$

Fig. 3.6 shows the shapes that the built forms take to minimise heat

† See, for example Hardy (1966).
‡ For such a measure see T. A. Markus *et al.* (1970).
§ To nearest whole number for the purposes of illustration.

losses. The clear trend – as can be seen algebraically from Equation 17 above – is for both length (x_2) and height (x_3) to decrease with increasing width (X_1). This is true whatever constant values of U_2, U_3 and V are chosen for the comparative exercise. However, while particular values of these independent variables might lead to buildings which use artificial lighting being 'more cube like' (Hardy 1966), in *general* there is no justification for this statement. Thus, within the limitations of our model, the only general remark that can be made is that blocks of similar construction† would need, as planning became deeper, to be both lower and shorter if heat losses were to be minimised.

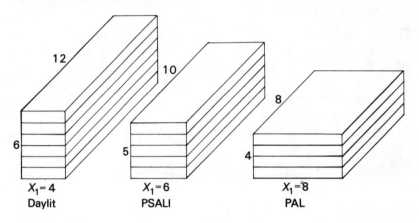

Fig. 3.6

Example two

What shape should a building be to reduce its cost?

Once again some crude simplifications must initially be made with only rectangular, block-like forms considered. And, to start with, the discussion will be limited merely to the cost of the external envelope, including the groundworks, of the form. Suppose that consideration includes a range of shapes to accommodate the same floor area, which for a given floor-to-ceiling height will produce a constant volume. The discussion will continue, as above, to treat height as a continuous variable although in practice it will be step-like depending on the number of floors.

The argument for costs follows the same lines' as that for thermal performance. Let the dimensions of the block be x_1, x_2 and x_3 as before. Let C_1 be the mean cost, $\frac{1}{2}(C_{11} + C_{12})$, of the two faces with dimensions x_2 and

† Excepting the principal walls whose manner of construction does not affect shape, but does modify thermal performance.

x_3 respectively, and let C_2 and C_3† be similarly defined. Then the least cost solution is given by

$$x_1:x_2:x_3::C_1:C_2:C_3 \tag{18}$$

with each x_i given by

$$x_i = C_i\left(\frac{V}{C_1C_2C_3}\right)^{1/3}. \tag{19}$$

Thus another theorem may be stated:

THEOREM 2. *The envelope of a simple rectangular block of given volume has a minimum cost when the dimension of each edge is proportional to the mean cost of the faces defined by the other two.*

The form of this theorem is the same as Theorem 1 above. Within the limiting simplifications of our assumptions it implies that buildings which are cube-like or which minimise surface area are not in general less costly to build. It is the *cost image* which matters, not the physical form of the building; and it is when the *cost image is a cube* that costs are least. An example will make this clear. Consider the four cost situations given (Table A) for a block with a volume of 216 units.

TABLE A

Situation	Ratio of costs C_1: C_2: C_3	Note
(a)	1:3 :9	Extremely expensive foundations, or high land costs
(b)	1:1.5 :2.25	
(c)	1:1 :1	
(d)	1:0.5 :0.25	Low cost roofing and ground slab, or low land costs

TABLE B

Situation	Dimensions of block x_1	x_2	x_3	Total surface area	Surface area less ground slab area
(a)	2	6	18	312	300
(b)	4	6	9	228	204
(c)	6	6	6	216	180
(d)	12	6	3	252	180

† C_3 includes C_{13}, the cost of the foundations and slab *less* the cost of the groundfloor at the same rate as the suspended floors, and C_{12}, the cost of the roof *less* the cost of the ceiling.

Using formula 19 the dimensions in Table B are derived for the least cost solution in each situation (Fig. 3.7):

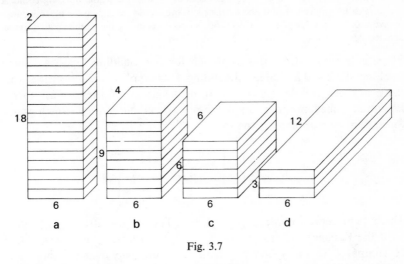

Fig. 3.7

There are a number of points that might be made about this example. Firstly, the possibility has been introduced that the form of the building may be influenced by land costs. The discussion can return later to the study of the way in which different built forms 'use' land. Secondly, it should be noted that, although in the context of this particular example the cubic form (c) does have the least surface area, there are two forms which have the least exposed surface areas. One of these is the cubic form, but the other is the squatter, spread-out form (d). If maintenance costs were, for example, directly proportional to the exposed surface area then as in Example 1 it would be clear that the half-cube is the best form to minimise these costs. Thirdly, it is important to remember that only the 'envelope' costs have been considered and not costs which arise because of the form, for example, the provision of lifts and staircases in tall buildings and air-conditioning in deep buildings. Fourthly, the 'envelope' costs are part of the capital cost of a building which in itself may be a fraction of the total cost of the building in use (Stone 1967). In fact, the cost of the envelope may not account for much more than about 10% of the capital cost.

To investigate the relationship between cost and form more deeply it will be necessary to construct more complex models as suggested by Bullock, Dickens and Steadman (1968):

If... we could cost the *range of buildings* obtained by a systematic transformation of the overall form..., it would be possible, in theory, to plot the cost for all different possible variations of the factors that have been isolated. If carried out on a sufficiently large number of examples, our understanding of which elements are most significant from the cost point of view would be considerably enlarged. In the first place changes in the factors controlling the cost of individual elements and of the whole building could be systematically explored. And in the second place this would make possible more accurate *forecasts* of the results of design decision, without requiring the architect to produce detailed designs for every variation. (See also Harper 1968.)

These authors illustrate this approach for two building types, a science teaching block and a residential building. Our simple model illustrates what these authors call 'a systematic transformation of the overall form'. Essentially, they propose a volume-preserving, three-way stretch transformation, or mapping, of the form

$$M: \begin{bmatrix} x_1 \\ x_2 \\ x_3 \end{bmatrix} \rightarrow \begin{bmatrix} a_{11} & \cdot & \cdot \\ \cdot & a_{22} & \cdot \\ \cdot & \cdot & a_{33} \end{bmatrix} \begin{bmatrix} x_1 \\ x_2 \\ x_3 \end{bmatrix}. \tag{20}$$

where, to preserve volume, $a_{11}a_{22}a_{33} = 1$. The scalar matrix $[a_{ij}\delta_{ij}]$, where δ_{ij} is the Kronecker delta so that $\delta_{ij} = 0$, $i \neq j$, and $\delta_{ij} = 1$, $i = j$, may be compared to the symmetric *tensor* of rank two in a principal axis transformation. With this in mind we may think of the built form experiencing orthogonal *strain* under orthogonal *stress* represented by such a tensor.† They then compare relative costs of the elements, in each transformation, per unit area of floor space. Now, if in our model the storey height is h the simple expression results:

$$V = Ah, \tag{21}$$

where A is the total floor area of the form. However, $V = x_i x_j x_k$ and the cost of each opposite pair of faces of the block is given by $C_i x_j x_k$, so that if K_i is the cost of these faces per unit area of floorspace the following may be expressed:

$$
\begin{aligned}
K_i &= \frac{C_i x_j x_k}{A} \\
&= \frac{C_i x_j x_k h}{x_i x_j x_k} \\
&= \frac{C_i h}{x_i}.
\end{aligned}
\tag{22}
$$

† This mechanistic analogy is related, as Philip Steadman has reminded me, to the work of the biologist D'Arcy Thompson (1917) which in its turn made use of H. de Parsons (1888) and Selig Hecht (1912). This early work was mainly descriptive with little explanatory power, but recently Robert Rosen has indicated a more functional approach (1967).

From this our previous condition (Equation 18) for the optimum (least) cost of envelope reduces to the simple rule:

$$K_1 = K_2 = K_3 \tag{23}$$

and

THEOREM 3. *The envelope of a simple rectangular block of given volume and floor area has least cost when the costs per unit area of floorspace of the pairs of opposite faces are equal.*

In the case of the study by Bullock, Dickens and Steadman of a university teaching block, they found

rather surprisingly perhaps, from this limited examination that other factors being equal, the *form* of the building – even allowing for the necessary variations in gross area – does not as such have an important effect on *capital* cost: although it might considerably affect the running costs. The cost of heating a tall thin building, or the costs of ventilation and lighting in a deep section building might be very significant. The variation in the cost of the particular elements that we have studied – the structure and the lifts – has more effect in some cases on the total capital cost than changes in the building form.†

On that note our naive study of built form and cost must be left and our attention turned to another problem.

Example three

How should buildings be laid out in order to make good use of land?

Again the question is vague and raises many other questions. In 1930, at the third meeting of Les Congrès Internationaux D'Architecture Moderne in Brussels, Walter Gropius addressed himself to this problem as it related to housing in a paper entitled 'Flach-, mittel- oder hochbau?'.‡ In this paper, among other things, Gropius attempted to demonstrate certain relationships existing between building height, open space, sunlighting, and orientation. He developed Heiligenthal's rule-of-thumb§ that the dis-

---

† Bullock, Dickens & Steadman (1968), p. 169. They go on to demonstrate that the most significant factor is a variation in floor area and, as this is determined by the way in which the building is used, that a study of 'activity patterns' would seem worthwhile in order to develop a more comprehensive model. Such a model, of course, can no longer be manipulated by ordinary mathematical methods and requires automatic computation.

‡ Walter Gropius (1931), also translated as 'Houses, walk-ups or apartment blocks' in Gropius (1956). This paper should be compared with George B. Ford's contemporary Harvard City Planning Study (1931).

§ This rule (according to Kenneth Frampton, 'Notes on Soviet urbanism, 1917–32', in Lewis 1968) was 'categorically applied in all finally approved town plans during the period 1930–32' in the Soviet Union. For recent Soviet work on this problem see the review by V. G. Davidovich, 'Interdependence between height of buildings, density of population and size of towns and settlements' in Davidovich 1968.

tance between parallel blocks must be one-and-a-half times the building height in the case of blocks orientated north–south and two-and-a-half times in the case of blocks orientated east–west – a rule which favoured the north–south orientation in regard to efficiency of land use. On this kind of principle Gropius proposed the following rules for parallel blocks with north–south orientation having from two to ten storeys on a given site:

1. Assuming a site of given size and a given angle of sunlighting incidence (30°), i.e. a given illumination condition, the number of beds increases with the number of stories.
2. Assuming a given angle of sunlight incidence and distributing a given number of beds (15 sq. m or 161 sq. ft of area of bed) into parallel apartment blocks with varying numbers of stories, the size of the required site decreases with increasing number of stories.
3. Assuming a building site of given size and a given number of beds and varying the number of stories, the angle of sunlight incidence decreases with increasing number floors, i.e., the conditions of illumination improve with increased height. (Gropius 1956.)

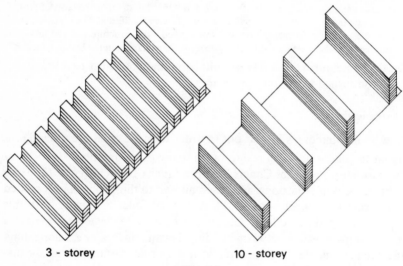

3 - storey   10 - storey

Fig. 3.8

These rules were used to counter the contemporary legislation which imposed 'limits on building height instead of dwelling area of building volume' thus depriving 'the public of these obvious economic and hygienic advantages'.

The diagrams which Gropius used to illustrate his assertions (Fig. 3.8) became powerful images of a future and better environment.† In the late

† However, Le Corbusier was not convinced: 'When in the period before Hitler, the Germans wanted to build according to the laws of the sun...they set up an order which was systematically sterile: corridors, tedious, monotonous parallelism, and silhouettes against the sky that were poverty stricken and unbalanced' (Le Corbusier 1939).

thirties progressive planning schemes were being built on these principles, while, following the Second World War, many official reconstruction schemes throughout Europe were designed this way in accordance with new legislation framed around Gropius' rules, or variations of these. In England, a paper by H. E. Beckett (1942), an illuminating engineer, developed Gropius' work and was finally published in 1942 at a time when fundamental rethinking was going on in relation to post-war planning policies.†

As a first step it is necessary to formalise Gropius' model. The dependent variables are, in turn, the number of beds, the size of the site and the angle of sunlight. We specify the following:

y_1 = number of beds,
y_2 = area of site,
y_3 = tangent of the angle of sunlight.

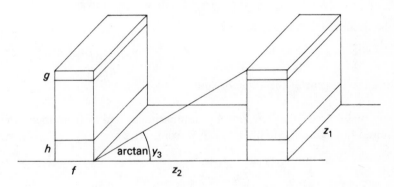

Fig. 3.9

In each rule *one* of these variables is the dependent variable, while the others are given.

The remaining variables are (Fig. 3.9):

z_1 = length of block,
z_2 = space between blocks,
f = width of block (assumed to be given),
h = storey height (assumed to be given),
g = parapet height (assumed to be given),
β = number of beds per unit floor area (assumed to be a given ratio),

† This paper is referred to in W. Allen and D. Crompton (1947), which set out the general principles upon which post-war legislation and planning practice in England and Wales was based.

and the principal *independent* variable is

$$x = \text{number of storeys},$$

which can be assumed to be continuous, although only integral values have any architectural meaning in practice. Each of Gropius' rules may then be derived from the behaviour of a function:

$$y_i = \phi_i(x, y_j, y_k) = \phi_i(x), \tag{24}$$

where the variable y_i is found in terms of a function of x, the number of storeys, and given values of the other two variables y_j and y_k. The rules simply state whether y_i increases or decreases with increasing values of x. The first derivative dy_i/dx or $\phi'_i(x)$ can be inspected to find out which relationship holds, if any at all.

Our task now in 'building' this Heiligenthal–Gropius model is to establish the functions ϕ_i. By definition, and from the geometry of the forms, three equations relating the variables may be written down:

the number of beds is given by $\qquad\qquad y_1 = \beta f z_1 x, \tag{25}$

the site area is given by $\qquad\qquad\qquad y_2 = z_1(f + z_2), \tag{26}$

and the tangent of the angle of sunlight by $\quad y_3 = \dfrac{hx + g}{z_2}. \tag{27}$

Using these three equations, and by eliminating z_1 and z_2 from them, the required functions ϕ_i are obtained. For example,

$$y_1 = \beta f z_1 x,$$

but from (27) $\qquad\qquad z_2 = \dfrac{hx + g}{y_3},$

and from (26) $\qquad\qquad z_1 = \dfrac{y_2}{f + z_2}$

$$= \dfrac{y_2 y_3}{hx + f y_3 + g}.$$

Hence, $\qquad\qquad y_1 = \beta f y_2 y_3 \dfrac{x}{hx + f y_3 + g},$

or by multiplying up,

$$(hy_1 - \beta f y_2 y_3)x + f y_1 y_3 + g y_1 = 0. \tag{28}$$

From this equation the three required functions are derived, namely,

$$y_1 = \phi_1(x) = \beta f y_2 y_3 \cdot \dfrac{x}{hx + f y_3 + g}, \text{ as above,} \tag{29}$$

$$y_2 = \phi_2(x) = \frac{y_1}{\beta f y_3} \cdot \frac{hx + f y_3 + g}{x}, \qquad (30)$$

and

$$y_3 = \phi_3(x) = \frac{y_1}{f} \frac{hx + g}{\beta y_2 x - y_1}. \qquad (31)$$

The first derivatives are obtained in the usual way,[†]

$$\frac{dy_1}{dx} = \phi'_1(x) = \beta f y_2 y_3 \cdot \frac{f y_3 + g}{(hx + f y_3 + g)^2} > 0, \qquad (32)$$

$$\frac{dy_2}{dx} = \phi'_2(x) = \frac{-y_1}{\beta f y_3} \cdot \frac{f y_3 + g}{x^2} \qquad < 0, \qquad (33)$$

$$\frac{dy_3}{dx} = \phi'_3(x) = \frac{-y_1}{f} \cdot \frac{hy_1 + \beta g y_2}{(\beta y_2 x - y_1)^2} \qquad < 0. \qquad (34)$$

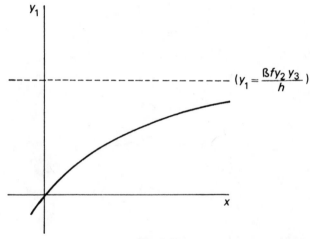

Fig. 3.10

Equations 32, 33 and 34 are true for all the positive values of the variables that are our concern. The first confirms that bed spaces *increase* with the number of storeys, the second that the site area required *decreases* with increasing storeys, and the last that the angle of obstruction *lessens* as the blocks increase in height (always assuming that in each case the other 'variables' are held constant).

Each function may be plotted graphically (Figs. 3.10, 3.11, 3.12). In fact each function may be represented by a hyperbola.[‡] (Only that part of the

[†] See any standard work on differential calculus, or Montgomery and Jones (1970), p. 132.

[‡] See any standard work on analytical geometry.

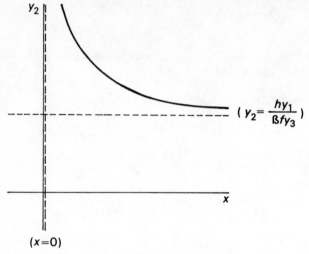

$$\left(y_2 = \frac{hy_1}{\beta f y_3} \right)$$

$(x=0)$

Fig. 3.11

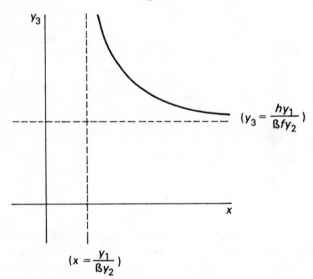

$$\left(y_3 = \frac{hy_1}{\beta f y_2} \right)$$

$$\left(x = \frac{y_1}{\beta y_2} \right)$$

Fig. 3.12

curve which lies within the positive quadrant, of course, is of interest.) The horizontal asymptotes set limits on extreme values of the y_i as x becomes very large. They are then related by the equation

$$hy_1 - \beta f y_2 y_3 = 0, \quad \text{for } x \to \infty. \tag{35}$$

This may surprise the unwary. It means for example that, with this form of development, there is an upper limit on density no matter how high the project is built. To take a specific example: if the bed space ratio is one bed to 15 sq. m of the gross floor area then $\beta = \frac{1}{15}$, if the block width is 9 m then $f = 9$, if the storey height is 3 m then $h = 3$, and if the angle of obstruction has a tangent value of $\frac{2}{3}$ then $y_3 = \frac{2}{3}$ (Heiligenthal's rule of thumb for north–south orientation). The density of bed spaces per *hectare*† is then given by

$$\frac{y_1}{y_2} = \frac{\beta f y_3}{h} \cdot 10{,}000 \tag{36}$$

$$= \frac{9.2}{15.3.3} \cdot 10{,}000$$

$$= 1333.$$

Thus with these values (close to Gropius' recommendations for 'hygienic' dwellings) the maximum possible density that could be achieved *no matter how high we built* is 1333 bed spaces per hectare, or about 533 persons per acre. Higher densities than these, using parallel blocks, could be achieved only if less space were allocated to every bed, or if the building depth were increased (perhaps windowless rooms as the old railroad tenements in New York used to have‡), or by diminishing the amount of light reaching the facade of the building, or by reducing ceiling heights. Each of these measured would be detrimental to housing quality and below acceptable standards.§

Another point to notice is that although the number of bed spaces does increase with building height (Fig. 3.10), the *rate* at which it does so *decreases* quite rapidly. This is to be seen from the second derivative

$$\phi_1''(x) = \frac{-\beta f h y_2 y_3 (f y_3 + g)}{(hx + f y_3 + g)^3} < 0, \tag{37}$$

which demonstrates that the order of the rate of increase of density with height changes (decreases) inversely with the cube of x. By far the greatest gains in density are to be made with the lower number of storeys, from one to six, say. The returns beyond this diminish very rapidly indeed. For

† 1 hectare equals 10,000 sq. m or 2.47 acres: roughly, 4 hectares equal 10 acres.
‡ These tenements were approximately 22.5 m deep with eight out of twelve of the rooms on each floor with no windows. In 1894, New York's worst ward had a density of 986.4 persons per acre. See Gray (1947).
§ Note that with the angle of obstruction employed in British planning controls for this kind of development (daylight indicator D1), the value of y_3 is approximately $\frac{1}{2}$. This means that the maximum density of bed spaces per hectare with these values of β, f and h is reduced to 1000, or 400 persons per acre.

example, using the values of β, f, h, y_3 above, and setting the parapet height to zero for simplicity so that $g = 0$, from Equation 29 the following can be derived:

$$\frac{y_1}{y_2} = \beta f y_3 \cdot \frac{x}{hx + f y_3 + g} \tag{38}$$

$$= \frac{9.2}{15.3} \cdot \frac{x}{3x + 9.2/3} \cdot 10{,}000 \text{ (beds per hectare)}$$

$$= \frac{x}{x+2} \cdot 1333.$$

The ratio $x/(x+2)$ is thus the *proportion* of the limiting density (1333 beds per hectare) achieved at x storeys. The table below shows values for various storey heights:

	No. of storeys				
	1	2	3	4	6
Proportion of limiting density	33%	50%	60%	67%	75%
Density per hectare	444	667	800	888	1000
Density per acre	178	267	320	355	400

Note the extremely high densities achieved with even 1- and 2-storey blocks: this is because of oversimplifications in the model. The Heiligenthal–Gropius model does not allow for other residential land uses such as roads and parking areas which become critical with low-rise high-density housing, nor are any constraints, other than the obstruction angle, placed on how close the blocks can be to one another to ensure, for example, fire protection and adequate privacy (Croghan and Hawkes 1970). Nevertheless the simplicity of the model does demonstrate the 'structural' properties of the relationships within the limits of the assumptions. Gropius used his model polemically to demonstrate the advantages of *hochbau*, 10- to 12-storey apartments, but a more discerning appreciation of its 'structure' might have convinced him that the greatest gains were to be found in *flachbau*, low-rise housing.† Before discussing Beckett's modifica-

† For forty years, modern planning and architectural practice has been influenced by the Gropius doctrine. Only recently have designers returned to a serious consideration of low-rise high-density housing: not on the whole, however, for intrinsic geometrical reasons, but out of sociological concern. Nevertheless, two critics in England have persistently pointed at the geometrical weaknesses in the high-rise doctrine: see A. T. Edwards (1968) and W. Segal (1964). See also Davidovich (1968), pp. 68–9, who on the basis of a more comprehensive model states: 'it can be concluded that there is no economic justification for planning buildings over five stories high...There is no justification for skyscrapers in a socialist society. The high cost of land, the concentration of capital and commercial life and the hunger for publicity – these factors have caused the erection of skyscrapers in the cities of the USA.'

tions of this model it is perhaps worth stating formally three theorems concerning the land use performance of simple rectangular blocks, or built forms, arranged in parallel rows as defined above. Note that these theorems are a little more general than Gropius' original rules: they are not dependent on particular values of the angle of obstruction, or particular values of the bed density β (in fact since the number of bed spaces is directly proportional, in the model, to the total floor area we shall use the latter instead). We also add corollaries.

The Heiligenthal–Gropius theorems

THEOREM 4. *Assuming a rectangular site of given size and given a fixed angle of obstruction between parallel and equal built forms, the total floor area increases hyperbolically with the number of storeys.*

Corollary. *The order of the rate of change of this increase varies inversely to the square of the number of storeys, the floor area asymptotically approaching an upper limit given by the products of the ratio of building width to storey height, the site area and the tangent of the angle of obstruction.*

THEOREM 5. *Assuming a given angle of obstruction between parallel and equal built forms and a constant floor area to be distributed within these forms, the size of the required site diminishes hyperbolically with the number of storeys.*

Corollary. *The order of the rate of change of this decrease varies inversely to the square of the number of storeys, the site area asymptotically approaching a lower limit given by the product of the ratio of storey height to building width, floor area and cotangent of the angle of obstruction.*

THEOREM 6. *Assuming a rectangular site of given size and constant floor area distributed within equal and parallel built forms, the angle of obstruction decreases hyperbolically with increasing number of storeys.*

Corollary. *The order of the rate of change of this decrease varies inversely to the square of the number of storeys, the tangent of the angle asymptotically approaching a lower limit given by the product of storey height to building width, and the ratio of the floor area to site area (floorspace index).*

Beckett's paper 'Population Density and the Heights of Buildings' (1942) was the first attempt, to the author's knowledge, to apply the formal apparatus of mathematical modelling to land use and built form problems. The paper's summary reads:

Although it is nowadays generally accepted that, for a given population density, rehousing in higher and more widely spaced buildings is likely to result in improved natural lighting conditions, ideas have hitherto remained somewhat vague.

In the present paper the truth of the above statement for the special case of tenement blocks arranged in parallel rows, is established by a simple mathematical analysis. It is shown that, except in very open developments such as are rarely encountered in towns, an increase in the height of the buildings will, for a given population density, always improve the lighting conditions; or, less desirably, that more people can by this means be

housed on a given site without making the lighting worse. In the latter case it can frequently happen that the increase in population density is accompanied by an *increase*
in the amount of open space per person.

The analysis rests on the assumption that, for a given orientation of the blocks, the
lighting conditions are defined by the angle of obstruction (determined by its tangent
[y_3, in the above notation] at the ground-floor windows). The latter part of the note is
concerned with an examination of the amounts of daylight and sunshine which can be
received with various values of y_3.

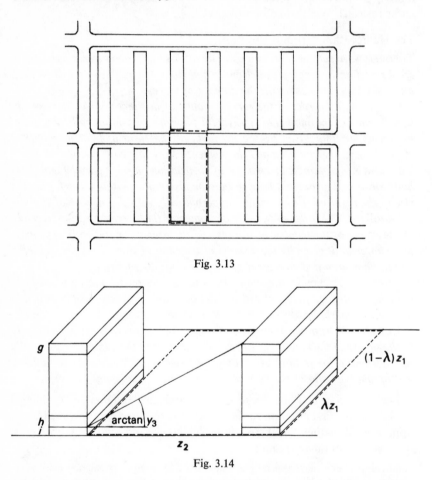

Fig. 3.13

Fig. 3.14

Beckett's model considers equal rectangular blocks arranged in parallel
rows with intersecting streets (Fig. 3.13). The intersection of streets is a
refinement on the Heiligenthal–Gropius model. Beckett's own section
through the blocks differs in one small, but significant, way from the
previous model (Fig. 3.9). Instead of a parapet at roof level, there is, as it

were, a 'negative parapet' at ground level: the angle of obstruction is read from a point above the ground on the façade of the first floor. The Heiligenthal–Gropius section can be used with the parapet, but the equations to measure the angle of obstruction should be modified in the way proposed by Beckett (Fig. 3.14). In plan, let z_1 be the length of the 'unit' site and define the length of the block as a proportion, λ, of this.

The variables may be listed

z_1 = length of site,
z_2 = distance between blocks,
f = width of block,
h = storey height,
g = parapet height,
i = height at which the angle of obstruction intersects the façade $(0 < i < h)$,
β = number of beds (persons, etc.)[†] per unit floor area,
λ = proportion of site length to given block length;

thus λz_1 = length of block,
$(1 - \lambda)z_1$ = longitudinal space between blocks;

and x = number of storeys,
y_1 = number of beds (persons, etc.),[‡]
y_2 = site area,
y_3 = tangent of the angle of obstruction,
y_4 = area of open space.

The principal dependent variables studied by Beckett are

$u_1 = y_1/y_2$ = bed space (population, etc.)[‡] density in relation to site area,
$u_2 = y_4/y_2$ = open space index,
$u_3 = u_1/u_2$ = bed space (population, etc.)[‡] density in relation to open space.

As before the relationships between these variables are established by definition and from the geometry of the layout.

For the number of bed spaces (persons, etc.), $\quad y_1 = \beta \lambda f z_1 x,$ \hfill (39)

[†] The 'dimension' of β determines the meaning of y_1, u_1 and u_3. Thus, if it is a measure of bedspaces per unit floor area, then y_1 is the number of bedspaces (as studied by Gropius); if it is a measure of population per unit floor area, then y_1 is the number of people, u_1 is the site density and u_3 is the number of persons to a unit area of open space (as studied by Beckett); if, however, it is set equal to 1 simply as a number, then y_1 is the area of floor space and u_1 is the floorspace index (Beckett's measure). Leaving the meaning of β open like this allows us to interpret the model in a variety of ways.
[‡] See preceding footnote.

for the site area, $y_2 = z_1(f+z_2),$ (40)

for the tangent of the angle of obstruction, $y_3 = \dfrac{hx+g-i}{z_2},$ (41)

and for the area of open space, $y_4 = y_2 - \dfrac{y_1}{\beta x}.$ (42)

The equation which relates y_1, y_2 and y_3 is found by eliminating z_1 and z_2 as before. This gives

$$(hy_1 - \beta\lambda fy_2y_3)x + (fy_3 + g - i)y_1 = 0 \tag{43}$$

which may be compared with Equation 28. The Heiligenthal–Gropius model is seen to be a special case of this Beckett model for the values $\lambda = 1$ (the blocks are continuous) and $i = 0$ (the obstruction angle is measured at the point where the building and ground meet). Beckett's equations follow:†

$$u_1 = \psi_1(x) = \beta\lambda fy_3 \cdot \frac{x}{hx + fy_3 + g - i}, \tag{44}$$

$$u_2 = \psi_2(x) = 1 - \frac{\lambda fy_3}{hx + fy_3 + g - i}, \text{ with varying } u_1, \tag{45}$$

$$= 1 - \frac{u_1}{\beta x}, \text{ with varying } y_3,$$

$$u_3 = \psi_3(x) = \beta\lambda fy_3 \cdot \frac{x}{hx + (1-\lambda)fy_3 + g - i},\ddagger \text{ with varying } u_1, \tag{46}$$

$$= \frac{\beta u_1 x}{\beta x - u_1}, \text{ with varying } y_3$$

and $y_3 = \phi_3(x) = \dfrac{u_1}{f} \cdot \dfrac{hx + g - i}{\beta\lambda x - u_1}.$ (47)

The behaviour of $\psi_2(x)$ and $\psi_3(x)$ may be investigated in terms of either u_1 or y_3. Again the functions may be plotted graphically as hyperbolae (Figs. 3.15, 3.16, 3.17, 3.18 show original graphs worked out by Beckett for specific values of the independent variables: $g = 0$, $f = 3h$, $i = 0.6h$, $\lambda = 0.75$). In some cases the behaviour of the functions is not so predictable: for example, under some conditions $\psi_1(x)$ increases with the number of storeys, but under other conditions the function decreases.

† Our own notation differs from Beckett's.
‡ Beckett, in fact, studied the behaviour of u_3^{-1}, the amount of open space per person.

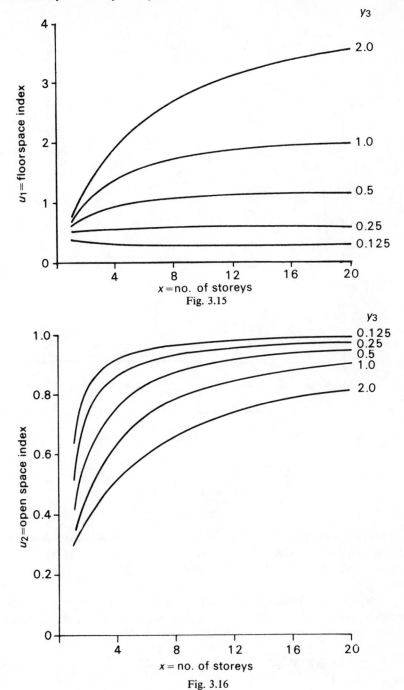

Fig. 3.15

Fig. 3.16

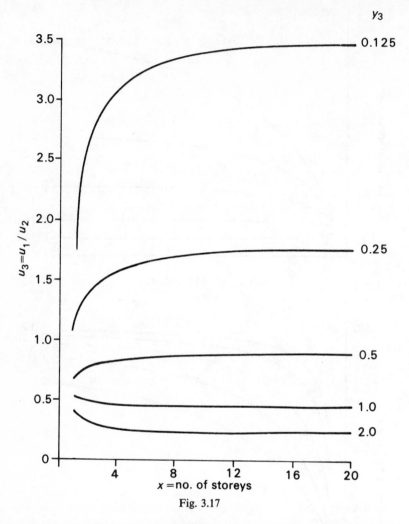

Fig. 3.17

This difference from the Heiligenthal–Gropius model is *entirely* due to the decision to measure the angle of obstruction at a point above the ground level. This is why the change from one model to the other 'is small, but significant'.

Once again the functions tend to finite limits as the number of storeys increase, but whether the function approaches this limit from above or below depends on the value of the derivative. Thus

$$\text{for } \psi_1(x), \frac{\mathrm{d}u_1}{\mathrm{d}x} = \psi_1'(x) = \beta\lambda f y_3 \cdot \frac{(fy_3+g-i)}{(hx+fy_3+g-i)^2}, \qquad (48)$$

and $\psi_1'(x)$ is greater than, equal to, or less than ($>$, $=$, or $<$) according to whether $fy_3+g-i>$, $=$, or <0; that is, whether $y_3>$, $=$, or $<(i-g)/f$. The behaviour of the function depends then on the relationship between f, g and i. Note that with $i=0$, the unequivocal Gropius rule is reconstructed that the floor space increases with the number of storeys. In any case $\psi_1(x)$ approaches a limit as the number of storeys becomes very large:

$$\lim_{x\to\infty} \psi_1(x) = \frac{\beta\lambda fy_3}{h}. \tag{49}$$

With β set to 1 this means that the limiting floorspace index is $\lambda fy_3/h$, or approximately 1.12 when $\lambda = 0.75$, $f = 3h$ and $y_3 = 0.5$, that is when

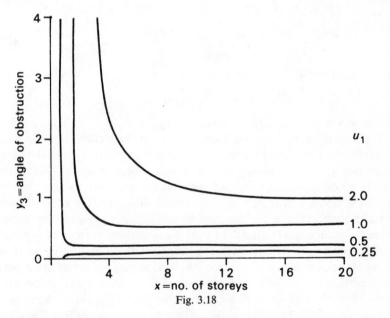

Fig. 3.18

the angle of obstruction is about $26°$ which is reasonable in residential developments.

$$\text{For } \psi_2(x), \quad \frac{du_2}{dx} = \psi_2'(x) = \frac{\lambda fhy_3}{(hx+fy_3+g-i)^2}, \text{ with varying } u_1, \tag{50}$$

$$= \frac{u_1}{x^2}, \text{ with varying } y_3,$$

and $\psi_2'(x)>0$ unequivocally in both cases, so that the open space index increases, as might be expected, with increasing number of storeys. In both cases the open space index approaches a limit

$$\lim_{x \to \infty} \psi_2(x) = 1. \tag{51}$$

This is a nice mathematical limit: it means that when the built forms 'are' infinitely high they occupy no land so that the whole site is open space.

$$\text{For } \psi_3(x), \frac{du_3}{dx} = \psi_3'(x) = \beta\lambda f y_3 \cdot \frac{\{(1-\lambda)fy_3 + g - i\}}{\{hx + (1-\lambda)fy_3 + g - i\}^2}$$

$$= \frac{-\beta u_1^2}{(\beta x - u_1)^2} \tag{52}$$

and when the angle of obstruction is held constant $\psi_3'(x) >$, $=$, or < 0 according to whether $(1-\lambda)fy_3 + g - i >$, $=$, or < 0; that is, whether $y_3 >$, $=$, or $< (i-g)/(1-\lambda)f$. The function tends to a limit

$$\lim_{x \to \infty} \psi_3(x) = \frac{\beta\lambda f y_3}{h}. \tag{53}$$

This is the same as $\lim_{x \to \infty} \psi_1(x)$ because

$$\lim_{x \to \infty} \psi_3(x) = \lim_{x \to \infty} \psi_1(x) / \lim_{x \to \infty} \psi_2(x)$$

and as was seen from Equation 51 $\lim_{x \to \infty} \psi_2(x) = 1$.

Note that if $i = 0$, $\psi_3'(x) > 0$. That is to say, in the Heiligenthal–Gropius model the density of persons to open space always *increases* with the number of storeys when the angle of obstruction is held constant. This means that the amount of open space per person diminishes with building height. Beckett's model contradicts this statement, and yet this contradiction arises solely because of a refinement to measure the angle of obstruction above the ground level rather than at it! Beckett, as has been noted, ignored the parapet height, g, and with the values of the variables he used he obtained the condition $y_3 >$, $=$, or < 0.8. In most planned urban situations† the condition $y_3 < 0.8$ will hold – the angle of obstruction will be less than $38°40'$. But if it is assumed with Gropius that the built form has a parapet, let us say $g = 0.3h$, then the condition becomes $y_3 >$, $=$, or < 0.4, and the critical angle of obstruction becomes $21°48'$, an angle less than that which might be expected in most urban situations where a choice is to be made between low-rise or high-rise building. In this case, the open space per person definitely *decreases* with higher development. It may seem curious that policies about high or low building may hinge in the end on the detailed design of the roof fascia, but such is the case. Yet this exaggerates the real situation in practice. The point is that the increases or decreases are likely to be slight anyway, especially beyond four or so storeys. When the floorspace index is held constant then the amount of open space per

† This may not be true in tropical cities where larger angles of obstruction are acceptable.

person unequivocally increases with height: this is demonstrated by the second expression

$$\psi_3'(x) = \frac{-\beta u_1^2}{(\beta x - u_1)^2} < 0.$$

(Remember that $\psi_3(x)$ is the density of population to open space, as this decreases so the amount of open space per person increases.)

For $\qquad \phi_3(x), \dfrac{dy_3}{dx} = \phi_3'(x) = \dfrac{-u_1}{f} \cdot \dfrac{hu_1 + \beta\lambda(g-i)}{(\beta\lambda x - u_1)^2},$ $\qquad$ (54)

and $\phi_3'(x) >, =,$ or < 0 if $hu_1 + \beta\lambda(g-i) <, =,$ or > 0; that is, if $u_1 <, =,$ or $> \beta\lambda(i-g)/h$. With $\beta = 1$, $\lambda = 0.75$, $i = 0.6h$, $g = 0.3h$ as before, this condition says that the angle of obstruction increases, is stationary, or decreases with height depending on whether the constant floorspace index is less than, equal to, or greater than 0.225. Thus except in low-density situations the lighting conditions can be expected to improve with increasing number of storeys. Setting $i = 0$ confirms the earlier Heiligenthal–Gropius theorem (6).

The Beckett theorems

THEOREM 7. *Assuming a constant angle of obstruction between parallel and equal built forms, the population density†* increases hyperbolically, is stationary, or decreases hyperbolically with increasing number of storeys according to whether the angle of obstruction is greater than, equal to, or less than arc tan $(i-g)/f$.‡

Corollary. *The order of the rate of change in the population density varies inversely with the square of the number of storeys, this density asymptotically approaching a limiting value for a very large number of storeys given by $\lambda f y_3/h$.*

THEOREM 8. *Assuming either a constant angle of obstruction between parallel and equal built forms, or a constant population density for such a development, the open space index increases hyperbolically with increasing number of storeys.*

Corollary. *The order of the rate of increase in the open space index varies inversely with the square of the number of storeys, the index asymptotically approaching an upper limit of 1 for a very large number of storeys.*

---

† See definition above, p. 81. When $\beta = 1$, the population density is the floorspace index, otherwise it is bed spaces, persons, rooms, etc., per unit area according to the precise definition of β.

‡ For this and following theorems the variables are as defined earlier, p. 81.

THEOREM 9. *Assuming a constant population density for a development of parallel and equal built forms, the density of persons to open space decreases with increasing number of storeys. (The amount of open space per person increases.)*

Corollary. *The order of the rate of increase of the density of persons to open space varies inversely with the square of the number of storeys, the density asymptotically approaching a lower limit equal to the population density.*

THEOREM 10. *Assuming a constant angle of obstruction between parallel and equal built forms the density of persons to open space increases hyperbolically, is stationary, or decreases hyperbolically with increasing number of storeys according to whether the angle of obstruction is greater than, equal to, or less than arc tan $(i-g)/(1-\lambda)f$.*

Corollary. *The order of the rate of change of the density of persons to open space varies inversely with the square of the number of storeys, this density asymptotically approaching a limiting value for a very large number of storeys equal to the limiting value of the population density, $\lambda f y_3/h$.*

THEOREM 11. *Assuming a constant population density for a development of parallel and equal built forms, the angle of obstruction increases hyperbolically, is stationary, or decreases hyperbolically according to whether the population density is less than, equal to, or greater than $\beta\lambda(i-g)/h$.*

Corollary. *The order of this change in the angle of obstruction varies inversely with the square of the number of storeys, approaching a limiting value for a very large number of storeys, arc tan $hu_1/\beta\lambda f$.*

The Heiligenthal–Gropius model showed that the relationships were not linear but hyperbolic, and in terms of the specification of that model the functions behaved consistently. The Beckett model demonstrates that a small refinement introduced into the model can significantly change the behaviour of the representative functions, and that detailed design factors, such as the height of the parapet, may be critical. As our models become more and more refined to take into account this and that factor the behaviour of these functions is likely to become more 'erratic', being dependent on a variety of *critical* relationships. The number of possible situations (defined by giving values to the independent variables) becomes very large and computing will usually have to be resorted to.†

But each refinement should be carefully considered. The reason Beckett chose a higher reference point for the angle of obstruction was in order better to estimate the level of daylight illumination in the ground floor

---

† See, for example, the environmental model described by Hawkes and Stibbs (1969) which can simulate highly complex architectural situations for the purposes of investigating lighting, heating and cooling, and acoustic performance.

rooms. Yet is this improvement in accuracy, if it be so, worth the considerable complications that it leads to? Recent work by Hawkes and Stibbs† on the effects of urban obstructions, such as motorways, on daylight suggests that the choice of reference point makes very little difference to the value of the external daylight factor (sky component and external reflected component) as measured on the vertical face of the ground storey. Thus, for practical purposes, the Heiligenthal–Gropius model is probably as good as Beckett's, and it is, of course, a good deal simpler to use and to understand. Nevertheless the Beckett model serves as an excellent illustration of the complex behaviour of a few variables describing a simple architectural system. There is no doubt that models can always be made more and more complicated, but the real challenge is to make them simple, stripped down until the quintessential structure of the problem is exposed.

Example four

Do other building forms use land differently from the layout of parallel blocks?

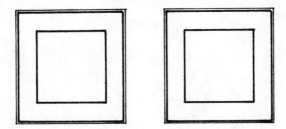

Fig. 3.19a. Ground coverage of 4-storey apartment buildings with interior courts.

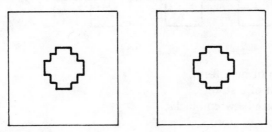

Fig. 3.19b. Ground coverage of 32-storey Sunlight Towers of same apartment capacity but with surrounding open areas.

† Private communication.

In 'Flach-, mittel- oder hochbau?' Walter Gropius demonstrates his main thesis by means of a diagram (Fig. 3.19) showing a 4-storey court development and a 32-storey tower scheme each of which contains the same number of apartments. This diagram can be taken as a starting point, simplifying the form of the 'Sunlight Tower' to a simple square plan. For the purposes of this demonstration the details of parapets and heights of reference points can be ignored, although, as has just been demonstrated, the models may be quite sensitive to these. Refinements, as always, can come later. Here the variables are defined as (Figs 3.20, 3.21):

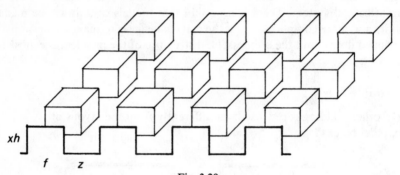

Fig. 3.20

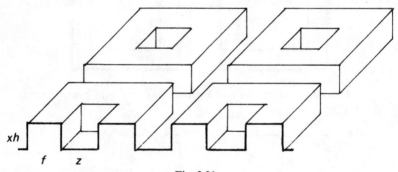

Fig. 3.21

f = width of built form,
h = height of a storey,
z = distance between blocks,
x = number of storeys,
y_1 = site area,
y_2 = total floor area,
y_3 = tangent of angle of obstruction.

The principal dependent variable is

$$u = y_2/y_1 = \text{the floorspace index.}$$

The other dependent variables for the two developments can be identified by the superscripts [0] and [2] for the tower and court respectively.† Thus $y_1^{[0]}$ represents the floor area of the tower; $y_2^{[2]}$ the site area of the court. In this exercise y_3 is treated as an independent variable. By the geometry of the arrangements, the following relations hold:

	Tower[0]	Court[2]	
For the site area	$y_1^{[0]} = (f+z)^2,$	$y_1^{[2]} = 4(f+z)^2,$	(55)
for the floor area	$y_2^{[0]} = f^2 x,$	$y_2^{[2]} = 4f(f+z)x,$	(56)

for the tangent of the obstruction angle $y_3 = \dfrac{hx}{z}.$ (57)

From Equation 57, $z = hx/y_3$ so that, eliminating z from equations 55 and 56, the expressions for the floorspace indices, $u^{[0]}$ and $u^{[2]}$, are derived

$$u^{[0]} = \left(\frac{fy_3}{fy_3 + hx}\right)^2 \cdot x \qquad (58^{[0]})$$

$$u^{[2]} = \left(\frac{fy_3}{fy_3 + hx}\right) \cdot x. \qquad (58^{[2]})$$

The form of equation $58^{[2]}$ is familiar. As in the previous example the function may be plotted as a hyperbola being a particular kind of quadratic expression in $u^{[2]}$ and x, in which the term of highest order is $u^{[2]}x$. This is not so in the case of equation $58^{[0]}$. Here the term of highest order is $u^{[0]}x^2$ which is 'cubic'. The behaviour of this function for the tower block is distinctly different from that of our earlier examples. Let us take a close look at $u^{[0]} = \phi^{[0]}(x)$. Note that $\phi^{[0]}(0) = 0$ and that $\lim_{x \to \infty} \phi^{[0]}(x) = 0$. Also, differentiating,

$$\frac{du^{[0]}}{dx} = \phi^{[0]\prime}(x) = \frac{(fy_3)^2(fy_3 - hx)}{(fy_3 + hx)^3}, \qquad (59^{[0]})$$

so that $\phi^{[0]\prime}(x) >$, $=$, or < 0 according to whether $y_3 >$, $=$, or $< hx/f$. For any given finite value of y_3 the function is stationary at $x = fy_3/h$ and this is in fact a maximum value. Thus, with a tower building an increase in the number of storeys at first increases the floorspace index, and then, passing a maximum value, decreases the index. The maximum value of the

† This notation derives from March and Trace (1968).

floorspace index for any given value of y_3 is then given by substituting fy_3/h for x in equation $58^{[0]}$:

$$u^{[0]}_{max} = \frac{fy_3}{4h}. \tag{$60^{[0]}$}$$

The behaviour of the court is, as has been said, more familiar. $\phi^{[2]}(0) = 0$, and $\lim_{x \to \infty} \phi^{[2]}(x) = fy_3/h$. Also, differentiating, it develops into

$$\frac{du^{[2]}}{dx} = \phi^{[2]'}(x) = \left(\frac{fy_3}{fy_3 + hx}\right)^2 > 0, \tag{$59^{[2]}$}$$

so that the function monotonically increases to a maximum value at infinity. That is to say, the court form tends to a limiting index of fy_3/h which is *four* times greater than the maximum achievable by the tower form. Perhaps a more realistic comparison is to see what the floorspace index of the court form is for the same number of storeys required to maximise the tower solution, namely $x = fy_3/h$.

$$u^{[2]} = \frac{fy_3}{2h} \tag{$60^{[2]}$}$$

which is just *twice* the value of $u^{[0]}_{max}$. Thus when the tower form's index is at its maximum, a court of similar height will achieve two times as much floorspace.

This can be put yet another way round. What height does a court have to be to achieve the same floorspace index as the maximum achievable in tower development? This requires that

$$u^{[2]} = u^{[0]}_{max}$$

or

$$\left(\frac{fy_3}{fy_3 + hx}\right) \cdot x = \frac{fy_3}{4h}, \tag{61}$$

whence we find

$$x = \frac{fy_3}{3h}.$$

Thus the number of storeys required is precisely *one-third* of those needed to maximise the index for the tower ($x_{max} = fy_3/h$, see above).

How do these forms compare with the land use performance of parallel rows? Similar notation is used to define the variables shown in Fig. 3.22 for parallel blocks. The following equations are then derived (the superscript $^{(2)}$ is used for this form):

For the site area $\qquad\qquad y^{(2)}_1 = (f+z)^2, \tag{$55^{(2)}$}$

for the floor area $$y_2^{(2)} = f(f+z) \cdot x, \tag{56$^{(2)}$}$$

and the tangent of the obstruction angle is as before (Equation 57). Thus eliminating z, the following is obtained:

For the floorspace index $$u^{(2)} = \left(\frac{fy_3}{fy_3+hx}\right) \cdot x, \tag{58$^{(2)}$}$$

which is exactly the same as for the court form's index, $u^{[2]}$ (see Equation $58^{[2]}$). The freestanding court and the street form behave in identical ways.

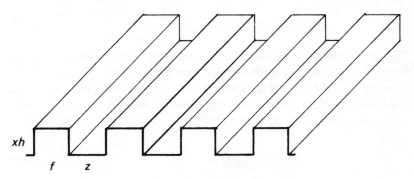

Fig. 3.22

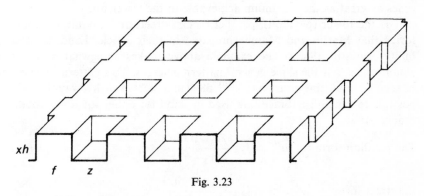

Fig. 3.23

The important point to recognise here is that any extrapolation from the performance of parallel blocks of the Heiligenthal–Gropius model to the behaviour of isolated towers with four incident faces is totally unwarranted. Yet such an extrapolation has been an essential part of the conventional wisdom on these matters.

Is there a form which can improve on the street and isolated court forms? Looking at the cruciform shown in Fig. 3.23, it is clear that many of these, by connecting, constitute a continuous series of courts. How does such a highly reticulated system behave in comparison with the more nucleated court and tower? Using a similar notation and defining the variables by Fig. 3.23 the following is obtained (a superscript $^{(4)}$ is employed for the cruciform):

For the site area $\quad y_1^{(4)} = (f+z)^2,$ $\hfill (55^{(4)})$

$$y_2^{(4)} = f(f+2z) \cdot x, \hfill (56^{(4)})$$

and once again $y_3 = hx/z$. Eliminating z, the result is

for the floorspace index $\quad u^{(4)} = \dfrac{fy_3(fy_3 + 2hx)}{(fy_3 + hx)^2} \cdot x. \hfill (58^{(4)})$

This is a third order expression in $u^{(4)}$ and x. But unlike equation $58^{[0]}$ the function $u^{(4)} = \phi^{(4)}(x)$ tends to a non-zero limit, in fact a maximum value given by $\lim\limits_{x \to \infty} \phi^{(4)}(x) = 2fy_3/h$ which is *twice* the limiting index of the isolated court or the parallel block (for example, see equation $60^{[2]}$). When the tower reaches its maximum value, the cruciform obtains an index value

$$u^{(4)} = \frac{3}{4} \cdot \frac{fy_3}{h} \hfill (60^{(4)})$$

for the same number of storeys $x = fy_3/h$. This is a floorspace index *three* times as great as the maximum achievable in the tower form.

It is the tower (pavilion), parallel block (street) and continuous court forms that Martin and March compared in their article 'Land use and built forms' in 1966.† The example above makes somewhat different assumptions, but the same general pattern emerges. This pattern can best be seen by re-writing equations $58^{[0]}$, $58^{(2)}$ and $58^{(4)}$ in such a way that it is possible to generalise (braces are used to stand for either square or round brackets):

The pavilion form $\quad u^{\{0\}} = fy_3 \dfrac{(fy_3 + 0 \cdot hx)}{(fy_3 + hx)^2} \cdot x, \hfill (61)$

the street form $\quad u^{\{2\}} = fy_3 \dfrac{(fy_3 + 1 \cdot hx)}{(fy_3 + hx)^2} \cdot x,$

the court form $\quad u^{\{4\}} = fy_3 \dfrac{(fy_3 + 2 \cdot hx)}{(fy_3 + hx)^2} \cdot x.$

The general equation

$$u^{\{2\alpha\}} = fy_3 \frac{(fy_3 + \alpha \cdot hx)}{(fy_3 + hx)^2} \cdot x, \quad \text{for } \alpha = 0,1,2 \hfill (62)$$

† See also parallel work by Eckhard Schulze-Fielitz (1968).

describes all the situations we have discussed above. From this it is easy to see that

$$u^{\{4\}} - u^{\{2\}} = u^{\{2\}} - u^{\{0\}} = \frac{fhy_3x^2}{(fy_3 + hx)^2} \qquad (63)$$

so that for all $x > 0$ the following may be written:

$$u^{\{4\}} > u^{\{2\}} > u^{\{0\}} \qquad (64)$$

a statement which says that the land use performance of arrays of built forms in this Martin–March model are ranked unequivocally: for a given number of storeys the floorspace index for the continuous court form is greater than that for an array of streets (parallel blocks) which, in turn, is greater than that for an array of pavilions (towers). And, in particular, for the number of storeys giving the maximum value of the index for an array of pavilions, the floorspace index of a street array is *twice* that of the pavilion array and that of the continuous court array *three* times that of the pavilion array. Two simple theorems may now be stated relating to the Martin–March model:

THEOREM 12. *Comparing infinite arrays of rectangular built forms controlled by a given angle of obstruction, the floorspace index of an array of continuous courts is always greater than that of an array of streets, which, in turn, is always greater than that of an array of pavilions for any given number of storeys.*

THEOREM 13. *There is a maximum floorspace index for an array of pavilions for some finite number of storeys, and for this same number of storeys the indices for street and continuous court arrays are two and three times the maximum achievable by the pavilion array, respectively.*

Of course, this model is a gross oversimplification in practical terms, and many objections can be raised. More and more elaborate models can be designed in an attempt to overcome some of these criticisms. March and Trace (1968),† for example, investigate a finer range of elemental built forms which can be combined to produce more complex arrangements; they look at systematic transformations of these forms, and they discuss the relation of their work to previous studies in this field including the problem of sidelighting to tower forms (the argument that the open development of high-rise towers gains far more in daylighting terms from light coming around obstructing blocks than is lost by increased vertical obstruction). Such elaborations lead to a more tedious mathematical discussion which would be out of place here, but it is not necessarily a more advanced one.

† For a more easily available digest of this work see Hutchinson (1970).

To bring more realism into such models is to lose generality (see Chapter 7). Nevertheless more sophisticated computer representations such as those by Hawkes and Stibbs (1969) allow a much more sensitive study of the environmental effects of buildings upon one another. Hawkes (1970) in a series of controlled experiments cautions against the indiscriminate use of generalisation in actual building design. As he points out there are many detailed points of design such as depth of window reveals, size and shape of openings, the specific physical properties of materials which affect significantly the environmental performance of groups of buildings. Nevertheless, simple models such as those described above do allow our more empirical experiments to be organised, do prompt important and serious questions, do act critically on our prejudices and the conventional wisdom, and do lead to speculations over far wider areas of study.

Elementary mathematical models are an excellent source of enquiry and are frequently suggestive of a systematic approach to computer-based experiment and investigation (Hawkes 1970, Tabor 1970). Finally, in practice they may help clear away some of the misleading 'rules-of-thumb' which frequently lurk behind design decisions, and they may help to replace these by more cautious generalisations, but, be warned – these may be equally misleading if results and conclusions are extrapolated beyond the simplifying assumptions of the original model.

4. *The use of models in planning and the architectural design process*[†]

NICHOLAS BULLOCK, PETER DICKENS &
PHILIP STEADMAN

Three classes of model have been distinguished in American city planning research; descriptive models, predictive models, and planning models, in ascending order of difficulty. Ira Lowry has enumerated the features of the descriptive model in urban studies as follows: 'The builder of a descriptive model has the limited objective of persuading the computer to replicate the relevant features of an existing urban environment or of an already observed process of urban change. Roughly speaking, the measures of his accomplishment are: one, the ratio of input data required by the model to output data generated by the model; two, the accuracy and cost of the latter as compared to direct observation of the variables in question; and three, the applicability of his model to other times and places than that for which it was originally constructed.' (1965).

The descriptive model provides the planner with an insight into the workings of city structure but it does not directly allow him to predict future trends or to determine the effects of particular planning policies. This is done by means of the predictive model, for which it is necessary to specify mechanisms of cause and effect governing the variables whose values are simply observed in the descriptive model. In some cases the predictions may take a conditional form; that is to say the model is designed to operate so that 'if X occurs, then Y will follow', but takes no

[†] This essay was written as an introduction to a report documenting work in progress in the Universities Study, in 1968. The main theme of the report was the necessity of finding some general framework whereby separate planning studies could be brought together and seen in a general relationship. The means for doing this was seen to be through the construction of mathematical models of university activity patterns, and the subsequent progress of this line of work is described in successive papers reproduced later in this volume. At the stage represented by this essay, however, it was felt necessary to try to make a general case for the use of models at all scales and in all areas of architectural and planning work, and for an experimental approach in environmental research as a whole. Hence the rather broad scope of the arguments, whose application goes beyond the narrower interests of university planning.

account of the actual likelihood of the occurrence of X. In this way the frame of reference of the model can be somewhat limited. It is nevertheless impossible to treat all external (exogenous) variables conditionally, since not all will operate independently of each other. We cannot assume both that 'if A occurs, then B will follow, and if X occurs then Y will follow' since the occurrence of A may preclude or affect the occurrence of X.

Planning models, the third type, form a class whose technology is not far developed. In planning models a measure of optimisation is introduced in terms of chosen criteria, in order to determine means of achieving stated planning goals. 'The essential steps are as follows: one, specification of alternative programs or actions that might be chosen by the planner; two, prediction of the consequences of choosing each alternative; three, scoring these consequences according to a metric of goal-achievement; and four, choosing the alternative which yields the highest score.' (Lowry, 1965). Since a wide choice of planning alternatives exists at each stage in the 'decision-tree' the number of overall possibilities rapidly becomes astronomic, but the use of computer programs to carry out steps three and four allows the examination of a fairly large number of alternative decision sequences.

The urban planning problems to which the American model-builders have applied their techniques have tended naturally to arise in the control and direction of powerful forces of change and growth in existing large cities. The future movements of a complex system are anticipated, and the effects of intervention from outside the system are measured – intervention in the form of public or private development programmes, or through planning controls and incentives of various kinds. What is important is that the model-building process takes up at a point in the history of the city's development when its 'design' or physical and organisational form is already well established. The model recognises the dynamic nature of a system in the process of change. The initial structure of the model is constituted by a current land use inventory by example, together with an analysis of the patterns of economic and social activity of the city's inhabitants at the present moment in time: trends are extrapolated forward as changes in this initial structure.

Such an approach has no application to the initial design of an accommodation for a new activity of whatever complexity on a virgin site. Not that the simulation of the performance of finished designs would not provide an invaluable means for their comprehensive evaluation and analysis. Nor can it be said that the study of urban models would not serve to illuminate the characteristic structure of the design problems of cities and acquaint the designer with the context for new solutions. It is in the creation of new forms that even models of the American planning type offer no direct help – for their role is in evaluation only, and alternative plans must be specified complete in advance of the model's operation. The truly inventive phase of the design process is that in which a form is synthesised in response to a programme. This will be discussed first in relation to the single building, since it is on the building scale that most of our work has so far concentrated, and the problems, though severe, are patently less so than those on the scale of the large development. The same principles will, however, apply in the larger problem, as in the smaller. Successful modelling of the single building is a necessary first step towards the goal of a complete model of an institution as a whole.

The debate on the process of derivation of architectural forms is an old one. This is not the place for a historical account of functionalism. But it is important for our purposes to distinguish two very different functionalist standpoints, the one determinist, the other we might call 'moral'.

Extreme apologists of rationalism in architecture have claimed that the form of a building proceeds directly and logically from the technique of its construction and the purpose to which it is put. They have suggested particularly of the engineering structure that its design follows an inevitable process, through a kind of 'constructional fatalism'. Representative of this determinist attitude in architecture was Auguste Choisy, who in his 'Histoire de l'Architecture' (1899) saw building form as a logical consequence of a *technique* and *methode*, signifying not simply the tools and methods of the building trade but 'aspects of society as a whole'. Thus 'buildings classify themselves as witnesses fixing the way of life and the moral condition of humanity, age by age.' The Gothic cathedrals were ideal for this form of treatment, since the lack of historical documentation of individual architects and particular technical inventions allowed Choisy to assume 'a kind of abstract necessity' as instrumental in their design. 'L'arc-boutant (the flying buttress)...ne fut point inventé, il s'imposa.'

This is something rather different from simply applauding the design of buildings which are contrived, either consciously or unconsciously, to exemplify the principles of their construction and to characterise the function they are to perform. That is a moral attitude, a kind of aesthetic puritanism which is as old as Aristotle. Classical functionalist theory seized on the analogy of the natural organism as a perfect paradigm of the relation of form to function. 'Living organisms and works of art are definite after their kinds, which Nature and Man respectively form by qualifying matter. The quantity of matter used in any case is determined by the form subserved; the size of a particular organ, or part, is determined by its form, which again is determined by the form of the whole organism or work.' Emphasis on fitness for purpose, inner consistency in relating the parts of the whole and forming the whole from the parts, and above all the organic analogy, are themes which recur throughout functionalist theory in its many phases and guises.

The development of nineteenth-century biology provoked a deeper examination of the parallels between natural and artistic organisms, especially in terms of structure and process as well as just outward appearance. 'In art as in nature an organism is an assemblage of interdependent parts of which the structure is determined by the function and of which the form is an expression of the structure' wrote the American critic Montgomery Schuyler (1894). Just as the palaeontologist could reconstruct the whole organism from a few bones, so with the architectural organism 'a person sufficiently skilled in the laws of organic structure can reconstruct, from the cross-section of the pier of a Gothic cathedral, the whole structural system of which it is the nucleus and prefigurement. The design of such a building...is an imitation not of the forms of nature but of the processes of nature.' (Schuyler 1894.) It was for the theory of biological evolution to show how the 'design' of living organisms occurs through an immensely protracted process of trial and error. Genetic mutations occur accidentally, at random. Some are unfavourable, some neutral, some favourable. In the struggle for existence, natural selection eliminates the unfavourable mutations; the favourable ones, on the contrary, are preserved, and the organisms possessing them will more likely reproduce themselves. Later nineteenth-century theorists of architectural rationalism like Schuyler held that the creation of new architectural forms was also a process of gradual evolution.

The distinction between approval of the manifestly functional qualities of a finished design and insistence on the inevitable logic of the process of design is important for the would-be user of theoretical model-building methods. It is only if he were able to accept the latter position that he could go on to conclude that architectural problems might be solved algorithmically, 'i.e. by the employment of a mathematical or logical construction that acts as a program or an instruction manual'. This is a problem discussed by Maldonado and Bonsieppi in an article entitled 'Science and Design' (1964). Once all the variables entering into the solution of a problem are summarised, is a mathematical formulation sufficient, they ask, to provide all detailed determinative data? They are inclined to conclude that mathematical techniques of problem-structuring are of instrumental rather than panacea value. 'For it is wrong to attempt to simulate the relationship of the designer to the problems facing him in the form of a simply determined system, because, after all, the process here discussed – as in every creative and inventive human behaviour – can, if at all, only be simulated with models on the level of complex probabilistic systems.'

It is not difficult to find many reasons for the indeterminacy of the architectural design process. It arises because even an explicit and apparently rigorous statement of the aims of the design is necessarily still vague on some points. Even performance standards of a technical, quantifiable nature can be variable within wide ranges and the results still quite acceptable. Minimum daylight levels can be fixed for the performance of visual tasks: or maximum levels to avoid discomfort from glare. Choice in the area between the two extremes is a matter of taste, or even indifference. Again one might imagine in theory that one particular configuration of rooms in a building would suit the pattern of intercommunication of the occupants best, and minimise their time spent walking: but in practice it will be immaterial to people within quite wide limits what distance they travel, so long as it is not too far and the journeys are not too frequent. In short, there is so much 'slack' in the system that even on the most clearly defined criteria a variety of solutions to each aspect of the design will be equally acceptable. As Alexander says 'for most requirements it is important to satisfy them at a level which suffices to prevent misfit between the form and the context, and to do this in the least arbitrary manner possible'. (1964, p. 99.)† For this reason Alexander proposes treating both specific requirements, and requirements of less definable but nevertheless crucially important character – 'comfort', 'security' or 'variety', in different contexts, for instance – as binary variables, that is to say taking one of two possible values only. Either the requirement is satisfied ('fit') or it is not ('misfit'). A continuous variable taking a range of values would be treated as a 'fit' for all values lying above the required standard, and for all values below as a 'misfit'.

A great part of the systematic and detailed study of design problems is devoted to the establishing of minimum or maximum standards and thereby the ranges within which variables operate. It is, in the nature of the problem, only the extremes which are susceptible to accurate determination. The fact that discussion may often dwell on minimum standards does not mean to imply that these are reckoned to be desirable or even, in the light of other considerations, acceptable. The same is true of the measurement of average conditions as found in present practice. The intention is simply to demonstrate the cost or savings involved in lavish or parsimonious allowances, or the implications of a raising or lowering of present standards.

As has been emphasised before, it is by no means necessary that in taking the optimum solution (indeed if one can be defined) to each subsidiary problem, a satisfactory result will be achieved in the total design. Advantage must be weighed in one area against consequent penalties in another: and this may be a matter of fine judgement. Where the benefits

† Cf. his note 6 on Herbert Simon and the concept of 'satisficing'.

and the costs are purely economic or can be expressed as such, a means of comparison exists; as Ira Lowry says 'the most comprehensive metric available in our society, whether we like it or not, is money'. (Lowry 1965, p. 161.) But where he must weigh comfort or convenience against monetary costs, every man's scale of values will be different.

It is easy to see why by contrast it was precisely in the area of engineering structures that the idea of the inevitability of the process of design arose. For it is here that performance requirements are most fully and accurately stated in advance, and where the criteria by which the success of the design is judged are unequivocal. A mechanism works or it does not, a structure either stays up or falls down. But Le Corbusier, for example, while admiring the integrity and economy of means of engineering works, recognised that although the engineer was guided by 'natural law' and mathematical calculation, he nevertheless did exercise an intuitive skill in design. 'The engineer...has his own aesthetic, for he must, in making his calculations, qualify some of the terms of his equation; and it is here that taste intervenes. Now, in handling a mathematical problem, a man is regarding it from a purely abstract point of view, and in such a state, his taste must follow a sure and certain path.' (1927, p. 19.)

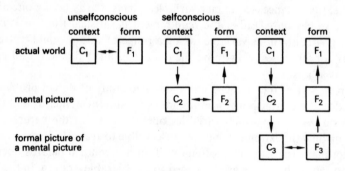

Fig. 4.1

Christopher Alexander attributes the very successful architecture of primitive cultures, as have critics before him, to the slow process by which its forms are evolved. He demands, however, a more explicit theory of adaptation than the 'vague hand-waving' of architectural Darwinism (1964, p. 37). Alexander draws a distinction between the 'unselfconscious' culture of primitive society, where the activity of 'design' is not recognised, where the user of a building is his own architect and the form evolves through the correction of individual technical failures as they occur; and the 'self-conscious' situation which obtains in our own culture, where design is the province of professionals, and is communicated through abstract principles and schemata. The 'unselfconscious' process relies on design being evolutionary rather than anticipatory, and on the existence of substantial forces of traditional taboo, as well as the slow movement of technical progress, to hold the evolving design steady. In the 'self-conscious' situation, instead of the form being shaped directly as a process of adaptation to the environment, this 'complex interaction between form and context' is modelled as a mental picture in the mind of the designer (Alexander 1964, ch. 6).† See Fig. 4.1.

Alexander argues that the unselfconscious process achieves success by virtue of the property of *homeostasis*, that is to say through being self-organising. The structure of the form-making system consists in a series of variables, or conditions which must be met to ensure 'good fit' between form and context; and the interaction between variables – causal linkages between one and another. See Fig. 4.2. (Alexander 1964, p. 43.)

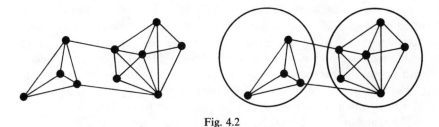

Fig. 4.2

'Since not all the variables are equally strongly connected (in other words there are not only dependences among the variables, but also independences), there will always be sub-systems...which can, in principle, operate fairly independently.' (Ibid.) These sub-systems, although interlinked, are yet 'sufficiently free of one another to adjust independently in a feasible amount of time'. The unselfconscious process works, 'because the cycles of correction and recorrection which occur during adaptation, are restricted to one sub-system at a time'. These kinds of dynamic systems

† See also diagram p. 76 reproduced here as Fig. 4.1. The designer imagines such interaction: the interaction takes place between a conceptual picture of the context and a conceptual picture of the form (diagrams and pictures which stand for the form). The success of the method is plainly dependent on the ability of the designer to comprehend the total problem context, and to model the proposed form effectively in order that he may examine properly its inadequacies or advantages in relation to this context. As Alexander says 'in the unselfconscious process there is no possibility of misconstruing the situation: nobody makes a picture of the context, so the picture cannot be wrong'. But in the self-conscious process the context is only pictured, and the designer's difficulty is in making this picture as complete and accurate as possible.

also characterise the biological world. Each system consists of many sub-systems loosely coupled; and the sub-systems themselves tend to consist of yet smaller systems, again more closely coupled internally yet less closely coupled between one another.

In the unselfconscious process any failure in the design, any 'misfit' will tend to affect strongly only those variables encompassed in the particular sub-system, and the failure will be resolved by an appropriate re-organisation of that sub-system. The self-conscious designer, in order to reduce his task to manageable proportions, attempts to pick out these sub-systems and attach a nomenclature, and then manipulate areas of the design in relative independence of each other in a similar way.† The trouble as Alexander sees it is that in practice the traditional categories, into which the design problem is intuitively analysed, tend not to correspond to its real structure.

His remedy for the failings of generalised concepts and categories, and their arbitrariness, is to reduce the listed variables making up a design programme to the level of specific detail. They 'must be chosen (1) to be of equal scope, (2) to be as independent of one another as is reasonably possible, and (3) to be as small in scope and hence as specific and detailed and numerous as possible'. (Alexander 1964, p. 115.) The design process is seen as one of error reduction and the variables have to do with anticipated causes of stress or misfit between the context for a design and the 'domain of forms' which could conceivably be placed in this context.

The domain 'may be thought of roughly as the set of all those dis-criminable forms (good and bad) which might possibly be placed in contact with the given context to complete the ensemble'. (Ibid., p. 103.) The variables are to be equal in scope so that some requirements are not sub-sumed partly or entirely within the broader frame of reference of others: and so following from this that they are independent of each other. Small in scope also because in this way the prejudice of ready-made semantic categories – 'acoustics', 'economics' and so on – is avoided.

The discussion so far concerns Alexander's account of the analytical phase only of the design programme. When it comes to the synthetic phase, or the realisation of the programme, Alexander seems to imply a degree of

† Alexander 1964, ch. 5. Alexander's analogy is that of a children's puzzle – one of those shallow glass-topped boxes, where balls must be rolled into sockets. An impatient child might well give the box a great shake and put it down, hoping for all the balls to fall in at once. His chances of success would be small, even if he repeated the process hundreds of times. More sensibly he would tap gently, moving one ball at a time, taking care not to disturb those already in place. The designer must adopt similar tactics, solving each independent area of the design in turn, so that decisions taken at a later stage do not invalidate the solutions to other 'sub-problems' already achieved.

functional determinism, in introducing the notion of a 'unified description' of form and context. For some very simple objects, he says 'there is virtually no rift between formal and functional descriptions Take a soap bubble for instance...

'The behaviour of soap films is so thoroughly understood that we know what shapes and sizes of bubbles different external conditions lead to. In this case, the formal descriptions and the functional descriptions are just different ways of saying the same things; we can say, if we like, that we have a unified description of a soap bubble.' (Ibid., p. 90.) Another example he takes is that of a road junction, where a diagrammatic representation of traffic flows as lines of different widths indicates directly the form the junction should take. The diagram is both a requirement diagram and a form diagram.

As he points out, however, there are few instances one can point to in the realm of man-made objects where the form has been uniquely determined by its requirements – the crane hook being thought to be one example (Archer 1956). The 'form diagram' can, in most design problems, be regarded as an exploratory tool, a tentative hypothesis about the matching of form to context, and like all hypotheses, derived through abstraction and invention. The process is that of the scientific method, where the hypothesis stands until shown to be false. It is measured against the requirements, by experiment, until a discrepancy between form and context is found. The hypothesis/diagram is then revised, and tested again.

It is important here, however, to emphasise the role in design of what might perhaps be called 'happy fit' as distinct from 'good fit': that is to say the possibility of finding a formal solution whose structure is particularly appropriate to the problem in hand but only through happy accident and not any kind of cause and effect. Such a possibility only arises through the relative 'slackness' of the programme requirements, whereby many alternative solutions are feasible. In this light, the soap-bubble example is misleading since no external purpose is recognised which the bubble fulfills; it exists as a natural phenomenon in its own right. It is a tension structure whose form is described completely by mathematical laws associated with the pressures exerted by the air. In the world of living organisms, similar tension structures are used for definite purposes to which they are admirably suited. But their forms cannot be ascribed simply to the moulding pressures arising from their functions: they are governed both by these *and* by independent structural laws of a general nature.

To take D'Arcy Thompson's classic example which approaches closest perhaps in the natural world to the problems of architecture: the honeycomb (Thompson 1942, pp. 499ff). The 'requirements' can be examined for an assembly of roughly cylindrical cells, stacked to fill space, strong and economical of material. The process of the comb's construction can be observed: how cylinders, stacked, will tend to get moved into a hexagonal array and six sides be flattened out as the bees work, pressing against each other from opposite sides. But it can also be seen, at the same time, how the symmetrical forces of surface tension, working on the warm wax, will pull the comb's wall into the same configuration. The final form represents a resolution of structural forces as well as a consequence of the purpose for which it is made, but one does not necessarily follow from the other.

A vivid example of the same thing in architecture is in the uses made of the Buckminster Fuller hemispherical dome which is patently unsuitable as a house, despite Fuller's own personal example. It has a rigorous structural logic and virtually no flexibility of form: yet it has applications to which it is particularly appropriate, as for example in housing rotating radar scanners, or a use to which it is put in Cambridge – as an 'artificial sky' for architectural lighting experiments.

It is not only for 'engineering' structures that this fortuitous match between form and function is found. A similar match exists in the problems of the university teaching timetable: in how, given a structure of courses and thus a division of the student body into groups which must attend separate series of teaching 'events', these 'events' are then assigned to rooms so as to fulfil a number of limiting criteria, the most important of which will generally be economy in space (though not at the expense of some other educational considerations). Although these criteria can be stated with mathematical precision, timetabling problems do not allow of unique solutions. Instead a sensible strategy must be devised for searching through feasible alternatives, and a basis established for selecting better solutions. These better solutions will rely, in particular when a timetable is designed to suit an existing set of rooms, but also when a set of rooms is designed to suit a given structure of courses, on the particular combinations of class size and the fact that these happen to correspond, fortuitously, with room size.

Another example which is familiar to architects is the problem of planning a set of rooms of required sizes in a tight or limited configuration. Successful solutions may depend on purely fortuitous coincidence of dimensions or groups of dimensions – the rooms happen to fit together just so. There is no way of going about the problem that does not involve a certain amount of trial and error.

Although the characteristics of the architectural design process so far described can be summed up, it is necessary first to have an understanding of the detailed structure of the requirements, or context, of the problem, without the distortions arising out of ready-made semantic categories. Some of these requirements may be difficult to measure and therefore indistinctly stated. The process of matching form to context is guided to a large degree by a correct interpretation of the structural nature of the problem; feasible alternative solutions are devised which are internally consistent and coherent in their own terms. These alternatives are then matched up to the context and their performance measured. Some solutions will be judged more successful than others, sometimes by virtue simply of a coincidental 'happy fit' of form and context. Where the scale of values by which performance is measured is essentially subjective and scientifically hard to define, or where performance on two disparate scales of value must be compared one against another, then opportunities must be presented to the designer or his client for the making of explicit judgement or choice in the matter.

The design process would therefore be considered to be largely a repetitive, cyclical one, in which the devising of preliminary solutions provokes a more explicit statement of the original requirements, and allows a progressively greater understanding of the structural nature of the problems in hand. Some of the choices and judgements which the designer or client must make only arise and only have meaning in relation to an intermediate solution, another reason why a measure of trial and error is inevitable. The fact that some requirements are mutually exclusive or work against each other in some way may similarly emerge only through the testing of alternative designs.

Now it is Alexander's contention that in architecture there is no means of generating ranges of alternative solutions symbolically (1964, p. 74), nor of expressing criteria for success in terms of a symbolic description of the form.

He instances certain kinds of problems which are capable of reduction to a matter of simple selection – 'like some of those that occur in economics, checkers, logic or administration, which can be clarified and solved mechanically'. It is impossible with architectural problems to generate a range of feasible, complete and finished solutions by a similar, single, uninterrupted, predetermined procedure of a mechanical nature. This, however, is no objection to a step-wise process, by which alternative preliminary forms or partial solutions are produced as a 'first hypothesis', evaluated, the terms of the problem somewhat revised, and a second series of appropriately modified forms tested again.

Now it is certainly true of a set of architectural drawings as a symbolic description that they present an inadequate means for a rigorous testing of the design against the programme requirements: building performance can only be assessed indirectly from them, by powerful exercise of the imagination or a great deal of prolonged and laborious calculation, depending on the characteristics of the design under consideration. As for the possibilities of full-scale experiment with real buildings, these are plainly limited since mistakes will be costly, and, in any case, identical circumstances are rarely repeated. But, as we have suggested before, the technique of simulating a design, either partial or complete, in the form of a computable model whose structure is mathematical, is exactly the way to evaluate its predicted performance with a high degree of realism. Calculations which were tedious and, in effect, impracticable for reasons of time become suddenly possible. Not only can external environmental conditions be simulated, but also the anticipated pattern of use of the building. Most important the pattern of use is not seen as something static and fixed, but as a dynamic process in time, over both the course of the day and the course of the years.

The unavoidably indeterminate way in which architectural problems are formulated, and the fact that as a consequence they may not be solved algorithmically, do not nevertheless imply that a strategy involving many successive alternate steps of design formulation and evaluation cannot be conducted in a perfectly logical, if not initially predetermined manner. The process allows the intervention of taste, judgement and invention at a series of intermediate stages; but with the cardinal advantage that these are exercised in relation to a clear statement of the structure of the problem and the issues at stake at each stage.

PART 2

ACTIVITIES, SPACE AND LOCATION

Introduction

From the more general work which has been indicated in the previous section, it seemed possible that studies might be developed at three different scales. The first is the scale of the individual building, at which level it might be possible to examine the internal and external relationships which affect the built form. The second is the scale of the urban sub-system, or, for example, the grouping of activities and buildings that are built up around the developing universities. The third scale is the major one of the urban system itself. All three of these programmes of work were in fact established by 1967. The first study to elaborate a method of work in Report form was the universities study, by Bullock, Dickens and Steadman, who produced their *Theoretical Basis for University Planning* in 1968.

The papers that follow were written at different points in that developing research programme. The first paper marked the end of the initial period of research. During this period, work on various parts of the programme was built up in some detail. An advance was made by the development of a method of studying timetabling and the relationship between numbers, intensity of use and space requirements of a given pattern of teaching (Toye 1968). Some of the earlier studies of the effect of different building forms on the use of land were given a more specific application, in which circulation and costs were taken into account. Some preliminary work was done on university residential accommodation and the effects of its location on the provision of other facilities on the campus itself.

But throughout all this work the main effort was to establish some means of examining the problem as a whole. What was required was the development of the kind of framework which would integrate hitherto isolated pieces of research and which, at the same time, would allow decisions made in one aspect of university planning, for instance numbers of students, to be seen in relation to the many other factors involved, for instance space. The proposal that a mathematical model should be used for this purpose had already been suggested in Chapter 4. But it was not at this stage clear what form this model could take: earlier models used for urban studies were on too large a scale for the problem in hand. The various sub-problems were, however, identified and the intention to provide an overall framework for the totality was graphically symbolised by a 'General Network' diagram which expressed the interrelationships involved.† By the time the second article had appeared (Bullock, Dickens and Steadman 1970) the work had been considerably advanced. It was now much more clear what form the model should take. The model was to be divided into two distinct parts: on the one hand it would describe the activities of the university (teaching, social activities, residential activities and so forth). And on the other, the model would also consist of a description of the physical context of the university – its floor space, the distribution of floor space over areas of land, and the relationship of the university to its surrounding urban areas. The timetabling studies previously made would be central to the description of activities, but the main need now was for a mathematical description of the 'non-scheduled' activities within the university.

From an examination of alternative approaches to the modelling of day-to-day activities, the authors came to the important conclusion that a distinction could be made between the amounts of time spent by different population-groups on various activities ('time budgets') and the locations in which these activities occur. Thus it is assumed that the time budgets can be considered as remaining relatively constant for comparable population groups independent of location; but that locational behaviour – movements to different geographical locations and the use of different facilities – is dependent on the range of facilities and the physical relationships to be found in a particular situation. These latter may include the layout of a university campus, the distribution of urban services and so forth. To illustrate the theoretical principles underlying such a 'two-stage' model, a simulation approach is demonstrated, in which highly simplified assumptions are made regarding the time budgets for different student groups and the factors affecting the choice of location. However, such an approach becomes impractical when applied to modelling the activities of large numbers of students in a more realistic situation, and the postscript outlines how an entropy-maximising approach overcomes some of the technical problems involved in handling large amounts of data. Nevertheless, the essential theory of activities modelling originally proposed – that of time budgets being independent of location – remains unchanged. Indeed, subsequent surveys of activities carried out at a series of

† See Fig. 5.1 on p. 118.

institutions confirm that such a theory should be borne out by empirical observation. It is clear that the intentions expressed in the original article of 1968 are now in sight of being achieved. At the same time it seems that in achieving this end the group has developed methods and approaches which would have important applications to problems other than those concerned with university planning.

Though this work has concentrated on the problem of the grouping of buildings within universities in which much of the statistical data necessary for the study was readily available, it clearly extends itself into a method of studying other more dispersed relationships such as those to be found in the grouping of polytechnics.†

But the problem extends beyond this into the subregion of the urban system. In the developing relationships between educational institutions themselves and in their possible interrelationship with the city of which they form a part there are no physical boundaries and no exact limits (Martin 1968). Consider the area between Boston and Cambridge (Mass.). The distance between them is about 4 miles. In this distance there exists a constantly changing and developing educational complex that includes the University of Harvard, the Massachusetts Institute of Technology, Boston University, North Eastern University, six or seven medical schools and a number of art schools. In this area the total student population alone is over 100,000 (Dober 1967). The internal relationship in each part will certainly change. But there is plenty of evidence that educational and research linkages (one of these with a particular relevance to the studies in this volume)‡ are now extending beyond single institutions and are increasingly involving the whole system.

The example nearer home is the University of Manchester. Forty years ago it centred around Owens College: the College of Art and the Technical College seemed remote and isolated institutions separated out by decaying housing. These considerable intervening areas have now been cleared. The expanding University and the new Institute of Science and Technology are to be related to the buildings controlled by the City Education Authority, that is, the Regional College of Art, the John Dalton College of Technology and the Adult Education College. The last three and the University Theatre and College of Music will offer educational opportunities to the surrounding community. All may share residential and dining facilities and will use a sports centre which no single institution could support in isolation. All this and the Whitworth Art Gallery, the major teaching hospital, the senior schools for boys and girls and various related residential areas

† The work has now been extended to include this problem.
‡ The Joint Centre for Urban Studies links Harvard and M.I.T.

form a band of development several miles long which is centred around higher education (Wilson & Womersley 1967).

Such developing clusters can no longer be thought of as a series of individual buildings. They are 'systems' within which we need to understand the basic framework of movement by which they are related, the interaction of the parts within this, the response of the building forms to the overlapping patterns of use that are constantly developing and changing. Cities are the main systems within which these sub-systems exist and operate.

5. *A theoretical model for university planning*[†]

NICHOLAS BULLOCK, PETER DICKENS & PHILIP STEADMAN

In the context of present controversy about the structure of university finance, of Government concern about the efficiency with which universities make use of buildings and sites, and of university dissatisfaction with the present way in which funds are allocated for new buildings and equipment, a clear need is felt for a basis of fact upon which rational discussion of the use of capacity and resources can be built. In Cambridge the relationships are being studied between university student numbers, amounts of building and the use of land. The work is being carried out in a university context and with the help of the administrative and academic staff of a number of universities.

What seems to be needed is a theoretical model of the physical planning of universities, a model similar to those used in economics and operations research, and of a kind now being developed, particularly in America, for use in the field of urban planning.[‡] The essential feature of such a model would be the establishment of a comprehensive series of mathematical relationships between the different parameters which affect the physical aspects of university planning. These would be based, in the first place, on the mechanisms of university expansion as they operate now. 'The simplest function of a mathematical model is to *explain*, in some sense, the present situation' (Wilson 1967), but shorn of many of the irrelevant complications that are always to be found in any actual case. Thus the model is primarily *descriptive*. The functioning of the actual system must be studied, as it has been possible to do for a large number of university buildings and sites, as

† This essay was originally published in *Universities Quarterly* for March 1968. The work was done in close consultation with the University Grants Committee and supported by the Department of Education and Science and the Gulbenkian Foundation.
‡ The Journal of the American Institute of Planners for May 1965 gives a very full picture of American work in this field. For an introduction to the use of models in planning, see Wilson (1967).

well as studying teaching patterns in detail at the London School of Economics and at the University of Newcastle. But once the model can be shown to represent adequately the relations of the variables as they are found, then its real value lies in its ability to *predict*, by the projections of the variables forward in time. Either it may be assumed that present trends continue, in which case the model is termed *predictive*: or else some variables may be controlled or planned, in which case it is called a *planning* model. Control of the variables may then be effected with some understanding of the implications of different decisions on the whole system – the university in this case – and the failings of piecemeal planning as it is now often carried on avoided. A mathematical model of the physical aspects of the university would serve therefore not only to describe the present use made of buildings and sites, but would also supply more precise information than is currently available about their potential capacity, and about the implications in physical terms of the massive expansion in student numbers which is taking place and will continue to take place over the next few years. Already, since the publication of the Robbins Report (Robbins 1963), the projected number of student places has been increased; in October 1967 a new target of 220,000 to 225,000 university places was announced for 1971 by the Secretary for Education and Science. Despite the doubling of government grants to universities in the last five years, the pressure of demand for places continues to increase and there is, therefore, a great need for universities to use their accommodation more efficiently. In this context a 'future state model' would supply evidence on which to base choices between urban, suburban and rural sites, to determine the effect of splitting the university teaching between different sites, or of undergraduate teaching separated from research, or to predict the amount of accommodation needed for new methods of teaching or new patterns of student residence.

Because of the mathematical nature of the model, and of the large volumes of numerical data involved, treatment by computer techniques is particularly appropriate.

There is in existence a considerable body of information, but largely unco-ordinated, on university planning, accumulated by separate organizations, firms and individuals. The Architects and Surveyors Group in the University Grants Committee, set up 'to advise the Committee on the universities' plans for individual buildings, and to develop systems of cost analysis which would provide norms, in the light of which such plans could be assessed', has in defining its cost limits done considerable research into student residence, libraries, playing fields, catering facilities, and the use of prefabrication in university building. Much work capable of general application has been done by firms of planning consultants commissioned by various universities to prepare development plans. The Committee of University Buildings Officers has started to pool the mass of statistical data in the possession of its individual members in a central information service. And there are contributions to the theory of planning made by independent firms, such as have grown out of Ove Arup and Partners' wide experience of university laboratory buildings (Dowson 1967); and by individuals, such as J. R. B. Taylor's work on the science lecture room (Taylor 1967). The list could be continued to great length: and a perhaps larger body of research done in America also has relevance for British university planning. The danger is that however many pieces of research are carried on, if they remain in isolation their value will be lost. Though perfectly consistent within themselves, they may fail to take into account the crucial effect of parameters outside their particular scope, and consequently be unable to provide the information with which to optimize in terms of the whole. Only by relating individual studies to the structure of their whole context can the universities become more efficient in their planning.

To take an example, the purchase of new building land and the capital cost of the building put on it are at present treated as separate transactions. So a high-rise or high density building is subject to the same kind of cost limits (with some extra allowance for lifts, etc.), as a low or spread-out building of equivalent floor area, irrespective of the consequent saving in land. Similarly capital and running costs are considered in isolation, as are the costs of buildings and the costs of staff salaries and equipment. One could imagine a situation in which a building, apparently wasteful in space, was nevertheless designed to allow a reduction in non-academic staff numbers, whose total salaries over the life of the structure constitute a sum which is large by comparison with the cost of the building. Again, great efforts might be made to cut down lecture room requirements by a reorganization of the teaching timetable; but with a resulting increased need for laboratory space, which student place for student place is much more expensive.

It would be extravagant to imagine that with limited resources and in a short time it is possible to treat in depth the whole range of studies which a comprehensive model would encompass. It is strongly felt though, that the advantages of taking the broader view are sufficient to compensate for an inevitable sketchiness and inadequacy in some areas, in the early stages.

Before describing the proposed model in detail, it should be emphasized that there is an important distinction between the making of the model, by defining the framework of the parameters and their interrelationships – a generalized process; and the formulation of a plan to solve a particular problem in which the parameters take particular values – a specific process.

Each parameter is allowed a reasonable range – at no stage are fixed ideal standards proposed. Nor is the model designed to optimize in terms of particular constraints (unless this is specifically required), but simply to demonstrate the effect of one variable upon another, and to outline the consequences of different decisions at each stage. These decisions, about patterns of teaching or about standards of accommodation or amenity, are plainly the province of academic planners, university administration, and their appointed architects. The model is based in the first place on standards, conditions and organization as they exist in universities now. But the assumption that such conditions are acceptable or desirable is not necessarily thereby built in.

The construction of the model falls into two parts: the relating of population – staff and student numbers – to amounts of space (measured in terms of floor area) required for their accommodation, and the relating of these floor area totals to the consequent volume of building and hence area of land used. To relate population to floor area involves a description of the patterns of activities which take place in these spaces, and of the patterns of movement between spaces: to relate floor areas to land area requires a description of the form and layout of buildings, and of the layout of areas between buildings. The principal types of accommodation involved are three: teaching, research and residential.

For 'formal' teaching, that is in fixed periods of any kind – whether they be lectures, classes, seminars, laboratory practicals or any other kind of teaching in groups at fixed times – the way in which space is used is subject to a general theory relating the size of groups and the structure of courses taught to the number and capacities of the teaching rooms. Most courses have typically a 'tree-like' structure, in which the total number of students is split down progressively into smaller and smaller groups, these corresponding to a series of options within the main subject. The courses may overlap to a greater or lesser degree, and have many or few 'branches', depending on whether a very catholic range of choices is offered or whether a rigid specialization is enforced. These cycles of 'teaching events', as Robbins calls them, are accommodated within the 'teaching week' (it may be a fortnightly cycle, or some other frequency, the principle is not affected), that is to say the total number of hours or periods available for teaching during the cycle. A typical teaching week (real week) might thus be thirty hours: six hours a day, five days a week.

The timetable is then designed to allocate events to rooms and periods, subject to a number of limiting constraints. The most obvious of possible constraints is the minimizing of the total number of rooms used. But there are considerations which work to increase the supply of rooms needed. It might not, for example, be thought desirable for any one group of students to attend more than two or three periods in immediate succession; there might be times at which a teacher was unable to attend, or there might be a limit on the amount of teaching he was prepared to do in one day; there might, according to the geographical layout of the buildings, be some rooms which it was impracticable to reach from others in the time allowed between periods. It may also be advisable to leave periods free for unscheduled events and sudden changes, and for the preparation of demonstrations and equipment – very necessary in teaching laboratories. P. N. Toye has been working at the Cambridge Mathematical Laboratory on a program for the automatic production of timetables, which allows for the introduction of such constraints (Toye 1968). Timetabling problems are necessarily indeterminate, and do not have unique solutions: Toye's program produces many timetables to fit one set of courses, but incorporates methods of working towards better solutions, and of rejecting trivially different alternatives.

Inevitably, even with the best timetables, some wastage will occur. To satisfy the constraints already mentioned necessitates some wastage in *time* – hours when rooms are not in use. And in general a complex course structure will also mean wastage in time. In addition the total wastage by *place* – seats vacant when a room is in use – is determined by the goodness of fit between group size and room size; and this depends on how large a structure of courses is programmed at once. At one extreme a very simple course, with few students, may be accommodated in a single room: in which case the room must be the size of the largest group. With many students, numerous groups and several rooms, there is a better chance of suiting group size to room size in each case, and reducing the wastage. The larger the scale, the better the fit. An example from Leeds demonstrates the point: 'a proposal for savings in capital expenditure by means of careful programme analysis was recorded in the University of Leeds Development Plan 1960. In it, lecture room requirements from departments of the New Medical School were shown to be subject to contraction of 50% if the principle of sharing and central control were acceptable.' (Taylor 1967.)

In a teaching laboratory, which it really is expensive to have standing empty, it may well be the availability of technical staff and the capacity of preparation and storage space which set the practical limits on its use. In some departments the greater part of the short vacations is presently taken up in preparing experimental apparatus for the next term's teaching, and this problem is one which would bear heavily on the feasibility of the four-term year. Despite these kinds of difficulties, Leeds, for example, has found it worth building 'multi-discipline' laboratories in which a greater initial outlay, on a more extensive provision of services and on more storage and

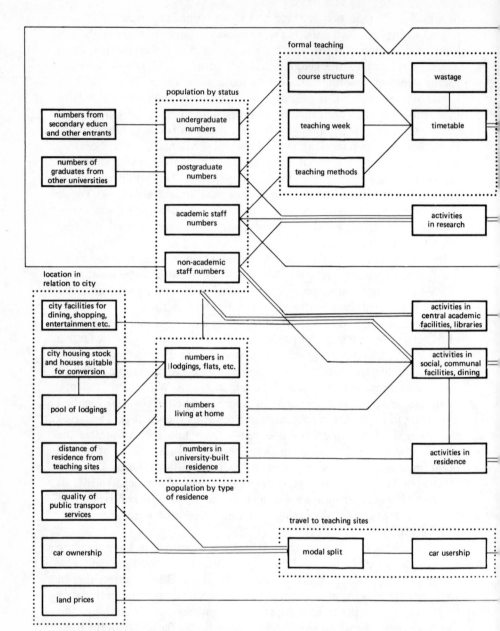

Fig. 5.1. The 'network' drawing is intended as an index of topics which enter into those aspects of university planning concerning buildings and sites. The boxes denote these topics, and the lines joining boxes indicate the existence of direct connections or relationships of some kind between topics. The object, in the construction of a computable model (for which this drawing is a kind of highly simplified blueprint), is to state such relationships as are quantifiable in mathematical or semi-mathematical form. The model is not completely closed: each parameter is allowed a reasonable range, and in

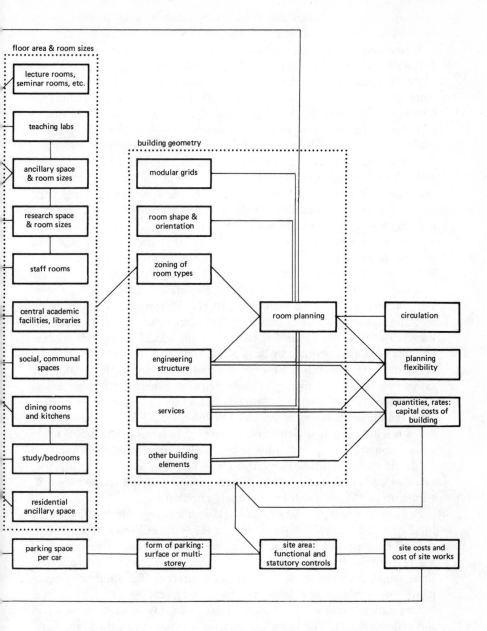

addition the process of computation is broken frequently to allow the introduction of 'policy' decisions on matters of fine judgement or taste – but with the cardinal advantage that these choices are exercised in the light of a clear exposition of the possible alternatives and their implications. The detail of the diagram is of necessity somewhat tentative in parts, and to some extent represents a plan for further work. For this reason not all the factors enumerated are to be thought of necessarily as equally important, and the structure of the 'network' is not entirely homogeneous.

ancillary space, is compensated for by the greater efficiency in use through the labs being shared between several departments.

In one case studied, the wastage in both laboratories and lecture rooms averaged over the whole university was found to be 84% by time, 80% by place: in other words each room was used on average five or six hours a week, and was less than a quarter full when in use. Such a performance compares badly with the full potential of that university. It may be due to complex course structures or to bad management – but, in either case, it is important to know how such low utilization figures have occurred.

So the space requirements for formal teaching are related to the student population through the timetable. It is through the timetable too that teaching staff numbers relate to student numbers, not as a simple fixed ratio but taking into account the teaching hours received by students, the teaching hours given by staff, and the sizes of classes. 'If it has been decided what teaching students shall receive, and in what size of class, it is then possible to calculate the teaching hours of the staff which will be implied by any particular staff/student ratio.' (Robbins 1963.)†

Robbins gives a statistical picture of the present distribution of total staff numbers between the various grades (1963). The relative emphasis on teaching and on research varies widely from department to department and university to university, and is treated in the model as an independent variable. The proportion can be expressed in terms of the ratio of post-graduates and research staff to undergraduates and teaching staff: or rather one should not distinguish research and teaching staff members as such, since in many cases these will be one and the same person, but rather the research and teaching activities of each individual. This in educational terms is a notoriously difficult distinction; but in terms of the use of space and equipment perhaps not quite so tricky. The proportion of technical to academic staff in scientific subjects is also a factor of the research/teaching ratio, as well as of the timetable. Non-academic staff as a whole may constitute up to 15% of the total university population.

For a given set of population figures, it would be possible to calculate the total space (floor area) requirements in teaching and research buildings. A number of 'room types' have been distinguished, that is, differentiated by *use* rather than by architectural characteristics. These are of two kinds, those which are capable of measurement in terms of a number of occupants – work places in a laboratory or library reading room, seats in a lecture hall, seminar or class room, members of staff in staff rooms – and those that are not. The latter are lumped together and called 'ancillary'

† Robbins uses the formula $C = (S/T) \times R$, where C is the average size of classes, S is the average hours of teaching received by each student, T the average teaching hours of each teacher and R the staff/student ratio.

rooms, something of a category by exclusion, and one which would cover all kinds of preparation and special rooms associated with laboratories, rooms housing special equipment, store rooms and workshops. As such the category covers a wide range of sizes of room and a heterogeneous collection of uses and service and environmental requirements. Together ancillary rooms form a large proportion – as much as a half – of the total area of a science department.

On the basis of key differences in room types it is possible to make a preliminary if crude division of the spectrum of academic disciplines into the three groups Arts, Pure Science and Technology. These distinctions are for our purposes architectural plain and simple, and indicate for the most part differences in the scale of laboratories – 'factory scale' for Technology, 'bench scale' for Pure Science, none at all in Arts. Thus mathematics becomes an 'Arts' subject. Within electrical engineering, for example, the teaching of electronics, while in academic terms an applied science, might, for our purposes, be treated as a 'Pure Science' because of the small scale of the experimental work involved. Conversely, the use of very large apparatus in physics might qualify it in part for treatment under 'Technology'.

The total floor area requirements in each 'occupied' room type may now be calculated by the specifying of 'space standards' for each appropriate activity. Space standards are derived using three closely interdependent methods. Anthropometric study is applicable in the case of simple, well-defined activities, as for instance the lecture room seat or the width of a laboratory bench. More problematic are the complex patterns of activities in research work, which may be varied and unusual. Still more intangible are those circumstances where questions of prestige and social distinction creep in. These difficulties are to some extent sidestepped by the second method, using surveys of existing standards, the assumption being that these are tried in use. And the third is on the basis of recommendations by the appropriate central administrative or advisory body, in this case, the University Grants Committee. The process is circular, in the sense that the derivation of the U.G.C.'s original standard was made, presumably, on the basis of standards as then observed in practice, and from anthropometric data: similarly a survey of existing standards in recent buildings shows for the most part merely the adoption of the U.G.C.'s recommendations. The best plan seems to be to represent space standards as variable within reasonable ranges, and to demonstrate the costs or savings involved in lavish or parsimonious allowances. In private space allotted for the exclusive use of one person, such as a staff room, the population multiplied by the appropriate space allowance gives the total net floor area direct. In rooms used for formal teaching the timetable in combination with space standards will give the areas required. In rooms with a sporadic and un-predictable pattern of use, such as libraries and common rooms, the space allowed will depend on a more statistical assessment of the amount of time spent by each student or staff member there, and the maximum use at peak times.

To determine suitable numbers and sizes for ancillary rooms an approach rather different from that of measuring work places must be used, since the rooms are in principle 'unoccupied'. A rather general statistical method has been adopted, since the uses of ancillary rooms are so many and varied: a survey of recently built university science departments has been made, to detect any systematic relationship that might exist between the *total* area of ancillary space in each department and the total areas for teaching and research; and to detect within this total a typical statistical distribution of ancillary room sizes. The proportion of ancillary floor area does not appear to vary much from subject to subject, at least in Pure Science, but it does vary considerably with the proportion of research to teaching, as one would anticipate.

The distinction between ancillary rooms and research rooms is in many instances a rather fine one, and it may prove better to treat the two in conjunction without distinction. There may be a lot to be said for designing a 'stock' of rooms in 'useful' sizes rather than to suit a very particular initial set of research and ancillary uses which will soon be superseded. A study made of the history of adaptation and change that has been undergone by the Cavendish Laboratory in Cambridge since the war shows that it is in these room types that the most extensive and frequent change tends to occur. The survey distinguishes changes in room type – e.g. from lecture room to lab, or from lab to office – and changes in size, either by throwing two or more smaller rooms into one large one, or by subdividing a large one into smaller. The most inflexible spaces are the largest, designed in the first place to fit very special needs and quickly becoming obsolete. By contrast there would appear to be a lot of smaller rooms, concentrated around the 200 square foot mark, which are readily adaptable to a variety of uses without structural alteration – an observation also made by Cowan in his work on growth and change in hospitals (Cowan 1962).

Present work on the 'population to floor area' calculations is concerned with measuring the flow of students (and staff) through the university from year to year, using methods of representation similar to existing dynamic models of the primary and secondary educational systems (Moser, Redfern 1965), (O.E.C.D. 1967). The problems of utilization and flexibility must be seen over the whole of a building's history; something that is clearly demonstrated in the Cavendish study is the difference in the patterns of growth of student population and the growth of buildings.

Student numbers increase steadily all the time; buildings by their nature grow in large increments infrequently. This means a constantly varying pattern of utilization: under-use when a building is first put up, tending gradually to overcrowding, until the congestion becomes intolerable and more space is built. One of the advantages of taking the timetable and utilization calculations through to their implications in floor-space terms is that it then becomes possible to follow this process in detail. A temporary space crisis in formal teaching may possibly be solved by adjusting the timetable through increasing the length of the teaching week rather than by building again. This may imply an increase in teaching staff numbers: the comparative economies of the two solutions can be assessed.

The detail of the model as described so far is cast in terms of the traditional forms of university teaching, and of room types and uses as they are found today. How far is the model capable of treating changes in these areas?

Some changes would be more of degree than of kind, such as the four-term year, or teaching in schools of study rather than by departments. The model would not need serious modification to cope with these. But more serious structural alteration would be needed for instance to accommodate the widespread use of teaching machines, or of mechanical aids in the library. Serious information on the detailed implications of such changes is hard to find, although American experience may provide indications. The speed of change is not likely to be so breakneck as to preclude a continual 'up-dating' of the model to keep pace: indeed the massive investment in plant and buildings which the universities represent acts as a kind of inertia in the process of innovation.

The next stage is to examine the implications of planning the total required floor area in different forms of building. Any kind of attempt at an exhaustive treatment is obviously a tall order, but to demonstrate some principles involved on a restricted scale, a single Pure Science department has been taken, with a population of about 1000 (students plus staff). At this stage, the restriction was made in order to isolate one kind of functional unit within the university, and for this purpose a department is manageable and typical. This choice for examination was made while bearing in mind many alternative plans for organization. For example, there are considerable economies to be made in the use of space in a centrally programmed organization rather than in a teaching structure that holds rigidly to separate departments.

For the Science Department example, a schedule of accommodation has been prepared to suit a typical teaching timetable, using a computer program developed for the production of schedules on the basis of population figures, the teaching pattern, space standards and assumptions about wastage. These areas are net, since the ratio of net to gross (gross including circulation space, etc.) varies with the actual planning of the building (something of which the U.G.C.'s standard allowances take no account). To start with, the geometrical forms under consideration have been limited to rectangular blocks, although projected future studies will include cross and court forms. In the present worked examples, the blocks are fixed in one dimension (length), but variable in width and height (number of floors). In all cases the total net floor area remains the same, exactly similar accommodation is provided, and the buildings range from a single-storey structure of extensive plan area to a thin ten-storey slab. The next step will be to allow the length to alter while holding the width constant.

By planning the same accommodation in these different envelopes it will be possible to make systematic comparison of graduated building shapes from low and flat to tall and thin. Cost comparisons being prepared should prove particularly interesting, since the quantity surveying profession finds it difficult to generalize in this way as a rule; individual building prices tend in practice to be idiosyncratic, varying with local conditions, the uncertainties of competitive tendering, different standards of finish, and so on. Here a constant standard of finishes is assumed, as are similar ground conditions so that foundation costs are comparable, and because the buildings are planned in detail, the cost comparisons should be realistic.

There are other comparisons to be made: for instance in the ratio of perimeter wall to floor area, and hence in the proportion of rooms with windows to internal 'core' rooms. This will have implications for the heating, lighting and ventilation of the building, and so for the running costs. Once the rooms are planned in detail, then the pedestrian circulation generated by the teaching timetable can be readily measured; a program has been written to do this for different plan layouts and patterns of teaching. Movement outside the timetable will be difficult to predict. On the other hand, one can expect peak flows to be associated with the changeover between lectures, and for other movement around the building to be random and sporadic by comparison.

Of course the number of ways in which the rooms might be planned within even this limited range of envelopes is very large. In the first place there are broad considerations governing the general overall distribution of room types between the various floors or parts of the building – for example rooms with heavy floor loadings or with which large volumes of circulation are associated which would sensibly be planned at ground level. There could be established a series of priorities whereby certain types of rooms would be planned on the building perimeter in order to afford a view or natural light – in this case perhaps the smaller work rooms such as staff or research rooms, with a less high priority for large research rooms and teaching laboratories, and lower still for ancillary space and lecture rooms. Within these general schemes there are infinitely variable permutations and combinations of room sizes and shapes.

It remains to be seen how widely building costs and pedestrian movement vary with different layouts. Meanwhile a number of programs are being devised to allow rapid evaluation of various aspects of these plans. One such program makes structural calculations, for a range of basic structural systems: a second is designed to calculate the lengths of service pipe runs, again for a variety of layout types. Both these provide essential data for the preparation of the capital cost estimates.

A final comparison is to be made in the use of land: first, ground area occupied by the building itself, then the use of surrounding land. This is difficult to describe exactly, but certainly one consideration must be the overshadowing of adjacent buildings, and studies using models have been conducted to measure light levels in 'rooms' opposite the model at varying distances. Surface car parking is a rapacious user of land, and the number of spaces required will be a factor of the building population, levels of student and staff car ownership, and the pattern of use of the building throughout the day.

The problems of student residence have received attention recently from various quarters, and information exists on space standards in student rooms and on appropriate furniture sizes, related to anthropometric data. This attention was extended to different forms of construction for residential buildings, and to the sociology of student housing and the comparative educational advantages of different types of accommodation and of different social groupings (Robbins 1963, Allen and Miller 1966, University Grants Committee 1967b). Robbins represents the most recent attempt to take a broad view over all of England, recommending 560,000 places in the whole of higher education by 1980–1, of which 350,000 would be in universities. The Report on Higher Education recommends that special residential accommodation should be provided for two-thirds of all additional students entering all sectors of higher education, the remainder going into lodgings or living at home. Under this policy the overall proportion of students in residence would rise from 32% in 1961–2 to 54% in 1980–1, an increase over the period of 225,000 extra residential places, 180,000 of those in universities.

The Robbins policy was based on the belief that the educational and social advantages of living in some form of university residence were considerable, and also on the observations that numbers living at home have been on the decline, and are unlikely to rise again, and that the supply of lodgings available in many towns was becoming extremely limited. The

Report gave a warning in conclusion, that the problem of finding sufficient residential accommodation could be one of the main barriers to the proposed expansion of higher education. Despite Robbins' prognostications however, the provision of purpose-built residential buildings has been placed low in the Government's priorities for university work, and with the squeeze, the building of U.G.C. financed accommodation falls a long way short of the Robbins target. The overall situation remains broadly as Robbins saw it, and the problems merely postponed.

It is intended that the model should represent for residential buildings, as it does for teaching, the relationship of numbers to floor space, of floor space to land use for different building forms, and of all these to total costs. By taking residence and teaching in conjunction, then the type and location of residential and communal accommodation will be seen in relation to teaching patterns and patterns of movement.

The cost per student in a traditional hall of residence may be as high as £1400. The present studies suggest that this figure could be reduced by up to half if alternative types of housing were adopted.† For example, flats without large central common rooms and dining rooms are considerably cheaper and may be more popular with students. A wide range of alternative types of residence has been examined, taking into account different space standards, building forms and constructional standards. These alternatives are evaluated in terms of capital costs, running costs and area of site required according to different criteria.

A survey of seventy-five residential projects in this country and abroad illustrates a very wide range in the size of basic student room, varying from 70 sq ft per student in shared double rooms – common practice in the U.S.A. – through the U.G.C.'s recommended allowance of 120 sq ft, to a typical figure of 170 in privately financed projects, mostly in Oxford and Cambridge. This single item, the student room, can account for a half of the total university floor area. Variations in space standards here are therefore of the utmost importance.

The use of student rooms out of term for conference delegates may make it worth building private bathrooms throughout. The provision of common and dining rooms will depend on decisions about social groupings, and often on the distance of the residence from the central teaching site. It may be too far for students to go back home at mid-day, but if lunch is provided centrally and an evening meal in the residence, then catering facilities and dining rooms are duplicated.

---

† The University of Lancaster is building student flats at a cost of £700 per student. 'The space standards achieved are comparable to the Residential Cost Unit formula, but the building costs have been achieved by using house building forms and standards.' Private communication from W. Chadwick, University Development Officer.

Conversions of existing houses are popular with students who find the traditional lodging house matriarchy oppressive. Studies at York and elsewhere suggest that the cost of buying and converting houses for students is also considerably less than that of building halls of residence.† The purchase and conversion of existing property is an important example illustrating the need to see university housing in relation to that of the surrounding area or the city as a whole. It is intended that the model might eventually operate in conjunction with city housing models, and in this way it is hoped to examine how city and university residential programmes might be combined.

The final stage of the model comprises a rudimentary representation of the urban context of the university, showing the distribution of student residence throughout the town in relation to teaching and research sites, comparative land values (and rent levels) in different sectors, and the overall traffic network. Projections of vehicle ownership figures will allow prediction of the commuting traffic volumes generated by the university population (dependent to some extent on the teaching timetable), total university transport costs (to the community), and total car parking requirements. On this basis it should be possible to make comprehensive comparison of the costs and advantages of a choice of teaching and residential sites.

Some preliminary work has been carried out on the distribution of student residence. Data has so far been collected for seven university cities. Of these, three have been selected for more detailed treatment, as being representative of three contrasting types: Manchester, on a central urban site, Birmingham on a suburban site, and Hatfield College of Technology, which although not a university is nevertheless an institution of comparable size, and which occupies an effectively rural site. The Hatfield students all live at home, and are drawn from a wide area around the college, from Welwyn Garden City, St Albans and even from north London.

In the two urban examples some evidence has been accumulated about the type, age and quality of housing in which student residence is concentrated – often in somewhat depressed areas of large late Victorian or Edwardian houses which lend themselves to conversion. And in all three cases data has also been collected on the frequency of public transport services to and from the sites. A strong motive for taking these particular examples is that they represent three of the very few universities for which detailed recent traffic surveys exist (Wilson and Womersley 1967, Richardson, Davies and Dunsford 1967, Rose 1966), and it is therefore possible to compare information on the location of residence and the quality of

† Crease (1967) gives figures of £485 and £696 per student room (unfurnished) for two actual conversions at York.

public transport with survey details of the so-called 'modal split'—that is how the numbers travelling to and from the university sites are divided between different means of transport—walking, cycling, by car, 'bus or train—for the urban, suburban and rural situations. In Birmingham and Hatfield it is also possible to compare the proportion of car users with statistics on levels of car ownership among students, academic staff and non-academic staff.

Plans for further study include more detailed survey work on patterns of student travel, and activities outside the hours of formal teaching. It is hoped that by establishing more accurate measures of accessibility to the teaching sites, it may be possible to make a measure of the comparative economies of rent as against travel costs at different distances from the university.

6. *The modelling of day to day activities*†

NICHOLAS BULLOCK, PETER DICKENS &
PHILIP STEADMAN

Alternative Approaches

The 'subsystems' of an urban system might be distinguished in several ways. They could be described as spatially defined areas of the city; alternatively they might be delimited as operational units – for example office organisations, industrial plants or educational institutions. In each case, a more detailed knowledge of how these sub-systems operate will assist in understanding the apparent complexity of the larger urban scene.

Equally of course, these parts or sub-systems – such as, for example, the particular institution here chosen to look at, the university – are deserving of study in their own right for the special planning and architectural problems they present at their particular scale, besides as components of the larger urban problem. The university is a relatively large, self-contained and well-defined institution, and is thus a particularly promising subject for study at this scale.

In moving from the urban scale to that of the institution, a much wider and more complex range of activities must be examined than just those distinctions between employment, service and home-based activities that might be made for an urban model. The study will have to examine how the various groups of people who engage in these varied activities choose the places which they do, and how these activities vary at different hours of the day and on different days of the week; in short, how detailed patterns of activity are arranged in time and space. For the university, the great variety of types of activity in which students and teachers engage, and the relative freedom which they have to organise their time as they please, makes this perhaps an especially complicated case to consider – by com-

† This chapter is a repreparation of two previously published papers: The first, originally entitled 'Activities, Space and Location,' appeared in *Architectural Review* of April 1970; and the second 'The Modelling of Day to Day Activity Patterns', in *Architectural Design*, May 1971. The attempt has been made in combining the two to show the principles adopted in a simple model of activities and then the complications that might apply to a more realistic case. A postscript describes the running of the developed model.

129

parison with the more regular routine of the factory or office worker, or the housewife. Nonetheless, academic life is not so different from the world outside that a model of university activities will not have relevance to other institutions or groups in the larger population, where the modelling job may indeed be a more simple one.

By analogy with economic thinking, the university, regarded as a system, might be divided into two parts – into 'demand' and 'supply' sectors. The activities of the university create a demand for space and for buildings of various kinds, and this demand is met with a supply of these different types of space. The activities or demand sector would cover for example patterns of teaching, patterns of activity in residential accommodation, the use of libraries and of social accommodation, and patterns of travel. In describing these detailed activities of the university population, a distinction is drawn between 'scheduled' activities governed by the timetable – lectures, classes and laboratory periods – and what have been termed 'non-scheduled' activities, which comprise all other activities outside the hours of formal teaching. Over longer time periods the activities sector concerns the flow of students from course to course, from one year of study to the next and from one place of residence to another.

The other half of the economic equation, the supply sector, is represented by the stock of buildings and sites in the university, and in addition some of the buildings and facilities of the surrounding urban area. In contrast to the urban situation though, where the disposition of floor space for different functions throughout different parts of the city is at least in part the result of the operation of market forces over a period of years, at the institutional level the layout of sites and buildings tends to come under some overall central planning control. At this scale there can therefore be no equivalent of the urban systems type of 'stock model', and the particular physical layout in each different situation must be regarded as a 'given', an input, for the purpose of a model of activities.

It is worth re-emphasising that the purpose of a model of university activities, as of the urban system, is in the first place to replicate or represent the workings of some selected aspects of the system as it is observed in the real world. A model is not to be confused with some kind of automatic design method for producing plans, nor is there any effort to optimise designs or layouts in terms of some function of cost, efficiency or satisfaction of any kind. A model of economical and concise form which describes the activities system as it exists, though, serves to increase our understanding and knowledge of that system, and this in itself can contribute towards better application to a number of different situations; then we may begin to have confidence in its *predictive* powers. The practical significance for planning of a model of activities then lies in the way in which it can give indications of what activities would take place, what patterns of use of space and buildings, in hypothetical situations. Thus the likely effect of different plans, or of different decisions on questions of academic and social organisation, for example, in the university case, can be explored and evaluated.

In attempting to deal with the activities of individuals or of small groups, rather than with populations at the city scale, we are faced with a choice of an appropriate mathematical tool from among a number of possibilities. The normative principles applicable at a large scale as in the urban systems type of model, although not deterministic, rely on statistical approximations of high probability based on very large numbers. As we move down the scale towards the level of small group activities and ultimately to the behaviour of the individual we are faced with greater variability and an increasing number of differences in types of activity, in the sequences by which activities follow one on another, and in the choice of locations for each different type of activity. The analogy from thermodynamics is put graphically by Bronowski (1960): 'A society moves under material pressure like a stream of gas, and on the average, its individuals obey the pressure; but at any instant, any individual may, like an atom of gas, be moving across or against the stream.' It might appear at first sight that the type of statistical descriptions applicable to mass behaviour, using the theoretical apparatus of statistical mechanics, would not apply to activities studied at the level of the small group.

It has been suggested by several authors in the past that the branch of applied mathematics which would lend itself most particularly to the modelling of the behaviour of individuals for the purpose of geographical or planning studies would be the *theory of games*. Developed largely by von Neumann and Morgenstern (1953) in the 'forties, game theory provides a means of representing the actions of the individual and his attempts to make 'optimum' decisions according to some measured scales of value, in a situation where he has some range of choice of possible actions with known or probable outcomes. There have been many applications of game theory in the fields of economics, business 'games', military planning and so on. Of the applications in geography and regional science, Isard and Dacey (1962) have used game theory to restate, from the point of view of the individual decision maker, some of the basic tenets of location theory. Gould (1963) illustrates its use in deciding the optimum strategy for raising crops and in choosing the best market for selling cattle in Ghana. And Marble (1967) has used game theory to model the travel behaviour of individuals between shopping and the home.

Despite its pre-eminent position as an elegant model of decision-making behaviour, however, there are serious drawbacks in the use of game theory for the present purpose. First there is the problem of the extent of the 'player's' knowledge and the degree of rationality that can be expected from him. The range of alternative courses of action – by analogy with possible 'moves' in some game – is very large, as is the number of possible conditions applying at each chosen location, or 'states of nature', of which the player must have at least partial knowledge. The number of possible outcomes of the player's actions increases proportionately. Yet the theory demands that the player must know not only all possible outcomes, but also the probability of the occurrence of each state of nature, if he is to make an 'optimum' decision. The player is said to act rationally only if he seeks to optimise his good, but if he cannot know all possible outcomes, how does this affect the rationality of his choice? Even von Neumann and Morgenstern admitted that 'it may be safely stated that there exists, at present, no satisfactory treatment of the question of rational behaviour'.

A second difficulty is in the estimation of the 'pay-offs', in the way in which the player attaches a significance to any outcome in terms of his own internal accounting system. In military or business applications the goals are clear and the estimation of pay-offs is generally simple. The goals of maximising profit, or of killing as many enemy as possible, and the calculation of pay-offs that these involve, are simple by comparison with some representation of a student's optimum decision, when in quick succession his overriding preoccupations might be to get a first-class degree, to date a girl, or to achieve maximum effect in a sit-in. Indeed the search for some common and generally workable metric against which to measure the value attributed by people to the pay-offs resulting from a choice of actions in such a situation, would appear to be sheer utopianism.

As an abstraction, then, game theory may be robust and simple; but to model students' behaviour in the complex environment of an urban university we must turn to other methods. After all, for the purposes of representing 'which students are where when', which is what our present aim amounts to, we have no call to get involved in the intricacies of individual motivation. Our concern is not with the particular person's values or priorities, nor with the subtleties of internal accounting which might lead to this or that decision. It will be quite sufficient if we can estimate the probability of a person visiting this or that facility, or spending so much time in one activity and so much in another, so as to reproduce a likely pattern for his day – how he divides his time between activities, the sequence in which he engages in those activities, and the places he chooses for them. That is to say, we concern ourselves quite simply in *what* patterns of activity are observed to take place, without the attempt to determine *why* they are chosen, from the individual point of view. Instead we take a more probabilistic view, at a somewhat coarser level of analysis. Although we will not know whether a particular student x or y might be in this or that facility at a given time, we may nevertheless be able to attach a probability to there being a total of say 120 to 130 people in this building, or 50 to 60 in that location, at some hour of the day. It is this overall picture which a simulation approach, using stochastic methods, is intended to build up.

Stochastic methods have been used to represent activities at very different scales. The work of Donnelly, Chapin and Weiss (1964), Hemmens (1966), Nystuen (1967) and Marble (1964, 1967) illustrates the use of these techniques for modelling activities at a city scale. Similar techniques have also been used by Hägerstrand (1967) to model the spread of innovation, and by Morrill (1962, 1965) to model patterns of settlement spread and to 'postdict' the growth of Negro ghettos. At the scale of the individual building, similar methods have been used in a pioneer study of circulation in hospitals, Souder *et al.* (1964) and more recently in schools, Bazjanac (1968). In a simulation approach there is no intention, as there is with game theory, to try to reproduce exactly the behaviour of some particular person on some particular occasion. Instead the method consists in simulating the activities of a great many 'typical individuals', or representatives of groups, one by one, all of whose 'simulated behaviour' will be different in detail because of different characteristics attributed to each one (in the university case, for example, a different teaching group, a different place of residence, ownership of a car or not, etc.). Because of an element of controlled randomness in the process of simulation, and by putting all the simulated individuals together, the result is that aggregate patterns of activity for the whole population will be approximated to with fair accuracy.

The first question which such an approach raises is whether various implicit assumptions of regularity in patterns of behaviour have any realism; whether in individual behaviour there is not too great a variation from one person to another and from one place to another – even taking an objective rather than a subjective view of behaviour – for the mechanisms of such a model to operate at all. If activities, viewed at the somewhat diagrammatic level of model-making, were to be crucially affected by the special characteristics of each particular place, then a general model of activities, freed from the peculiar features of any one unique spatial environment, would not be possible. However, the experience of other workers, as well as ourselves, with data from diary and other sources, describing activity patterns at varying scales, does suggest that considerable regularity is in fact observed empirically.

The work of Hemmens (1966) on patterns of linkages at the urban scale, for instance, suggests a similarity of travel behaviour between a number of different American cities. 'Linkages' in this context refers to the probability of trips being made between various origins and destinations in the city, taking into account round-trip journeys as well as simple place-to-place movements. Hemmens explores the degree of connection in this way between different types of activities at different locations, using data from transportation studies in Chicago, Pittsburgh and Buffalo. What is interesting, and gives this work general significance, is the similarity of the results for these three places. Hemmens warns that the 'linkage coefficients' would no longer remain valid as a means of predicting activity patterns if the number of trips per day per person were increased. But, by contrast, he is prepared to suggest that this pattern of linkages is not dependent on the particular physical context: 'The similarity of the percentage distribution of multiple leg journeys in Chicago and Pittsburgh suggests the possible hypothesis that the journey-making behaviour of residents of at least large urban areas may be independent of the size and character of the urban areas.'

At the site and building scale the studies of Souder *et al.* (1964) on internal traffic systems in hospitals would appear to have a direct relevance to the study of students' activities. Their work also suggests that the frequency of trips between different facilities, and the use of these facilities, may be independent of their relative location. From a survey of traffic in two hospitals, in Massachusetts and California, Souder and his colleagues determined statistical correlations between the numbers of trips in different categories – according to origin and destination, and trip purpose – and appropriate figures for the size of different groups in the hospital population. Thus the frequency of trips made by nurses to and from wards, for instance, is expressed as a simple function of the total number of patients; similarly the number of trips to the wards by outside visitors is expressed also as a function of the number of patients, and so on. These simple regularities in trip frequency, related to population numbers, are used by Souder *et al.* to simulate the anticipated traffic for various patient loads and facilities, and to relate this traffic to hypothetical hospital plan layouts, to predict peaks and to see where congestion might occur.

The studies of both Hemmens and Souder *et al.* indicate, for their respective areas of interest, the independence of activities from their physical context. At the city scale, a pattern of trip behaviour common to a number of cities emerges clearly and is confirmed in similar findings for cities of widely different form. In their study of hospitals, Souder *et al.* are able to show that the same kinds of similarities exists between the same type of hospitals, because of the way in which hospitals are run and the inherently regular nature of their activities. Can their approach be applied equally to the simulation of the students' activities? There are important differences in the activities of the university which suggest a somewhat different treatment; but nevertheless, at another level, the underlying regularities are still to be found.

Earlier, the degree of freedom open to a student in organising his day was remarked upon. He is not bound by a regular pattern of working from 9.00 to 5.00, nor is he or she, in general, responsible for looking after children, for cooking or shopping for a family. Lectures, it is true, do form a framework around which the student shapes his day, but for the remainder of his time he is free to do what he pleases and where. Comparing the typical student's day with that of most other people, his range of activities and use of facilities is possibly much greater. Teaching apart, he may study in the library, sit in the union, play football, talk over coffee until the early hours or just stay in bed. His pattern of travel, too, is very different. For many people most trips start and end at home: the trip to work and back, the trip to the shops and back, the trip to drop children at school and back.

An important consequence of the student's freedom of action is the possibility of choice open to him for engaging in the same activity in any of a variety of types of location. To take an obvious example: for 'private study', an urban university student could choose between his own room, one of the university's libraries, the city library or even the students' union. For many other activities there is a similar range of choices of location. For models of entire urban systems, where only a crude distinction might be made between activity types, the location is frequently used – quite justifiably – as a convenient label for the activity which takes place there; there are work places, and there are residential locations. However, in the study of hospitals the simulation approach described treats activities and locations together in a single operation.

Since this is not legitimate for the university case, an important distinction has been drawn in this approach between the questions of the choice of activity, and the choice of location for that activity. Furthermore, it was assumed that although there may be no consistency in the choice of particular locations for some activity, nor any regularity in the sequences in which students engage in activities, nor their exact timing during the day, there is nevertheless a regularity in the total amounts of time devoted to activities, summed over some fixed period such as a day or week. This overall division of time between activities is referred to as a 'time-budget'; and the sort of classification of activities made for this purpose might distinguish for example formal teaching, private study, sleeping, eating, athletic sport, social activities and club meetings, and so on. Different students or groups of students with various different characteristics might be expected to have different time-budgets. It is in this form that activities data may be found to be relatively independent of the particular physical environment of the population from whom it is drawn.

A worked example

A number of assumptions are necessary to illustrate by worked examples the possibility of day to day modelling of university activities.

First, that all students attend the scheduled classes, lectures, etc. for which they are enrolled – this irrespective of the time of day or the place at which the classes are given. For this formal teaching, then, a timetable may be regarded as a model of activities, in that it represents ideally who (which class or teaching group) is where (in which classroom or lecture theatre) when (for which teaching period) – although of course in the real situation the actual attendance will vary from these theoretical figures. The timetable is taken to form the backbone of the complete simulation of all activities; it is assumed that the student organises the pattern of his day around the fixed events of the teaching programme.

The second assumption has to do with the time-budget, and the regularity of variations characterising students. For a given student or group of students and over some repeated period, say a day or week, it has to be assumed that the proportions of time he or they spend in various activities, crudely classified, remains the same, although the sequence of activities and the locations chosen might change. One could expect variations in time-budgets between arts students and science students, or for a more detailed breakdown by subject studied. Further differences can be expected according to year of study, type of residence and distance of residence from the central site, ownership of bicycle or car, and probably with other more detailed distinctions still.

In the somewhat schematic but not completely uneventful pattern of life assumed for the students in our notional example, their time is taken to be divided, apart from sleeping and eating, between lectures, practical classes, supervisions, private study and sport. In addition the students drink and talk together (social): and finally they use the facilities in the town (these are unspecified, but might include perhaps shops, theatre, cinema, etc.).

To keep the example simple, it has been assumed there are only two groups between which the time-budgets differ – arts students and science students. Scientists spend more time in formal teaching and correspondingly less in private study than arts students. They also take part in more sports. The time-budgets vary for different times of the day; and the proportions of time spent in different activities for the two – arts and science – groups are shown in Fig. 6.1.

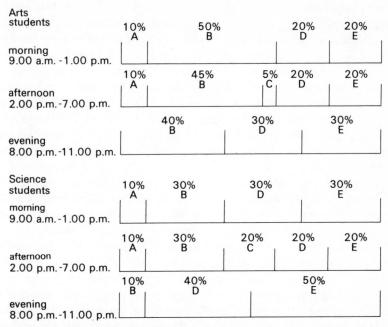

Fig. 6.1. 'Time-budget': the proportion of time spent in different activities by arts and science students, for different times of the day (A, library study; B, private study; C, sports; D, social activities; E, town-based activities).

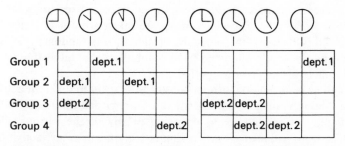

Fig. 6.2. The timetable for the four teaching groups, showing the department in which each teaching event takes place.

Each student belongs to one of four distinct teaching groups, and for each group there is a timetable of lectures, classes and practicals; these are assumed to be fully attended. Fig. 6.2 gives this timetable, with the times and places of each teaching event shown. In addition each individual is assigned a weekly supervision at a prearranged time and place. Finally he is assigned to a particular place of residence, of which there are only two in this rather meagrely provided university.

The plan of the university and its surroundings in this example is highly diagrammatic (see Fig. 6.4). It consists of a small number of square 'cells' into which the landscape is divided with a regular grid. The main university site consists of five cells and each of the various university facilities occupies one cell. There are two departments, one arts and one science, a student union building, and a library. The site is an urban one, and two alternatives are contrasted: A, where two of the cells in the town are occupied by the two halls of residence, and B, where one hall is brought onto the main university site. Of the surrounding town cells, only three are assumed to be visited by students ever, and these are taken to have differing powers of attraction: in other words, differing probabilities of any given trip into town being made to that particular cell, are assigned to each. There is no scale of distance given to this diagrammatic plan, but instead it is assumed that a journey from any cell to the adjacent cell takes ten minutes – all journeys being by the same means of travel, walking.

The actual process of simulation can now be shown. The mechanism used here is simple. The student is assumed to start the day in his place of residence; and the periods of formal teaching which he must attend, and supervisions if any, are entered in the appropriate time periods before any other non-scheduled activities are fitted around these. For the sake of economy in the arithmetic, different activities are chosen only for periods of a whole hour at a time, and the day is not broken down into smaller time-units – ten or fifteen minutes, say – as it would have to be in a more realistic simulation.

In this case lunch and dinner are assumed to be at fixed times for every student, but the places at which meals are taken are not in general predetermined. Otherwise the sequence of activities is random; that is, the activity chosen for a given time period is not affected at all by the choice of activity made in the previous period.

As well as recording the proportions of time spent in different activities, the time-budget for a given student can be regarded alternatively as recording the probability of his engaging in any of the various allowed activities at a particular time. To simulate a student's day, activities are selected at random for each time period in turn – with the exception of those already filled by scheduled events – according to the probabilities of the time-budget.

Once an activity has been picked, then an appropriate place is chosen in which the student is assumed to engage in that activity. In each case a variety of suitable places may exist: in this example the choice of where to eat is between the Union, a café in the town and the halls of residence. Table A shows which locations are allowed for which activities. In the simulation it is always the nearest location which is chosen for an activity,

TABLE A. *Locations allowed for different activities*

	Private study	Library study	Social: talking, coffee, etc.	Sports	Town-based activities	Eating
▨ Residence	□		□			□
▨ Café			□			□
◣ Library	□	□				
⅏ Department						
■ Town					□	
▨ Union			□			□
‖‖ Sportsfield				□		

Notes: No eating facilities are provided in residence on the teaching site. All lectures and practicals, as well as supervisions, are taught in the departments.

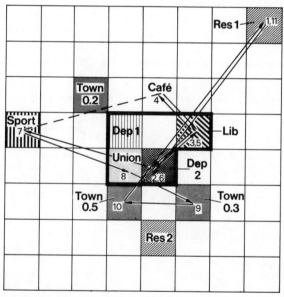

Fig. 6.3. Sample simulation: one student's activities and journeys between facilities for one day (compare table B) plotted for university plan A. The numbers record the sequence in which the student visits facilities: the dotted line represents the choice of the activity 'sports' which had to be rejected because of a tutorial at 3.00 p.m.

following the 'principle of least effort' (Zipf 1949), so that the student's journeys from one activity to another are minimised. The mechanism of the simulation takes account of what can be regarded as a certain planning ahead on the part of the student. Supposing an activity and a location are fixed for a given time period – a lecture in the science faculty, for example –

and an activity is to be selected for the preceding period. The activity is chosen – let us say it is sport – and then the nearest appropriate location, the university playing field, at some distance away in the town. It happens though, that more than the whole hour period will be taken up with travelling, so that the student cannot return in time for his lecture, and has no time for his game either. The activity is therefore rejected, and another chosen. The accompanying Table B shows the simulated day of one student in detail, in which precisely this situation arises. Fig. 6.3 shows the sequence of journeys which this same student makes for the series of activities listed in the table. A day's activities are simulated for each student in this way in turn, and the total numbers engaged in each activity at each location for each hour period are added up (see Table B). A further elaboration of the planning ahead device could take account of overcrowding, so that a location would be rejected for a given activity, although it might be the nearest, if the number of students already placed there in the process of simulation had reached a fixed maximum figure. Another development would be to introduce probabilities governing the lengths of time likely to be spent in

TABLE B. *Sample simulations: one student's activities for one day* (*compare Fig. 6.3*)

8.00	Residence 1	(location 1)		4.00	Sports	
					Sportsfield	(location 7)
9.00	Lecture					
	Department 2	(location 2)		5.00	Sports	
					Sportsfield	(location 7)
10.00	Private study					
	Library	(location 3)		6.00	Social activities	
					Union	(location 8)
11.00	Private study					
	Library	(location 3)		7.00	Dinner	
					Union	(location 8)
12.00	Private study					
	Library	(location 3)		8.00	Town based activities	
					Town 0.3	(location 9)
1.00	Lunch					
	Café	(location 4)		9.00	Town based activities	
					Town 0.5	(location 10)
2.00	(Sports selected but rejected					
	because of a supervision at 3.00)			10.00	Town based activities	
	Private study				Town 0.5	(location 10)
	Library	(location 5)				
				11.00	Residence 1	(location 11)
3.00	Supervision					
	Department 2	(location 6)				

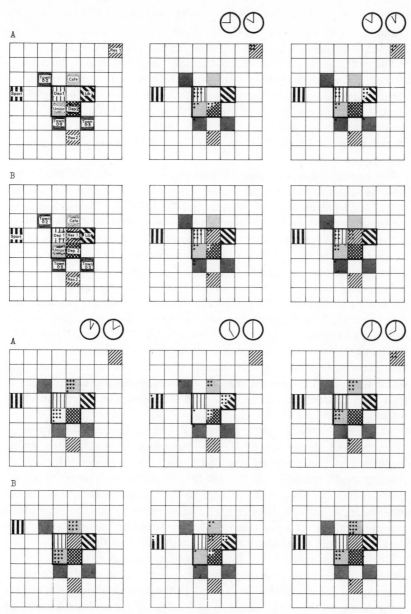

Fig. 6.4. Location of university facilities and patterns of students' activities: the results of the simple simulation. Central university site shown in heavy outline. Dots indicate numbers of students in each facility, for different times of the day. Only certain town cells are visited by students: figures give probabilities of a given trip to town being made to that cell.

given activities. A game of rugby would take generally two hours for example, a visit to the cinema the same perhaps, while the lengths of time devoted to private study or to social activities might vary widely.

The method is crude and with this greatly simplified model, the patterns of student behaviour found in the real world cannot be expected to be closely reproduced. It will be necessary to return to the weaknesses of this worked example and see how the simulation of student activities can be made much more realistic and accurate. But even with its crudity, the present example is capable of showing the kind of results which a simulation approach can yield.

For contrast, two situations are represented (Fig. 6.4): first where residence is at some distance from the university (A), and second with the one hall of residence brought onto the central site (B). Since the mechanism of the simulation dictates that in every case the location chosen for an activity is the nearest appropriate one, a change in the relative locations of the various parts of the schematic university plan will produce a resulting change in the overall patterns of simulated student activity.

Following the two alternatives over the whole day, it is apparent that by the 10.00 a.m. to 11.00 a.m. period, the differences are quite marked. (The dots in each cell in the diagrams indicate the numbers of students in each faculty, and the clocks show the time periods depicted.) The first lectures of the morning are over, and many students choose private study as their next activity. In A the nearest suitable place for this is the library; but where the residence is on the central site, in B, students prefer to study in their own rooms instead, and may use the library only for consulting reference books.

At lunch-time there is little apparent difference between the two situations, but the reason behind this is interesting. In A, although dining facilities would no doubt be provided in the halls of residence for serving evening meals, the halls are too far for the students to return there for lunch and the simulation sends them to the Union instead. In B, on the other hand, we assume that there is no need for the hall on the main site to provide meals at all, since this would only duplicate facilities already on the site; so again the students from that hall patronise the Union.

During the afternoon the library is used more in A than in B, for the same reasons as in the morning. By dinner-time a number of students are returning to their residence in A; and in the final time period there are fewer people on the central site than in B, since the library is assumed to be closed. In B, on the other hand, students remain on the site and there are more people in the town than in A, where the distance of the residence from town deters them from making the journey.

Even this thumbnail sketch of the workings of a university begins to show how a greater knowledge of patterns of student behaviour, affected by different plan layouts, might provide answers to some of the questions which have occupied the planners of new universities. Will the campus be deserted after the end of the day's teaching, or will the bringing of student housing on to the central site infuse some life into the university at night? Is separate study space needed on the central site for those whose place of residence is at a distance? Does it make sense to duplicate expensive dining and common rooms in residences and on the central site? The patterns of students' movement in this exercise are relevant to all these topics – though of course it will need a far more detailed and tested model to provide the real evidence needed to answer such questions.

Figures 6.5, 6.6, 6.7, illustrate the results of a simulation carried out at a more realistic level (though again a hypothetical case) – for a representative 10% sample of students in a university of 3,000 students in all, whose buildings and site layout are shown in the plans (Fig. 6.6). Although the general principles governing the working of the simulation are similar to the first example, the detail is much elaborated. There is a greater number of distinct student groups whose time-budgets differ correspondingly. The timetable is more detailed, and is typical of the real timetables actually operated in universities. The students' places of residence are widely scattered about the city to represent lodgings as well as halls of residence, and the distribution of lodgings is related to the age and character of the housing in different areas. Students travel by different means, and the range of locations available to car-owners, for instance, for a given activity is correspondingly larger than for those who travel by bicycle or on foot.

The heavy superimposed lines on the plans show the numbers of students travelling along each route (the thickness of the line corresponding to the number of students) totalled over each time period. The pedestrian routes shown in the plans of the central university site (Fig. 6.6) follow actual pathways and run from the entrance of one building to another. In the city-scale diagrams (Fig. 6.7) the movements are shown as 'bee-lines' only. It is clear that, besides tabulating pedestrian circulation and other traffic flows, it would be possible to present the results of the simulation in terms of the numbers of occupants of each building over the course of the day.

Despite the increased detail, the underlying assumptions about behaviour are, however broadly, the same as those described earlier. On what evidence are these assumptions based, how reasonable are they, and how might they have to be revised to meet observed facts? At present the notion that patterns of student activity might be accurately reproduced with a model of some kind is partly speculation. There is empirical evidence to suggest that time-budgets can indeed be derived for different student

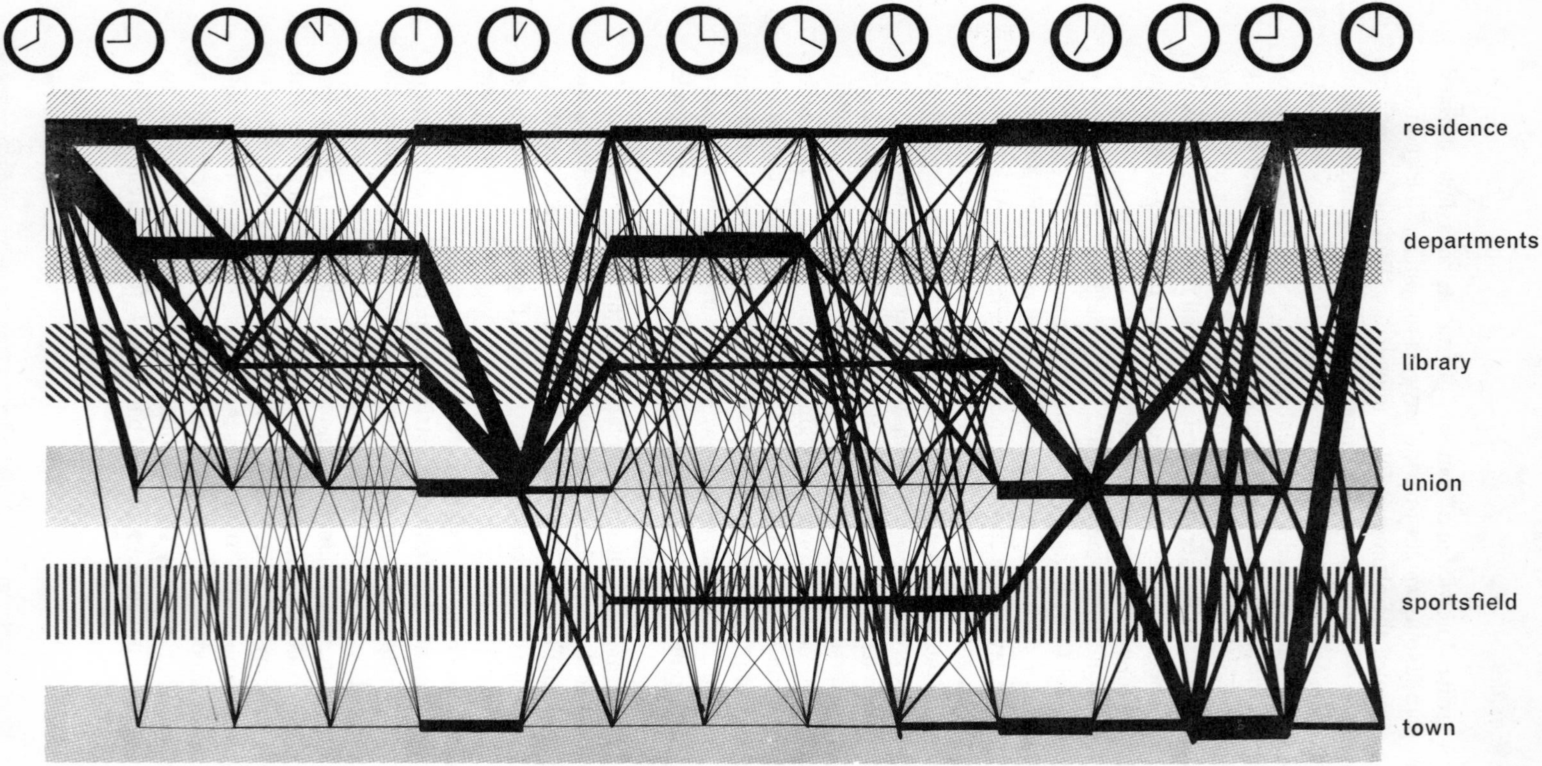

Fig. 6.5. Diagrammatic presentation of the results of a large-scale simulation of student activities for a 10% sample of a university of 3000 students in all. The tinted bands denote different facilities, the clocks the hours of the day: the superimposed black lines represent the numbers of students moving from one facility to the next, from one hour time period to the next (the thickness of the line being proportional to the numbers of students). Note lectures in the morning, the convergence on the Union for lunch and dinner, laboratory classes and sports in the afternoon, town-based activities in the evening.

groups.† The implication that an activity is decided upon, and then the nearest appropriate location chosen, is, on the other hand, clearly an extreme simplification. Models of activity patterns developed in planning research outside the university field suggest that journeys might instead be simulated according to a trip frequency distribution curve, with a higher probability of shorter journeys, and an increasingly lower likelihood of longer trips. The shape of such a curve might be found to vary for different activities, and especially for the users of different means of transport. The choice of somewhere to lunch, for example, might be expected to depend on the nearness of the eating place, the price of the food, and some estimate perhaps of overcrowding.

Other activities might be uniquely tied to particular locations: the cinema, or particular sports for example. In other cases a mass-distance effect might be observed, in which people were prepared to travel longer distances to facilities of correspondingly greater mass – to a library with more books, a shopping area with more and larger shops. On the other hand, the choice of convenience shopping, laundrette or telephone might correspond to the first simple model, of the nearest facility available.

More serious problems could arise through the effect which the location of some facility might have on the choice of activity. The previous assumption was that an activity was chosen, then a location. But with shopping or social activities one could imagine a person finding himself near the shops or near a common-room or coffee-bar, and taking advantage of that fact while he was there. It is quite conceivable that he might plan a series of activities taking him from one place to another so that his overall journey was minimised (although it is by no means essential that a day's activities be simulated in sequence; and one can imagine a gradual piecing together of the whole pattern, with some of these complicating factors taken into account). Against all these difficulties, however, must be set the fact that the purpose is not to reproduce any one person's movements with accuracy. This is worth saying again. The manager of a department store has no knowledge of what motives, what peculiar chain of circumstances brings each person to his shop, or how much each will spend. He can predict with some confidence, however, what his total takings will be in any day; and he will perhaps know this for different departments in the store, and for different days of the week. It is the overall pattern which is regular

---

† As for example in R. Drewett, P. Hall, J. Oram (1967) which contains some correlations between amounts of time spent in different facilities and the identifying characteristics of various student groups for Battersea College. The Robbins Report (1963) gives a limited amount of information, too, on the proportions of time spent in different activities by students in different years of study and reading different subjects.

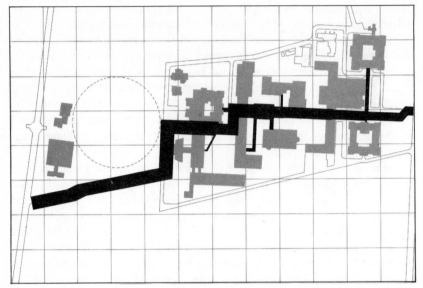

Fig. 6.6. Results of the large-scale simulation (compare Fig. 6.5), showing the pedestrian traffic movement on the main university site for 3-hour periods during the day, 8.00

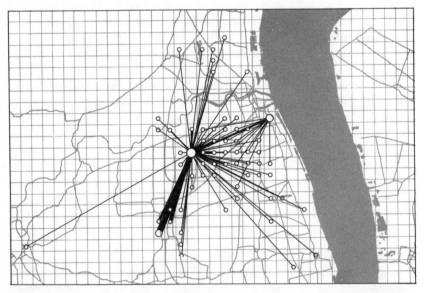

Fig. 6.7. Results of the large-scale simulation (compare Figs. 6.5 and 6.6), showing the movement of students (by all means of transport) through the city for 3-hour periods during the day, 8.00 a.m.–9.00 p.m., 1.00 p.m.–2.00 p.m. and 3.00 p.m.–4.00 p.m. (as in Fig. 6.6). Journeys are shown as 'bee-lines' from the centre of one city 'cell' to another (small circles). The thickness of the lines is proportional to the number of students

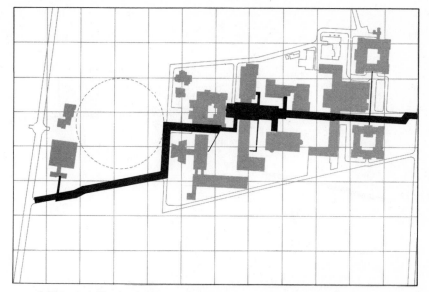

a.m.–9.00 a.m., 1.00 p.m.–2.00 p.m., and 3.00 p.m.–4.00 p.m. The heavy superimposed lines are proportional in thickness to the numbers of students moving along each route.

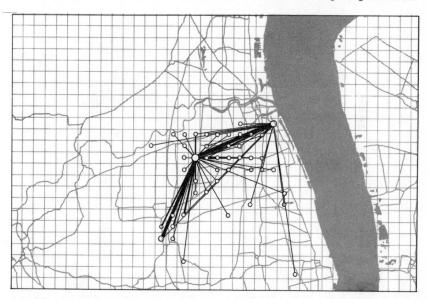

travelling. The large circle in the centre of the map is the main university site, the large circle upper right is the city centre, and the large circle lower left the principal group of halls of residence. The city is divided with a regular grid into half-kilometre square grid 'cells'.

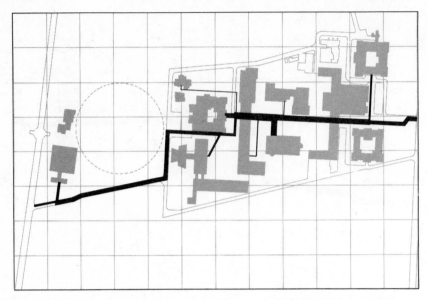

and predictable, and the same applies in the university, though for a more complicated and varied range of activities.

The type of model of university activities proposed here represents a series of hypotheses, and at present a large survey is being made of student behaviour in a real situation – at the University of Reading – in order to test these hypotheses. The survey takes the form of a 'diary', to be filled in by each of a 10% sample of students (500 in all) over a week, with a record of his activities, giving times and locations. Together with the diary the student is asked to complete a questionnaire which covers such subjects as his academic status, the courses for which he is enrolled, his marital status, his place of residence, whether he owns a car or bicycle, and so on. This information is used in determining different groups for the purpose of deriving time-budgets.

It may quite well prove impossible to extract from the survey data time-budgets for groups of students of any size. It may prove impossible to reproduce aggregate behaviour by the kinds of simulation methods described. Work in other areas, in particular studies of shopping behaviour and other household activity patterns, suggests, however, that such models can successfully be made, even at a surprisingly small scale of detail.[†] But to produce a model which works is only the beginning.

It is clearly the first requirement of a model that it should work, that it should approximate in its results observations made of the real world. But once a model is made to work, two questions must then be asked. First, how powerful and flexible is the model? That is to say, would it still work for different situations and in different circumstances? Would a model built to fit survey results from one university give an accurate picture of a university with a quite different layout, or with a student population broken down by quite different groupings?

And the second question to ask is: How simple is the model's mechanism, how economical? Does it give a real insight into the workings of the situations modelled: or is it so elaborated that it could be made to fit virtually any data whatsoever? Confidence may be placed in a model whose structure is simple and it can be expected that it may then prove powerful. But a model which, like the Ptolemaic theory of the solar system, is subject to endless qualification and reconstruction to fit new data, is in the end neither useful nor illuminating, although it cannot be proved that it does not represent the truth. It can always be patched up and made to work.

The theories of university activities modelling outlined here remain to be tried. But if it should prove possible to build a model which is reasonably robust, yet simple, then its uses in planning would be many and various.

[†] For instance: Hemmens (1966), Chapin and Hightower (1966), Bazjanac (1968), Farley and Ring (1966), Souder *et al.* (1964).

It has been indicated how the simulated patterns of student activity would give information about both traffic and pedestrian circulation flows, and about the extent to which each building or facility is used through the day. In a particular real situation this could give useful evidence for the siting and design of new buildings, and could provide a basis for the calculation of required capacity in, for example, dining-rooms or libraries. It would be possible to demonstrate the effects of increasing or decreasing the provision of space on the number of students using the accommodation.

At a more general level the model could be used, in a systematic series of experiments, to investigate the effects of broadly differing types of academic policy, of different policies for the social and residential organisation of the university, of different characteristic types of site layout and building form; and their implications one for another.

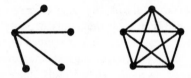

Fig. 6.8. A course with few 'linked' teaching groups compared with a highly interconnected course.

In terms of academic policies, one of the principal ways in which the new universities have differed from the old is in the breadth of the courses they offer. In contrast to the sometimes rigid compartmentalisation of the old departmental structure, each student is allowed in the 'schools of study' type of organisation a wide choice of options of courses he may combine together. The greater this choice, the more complex the interlocking of different courses becomes; and so the production of a timetable gets progressively more difficult. Measures, from graph theory, developed to express the 'connectivity' of transport and communication networks,† have been borrowed to describe this complexity and overlapping of courses in abstract mathematical form (Fig. 6.8). By using the timetabling programme mentioned earlier, experiments can be made to determine the correlation between these indices of complexity of courses, and the intensity of use of teaching space which can be achieved in their time-tabling. The differing effects on the use of floor space through the allocation of teaching facilities at the level of the department, the faculty or the whole university can be contrasted. In general, a more centrally controlled allocation of floor space can be shown to give a greater saving.

† Shimbel 1953; Kansky 1963.

Other experiments could involve the progressive shortening or lengthening of the teaching week – the total number of periods available for teaching in a week, usually about 30 hours – with its consequent effects on the timetables.

By representing in detail certain physical characteristics of the university: the layout of teaching rooms in the various buildings, the numbers of rooms of different types and sizes, and the distances separating one room from another, it would be possible to explore the consequences of particular plan forms for patterns of teaching and possible levels of space utilisation. These experiments make use of the timetable as a model of formal teaching patterns, but a complete simulation of the whole day's activities could be used to examine the effects of changes in academic arrangements and teaching programmes on the use of other facilities and on patterns of movement through and between sites.

To carry out experiments of this sort, the different types of university plan layout will have to be characterised in a general way and their salient features drawn out, while the irrelevant complicating detail of their particular idiosyncrasies is suppressed. Properties of layouts which might be measured and compared in a quantitative analysis are: first, the overall density of development, and the variations of density from one part of a site to another. Second, the zoning of different space uses and types of activity in different parts of a site (or between several sites). Third, the structural character of the route system which links these spaces and activities together. Routes would include paths and roads crossing the site, corridors in buildings, and the vertical routes – lifts and staircases.

To be able to measure particular properties of layouts – density, zoning and route structure – would be to characterise three most significant aspects of their varied designs. In terms of density of development one can see at the two extremes the very lavish spaciousness of some American rural campuses, and the tightly cramped central developments of the older English civic universities. The University of Illinois at Chicago Circle in which all space types are segregated, all laboratories in one building, all lecture rooms in another, all administrative offices in another, represents a zoning policy which is the complete antithesis of the University of Loughborough, for example, with its use of a single structural unit and a single building type to accommodate all academic activities. As for the varying possibilities in the structure of routes, the following can be cited: the linear type of system, with central spine and branching secondary routes, as typified by the design of the University of Bath (Fig. 6.9a); the 'nuclear' type of arrangement, where a number of sub-centres are linked by criss-crossing routes – York is an example of this (Fig. 6.9b); or the rectilinear gridiron plan used by Candilis, Josic and Woods in their design for the

Free University of Berlin (Fig. 6.9c). A model of activity patterns could show how different characteristic types of plan compare for different general types of teaching programme or for different compositions of the student population.

At a broader, town-planning scale, the kinds of problem which an activities model could treat are those attending the siting of new universities, the growth of existing campuses, or the amalgamation of a number of existing institutions of higher education to form some larger unit – this last being typically the situation of the Colleges of Advanced Technology,

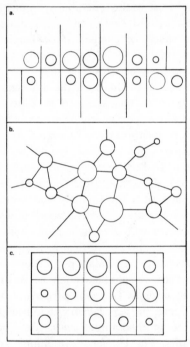

Fig. 6.9. Structure of routes at three universities: (a) linear at Bath; (b) nuclear at York; (c) gridiron at Berlin Free University.

of some of the technological universities, and of the new polytechnics, which find themselves with widely scattered buildings, mostly old and on small sites. The main concerns here, in a quantified comparison of alternatives, are the differences in land values between urban, suburban and rural sites; the costs of redevelopment, and the problems in the way of expansion and acquisition of sites in central city areas; the availability of a supply of suitable student lodgings, especially now when funds for purpose-built residence are short; and what the distribution of student residence means for patterns of travel.

In the problem of student residence, a start has been made on the construction of a new type of model whose purpose is to explain the present distribution of lodgings in a number of university cities, and which is intended, if successful, to provide a means for predicting the likely distribution in new situations. The factors affecting the suitability of different areas of housing for student lodgings which are covered by this model are: distances from the main university site or sites, the age of housing (Fig. 6.7 shows this kind of analysis by half-kilometre grid cells), housing density, household size and house size – these last four factors being often correlated one with another.

Another type of model represents an attempt to reproduce the movement of students, not in their day-to-day activities, as with the simulation exercises, but over the longer period of each academic year to the next. For this purpose some of the techniques of large-scale educational planning, the so-called 'input–output matrix' type models,† have been borrowed and applied to the description of flows of students from course to course and from year to year at the level of the individual institution. Simply, the input–output matrix is a table showing which students attend which courses and are in which year of study at some point in time. Then the likelihood of students moving in the next academic year to the next level of their courses, repeating their courses, changing their courses, or leaving the system altogether, could be predicted by a series of 'transition probabilities' derived from observation of the process in previous years.

Yet another, third new model will take this basic data on the yearly movement of students through the university, and use it, together with the housing data already mentioned, to reproduce their movements from one place of residence to another. This model would be able to plot the spread of student housing, and anticipate the saturation level when no more lodgings can be found. These two long-term models of student flow – through the academic courses of the university, and through their occupation of different places of residence and areas of housing – combined with the short-term, day-to-day modelling of student activity-patterns by techniques of simulation, will offer a solid basis for comparing policies of expansion, for planning building programmes, for actually measuring the flexibility of forms of building and site layouts and their ability to accept changes of use.

Higher education is one of the fastest growing major national enterprises. All the urgent measures recently proposed for the accommodation of an estimated doubling of student numbers' by 1980 mean that an increasingly scientific and less haphazard outlook on planning will be

† See in particular *OECD* (1966) and *OECD* (1967).

needed in the seventies. If space is to be used more intensively, residences
built more cheaply, and student intake increased at an accelerating rate,
then much more care is needed in planning to see that standards do not
suffer as a result. The possible meanings of expansion plans can be explored with a model approach, and at least some of their results predicted
before they are put into effect.

Postscript

Since the foregoing two papers were written, work on constructing a model
of university activities has rapidly progressed. During the intervening
eighteen months (up to October 1971), three activity surveys have been
completed: two at universities (Reading and Leicester) and another at a
polytechnic (Leicester). The two universities are similar both in size and in
their general relationship to the surrounding area – both have about 5000
students and are located on suburban sites some distance from the city
centre. The polytechnic, on the other hand, is located on a central site and,
although its student body is similar in size to the two universities, it is
characterised by a large proportion of part-time students who are employed
elsewhere on some days. The similarities among the three institutions
allow a model of activities to be tested against three situations in which as
many factors as possible are comparable, and also permit variations in
activity patterns to be studied in relation to the limited number of factors
which are not constant: location of the campus, different types of student
and so forth.

The diary technique previously outlined was adopted for all three surveys: students were asked to complete, in their own words, a description of
their activities and their location over a week. A high response rate was
achieved (approximately 80% at the two universities) covering in all about
650 students and a total of about 110,000 separately recorded activities.
Approximately 330 categories of activity were encountered in the diaries,
and in coding the information in a form suitable for computer handling,
this level of disaggregation was initially maintained. Complementary to
these activity surveys, further surveys have been made of the spatial context within which the activities occurred. These include the floor space of
the university, its location and its capacity for containing different activities, as well as the range of urban facilities – shops, cafes, etc. – which the
students might use.

To make the raw data in the diaries more comprehensible the original
330 activities were experimentally grouped into 48 categories. The next
step was to examine the composition of time-budgets to find different
groups of students who vary markedly in the total times they spent in each

of these 48 activities. The time-budgets were encouraging both in their differences and in their similarities. For example, the time spent in sleeping was not dependent on the student's faculty, whereas, the time spent in formal teaching varies significantly by faculties. Overall, it was found that of the 48 activity groups, under one third of them accounted for the greater part of the students' time.

Other aspects of the raw data were studied to gain an impression of the important factors affecting activities, and to provide a basis for the initial model. Amongst these factors were the ranges of durations of each of the 48 activity groups and the proportion of the sample population engaged in each activity group at 15-minute intervals during the day. This distribution of students to activities during the day was chosen as the first to be modelled, using the time-budgets and the durations of activities as input.

In formulating an operational model suitable for handling large amounts of data, certain changes have been made to the basic simulation approach. Simulation is particularly good for illustrating the theoretical principles involved in modelling students' activities, but the method raises a number of technical difficulties. The principal one concerns the excessive amounts of computation involved in handling the very large numbers of separate simulations. This is avoided through the use of an entropy maximising method of the type proposed by Wilson (1971). Essentially, this method requires an initial estimation of the overall distribution of the student population between different activities during each of the time periods. Then the program produces a distribution of population to activities, altered iteratively until the given constraints are satisfied. The initial estimation is determined from the time-budgets and duration of activity data derived from the diaries. The estimation and the subsequent iterated activity distributions are governed by restrictions that allow activities to take place only during appropriate time periods; these restrictions are similar to those used in the simulation approach. For an example of a restriction as distinguished from a constraint, formal teaching is limited to the hours between 9.00 a.m. and 1.00 p.m., and between 2.00 p.m. and 6.00 p.m. The constraints for the entropy maximising method are the same as those which were used implicitly in the simulation, i.e. the time-budget and the constant size of the population.

Given equivalent initial conditions, both simulation and entropy maximising should give the same results when a stable distribution for each has been achieved. For calculation by computer, however, the entropy maximising method has the advantage that, after each iteration, a direct and reliable measure of the accuracy of the current distribution can be obtained by finding the amount by which the constraints are not satisfied. Using the simulation method, however, the stability, and hence accuracy, of a given distribution can only be determined by running further trials and finding the effect on the distribution. Only a distribution that is not affected by further trials is stable and truly represents the effect of the initial conditions. As a further consequence, using the entropy maximising approach, two distributions which satisfy the constraints to the same degree but which were obtained with different initial conditions can be compared, and the differences are known to be due to the differences in the initial conditions. For the simulation approach, however, only stable distributions can be compared usefully, otherwise differences may be due to the different sequences of random numbers used in each case.

It was decided therefore to program an entropy maximising model. Initially this would be done for a single group of students whose time-budget approximately corresponded to an average of the Reading diaries.

In addition, certain activities were allowed to occur only at certain times of day. For example, the model only allowed shopping to occur between 9.00 a.m. and 6.00 p.m. Private study and social activities, on the other hand, were unrestricted in the times at which they could occur. Initially, each activity was assigned a single duration—this again being based on an average figure found from the diaries. The initial distribution was found by making the probability for starting an activity at any given time proportional to the number of instances of that activity per day, and inversely proportional to the number of times available for starting that activity. The initial distribution was then balanced in order to satisfy the constraints. The constraints to be satisfied were that the total population at each time period should remain constant, and that the number of man-hours spent in each activity should agree with the time-budget for the student group. Twenty iterations, taking about 1 minute of computer time, generally gave a total discrepancy of less than 1 % in the constraints. The results of this model reproduced fairly well the broad outlines of the distribution shown by the data. But details such as a peak in washing between sleep and breakfast and a peak in talking to friends before sleep are not reproduced. Such details could probably be improved by placing further restrictions over the activities, but it is important not to lose generality by forcing agreement with one set of data – the input for this initial model being based only on the Reading University survey.

The model described here is a tentative exploration: many extensions are possible, some of which are being implemented at the time of writing. In particular, physical location can be added to the activity model, so that the distribution obtained is the distribution of students over the campus and the town as well as over activities during the day. This would involve some measure of the relative attraction of the different facilities available as well as of the travel costs or 'friction' brought about by distance. At this point the students who own cars may have to be considered as a separate population group.

Although much still remains to be done, it will be clear that the intentions originally expressed in Chapter 5 'A theoretical model for university planning' are now in sight of being achieved. It will be clear too, that models of human behaviour at this smaller scale have obvious general applications to urban processes as a whole as well as to particular institutions such as universities. Models of behaviour which move towards increasing generalisation from a detailed understanding of a selected area are clearly complementary to the more aggregated approach implied by Echenique and his colleagues in developing a model of urban stock and behaviour on a larger scale.

PART 3

URBAN SYSTEMS

Introduction

The spatial structure of a city is a system. The motivation behind the studies that follow is the sense that before we can talk about the objectives and goals of planning we need to understand the process within which they might be achieved. The concern of these papers is therefore not with some desirable future end but with the attempt to understand and delineate what we have called the 'system': that is the complex pattern of constantly changing interactions which determine and are in turn determined by the spatial structure of a city. It is precisely this interaction within a system that traditional land use planning, concepts of density and zoning, and the 'closed' or static concept of the city plan have been unable to describe.

The difficulty is that in considering any complex problem we tend to tackle its various aspects in sequence: we have little means of examining them instantaneously. At worst when, as in planning, the problem becomes immensely complicated, it is separated out into isolated pieces incomplete in themselves and highly destructive to the overall unity of the concept.

To see a city as a structure of communities may be admirable. But a plan that considers the road system as independent and separable has already broken down the initial concept. To add to this the consideration of an overall pattern of densities is to distort the issue still further. What is left is an application of bits and pieces, each capable of destroying an existing pattern but incapable of establishing a new one in its place.

What is necessary is some method of assessing the related problems of traffic, housing, schools, shopping, recreation etc., (indeed the component parts of the environmental area) within a total unifying context. And somehow, that highly complicated pattern of uses...must be translated into a viable built form. (Martin 1967.)

By the time that these papers were written this critical attitude to traditional city and metropolitan planning had been expressed by research workers who approached the urban problem from a background of studies in the Social Sciences. (Webber *et al.* 1964.) In 1964 Foley and Webber in the U.S.A. produced essays which outlined some different ways of examining and describing the urban spatial structure. A year later in 1965, the work of Lowry and Britton Harris and their description of parts of the city structure by means of mathematical models was readily available. (Lowry 1965, Harris 1965.)

The work of Echenique in Cambridge proceeds from this point and from the background of earlier Cambridge studies. A preliminary attempt to work at the scale of the environmental area proved the inadequacy of examining a part of a system without seeing it in relation to the whole. Problems of transport, employment and residence interact beyond its boundaries. The system must be seen as a whole. The problem, then, becomes one of discovering the basic elements which form the interrelated structure of a city. It is then necessary within this total conceptual framework to ascribe values to these elements and to formulate theories as to their relationships. If these values can be obtained from the data relating to an existing city then the theoretical description can be tested by the closeness that it can achieve to the reality of the city that it describes.

The result is a model capable of describing an urban system. A model of this kind is not necessarily limited to describing the one situation for which it was constructed. As the model is built upon a theory of the interaction of parts of the urban structure, the theory of relationships can be applied to other situations. The nature of the relationships in the theory is such that to change the data in any one of the shapes inherent in the model's representation of reality will alter the entire range of interlocking geometries. Therefore, a model becomes an explorative model if any of the theoretical parts are changed to represent not another urban space, but the same one experimentally altered to correspond to possible planning decisions. Echenique's first paper (1968a) is an examination and classification of this model building framework. It identifies various types of model and clarifies definitions. It becomes clear that the model intended only to describe, is an essential first step from which other developments might be built up and it seems true that its presentation in mathematical terms is particularly appropriate. The mathematical presentation can formulate the interrelationships of the system accurately. The computer can then handle the immense quantities of data involved and can examine those simultaneous interactions, where a solution in one part (employment for example) depends on answers to problems in others (for instance in residential accommodation or in transport). The point has already been made that these interlocking presentations are an essential prerequisite in studies of the urban structure. In a later paper, Echenique proposed his first formulation of an urban model (Echenique 1968b) which brings into relationship various submodels of the urban spatial structure. Its relation to earlier work has been described as follows:

The Lowry model allocates residents about work-places and services about residences: these services in turn generate more residents and the model is iterated until equilibrium is reached. Echenique has adapted and improved this basic formulation by taking into account the physical infra-structure of a town (i.e. the stock of land, building and roads). (Echenique *et al.* 1971.)

The model has two interacting parts each with sub-sections. The first part of the model deals with activities and is similar to other spatial models of activity systems. But the unique contribution of the Echenique formulation is the way in which activities are realistically accommodated by the second part of the process: the stocks location models.

When in August 1968 Crowther and Lindsay came back to Cambridge from the Ministry of Housing and Local Government to join the Urban Systems Study, they brought with them the sources of data necessary for the testing of the theoretical formulation. They had been working on the assembly and analysis of data into grid squares for the town of Reading. With the helpful co-operation of the Ministry of Housing and Local Government much of this data became available and in a form particularly suitable for computer application. The simple theoretical model could therefore be tested against the real situation and its effectiveness proved by its capacity to describe Reading (Echenique, Crowther and Lindsay 1969a). The first version of the complete urban model and its mathematical formulation, together with the testing and trial runs for the town of Reading, are described in the L.U.B.F.S. Working Paper No. 12. The work on the model with the data for Reading revealed the need for refinements and the possibility of easier expressions. In the second part of this section, the model with its refinements is described. The first part of the paper explains the construction of each of the model's parts, and the second describes how the parts were integrated in the complete model.

Now that the model existed and had been tested by its capacity to describe a real situation, it became possible to develop its potentialities by using the data from three generations of new towns. At this stage the 'descriptive' model as devised for Reading was extended by the introduction of a set of evaluation indicators and a first attempt was made to compare, in a simple way, some aspects of the performance of different types of urban structure; in this case Stevenage and the proposed towns of Hook and Milton Keynes (Echenique, Crowther and Lindsay 1969c). This work, presented as the paper following the description of the model itself, provides a test for the validity of the model and its usefulness in evaluating planning proposals.

The theoretical effectiveness of the model has now been strengthened by two papers by March (1969, 1970). The development of a Cordon Model will allow greater complexity to be considered by more highly magnifying certain parts of a city to resolve greater detail, and yet this refinement can compensate mathematically within the model for the disparity of scale. It will make it possible, for instance, for district or action area proposals to be seen in relation to the total urban context (Baxter 1970). One necessary aspect of the effective working of the more complex model now being developed is the selection and collection of the vast amount of data that is necessary for its operation and the results of its analysis have been summarised in several papers published by L.U.B.F.S.†

Since its initial formulation in 1968 the model has been tested in six different towns of widely different size (populations of 57,000 to 2,000,000) and character. One of these is an unplanned town which has developed with little restraint: Reading. Three are planned towns, but each has a different set of objectives: Stevenage, Hook, Milton Keynes. The fifth is an ancient town with a developing area around it: Cambridge. The last is the large and rapidly expanding city of Santiago in Chile.

What seems to have been proved is that the model works. Given the data, it seems to be possible to describe the related elements of an urban structure with reasonable accuracy. In combination with evaluation procedures, certain types of alternative strategies can be assessed and the effects of particular developments within the total urban area can be demonstrated. The model then appears to be a useful tool for planners and the conclusion to the third essay emphasises this. What is impressive, however, is the speed with which these new techniques can be assimilated. In 1969 eight students in the fifth year of their course in the School of Architecture followed through the complete process of work necessary to understand the principles, assemble the data and run the model. They were able to operate the model in relation to the town of Cambridge. They followed this (with the agreement of the Cambridgeshire and Isle of Ely Planning Department and the City of Cambridge Department of Architecture and Planning) with an exploration which tested the internal consistency of the two different policies which these authorities had evolved and evaluated them in terms of accessibility and space standards that would result from each. The results are published in L.U.B.F.S. Working Paper No. 14 (Booth *et al.* 1970).

These things appear to be at least some useful aids. But there remains the deeper question of what we are trying to do when we study the urban region. Peter Cowan (1970) has recently made the observation that most of the development plans that we know normally follow the classical pattern set out by Abercrombie in his Greater London plan of 1944. They are in

---

† J. Anthony (1970a), Data on Household Income and Economic Group; H. Torres (1970), Accessibility and Residential Location; G. Lenzie (1970), A Study of a Road Network, 1. Data Base; J. Anthony (1970b), The Effect of Income and Socio-Economic Group on Housing Choice; J. Perraton (1970), Collection and Management of Data for a Complex Model; R. Baxter, and J. Anthony (1971), The First Stage in Disaggregating the Residential Model.

principle concerned with goals; with a desirable condition towards which the community may wish to move. The most recent plans, it is true, are no longer self-contained concepts, like the plan of London or the plans for the first generation of new towns. They have extended their range to the study of regions, as in the South East Lancashire or the Hampshire proposals. These set out a structural framework and leave much of the infilling free for future choices. They are in this sense open-ended. Indeed, in Milton Keynes, this open-endedness and the ability to adapt and change during the process of growth are themselves goals of the plan.†

But the goals are still there as objectives. In contrast to this the developing work which these papers present illustrates a different emphasis and a different attitude of mind. In the place of a body of goals to be worked for, there is an effort to understand and to describe a process. What is being attempted is much closer to the development of a method through which the nature of the total problem can be more completely grasped and the consequences of decision and alternative options or goals can be clarified and assessed.

We are brought back to the question of what it is in the urban structure that we can study effectively; and that surely must be the reality of the present situation and the alternative strategies and options that are available to meet its need for growth and change. For the rest, we need not hope that we can enforce an environment by planning. It has to be built. We cannot assume that it will be built with any common unity of ideas. It is more likely to result from different interests and choices. It will not all be beautiful, but people will have been free to shape it, to make their own decisions and to learn from their actions. The environment will then be educational in the widest sense, through the experience that all of us share in building it (March 1967).

† For a discussion of goals and processes see Foley (1964) pp. 56–7 and Webber (1964).

7. *Models: a discussion*[†]

MARCIAL ECHENIQUE

Without a theoretical framework of reference, factual information does not have any relevance: 'Descriptions are not written on the face of events to be transferred directly into language, but are already "interpretations" of events' (Hesse 1963). These interpretations depend on a set of already established assumptions. The collection and ordering of information also presupposes a theoretical framework of reference; as C. H. Coombs (1964) states: 'All knowledge is the result of theory – we buy information with assumptions–"facts are inferences", and so also are data, measurements and scales.' It follows, therefore, that such a framework is also necessary in partial studies of large and complex systems, where the nature of inter-actions between a number of factors and their context is to be specified.

The purpose here is to try to establish some definitions to facilitate the building of a framework or model that will make the observation–description process useful and partial studies possible. In establishing definitions, part of the problem is one of classification. Clearly a chart of sales trends differs from a quadratic equation, a popularity poll from an urban renewal site map, architects' plans or scale models from pressure gauges and thermometers. However, all are models and all are frameworks of reference interpreting reality.

A model is a representation of a reality, in which the representation is made by the expression of certain relevant characteristics of the observed reality and where reality consists of the objects or systems that exist, have existed, or may exist. Having broadly defined a model, it is now possible to discuss the selection of the relevant characteristics of reality and the means of representing them and from this selection to attempt a classification of all models.

† This paper is based on Land Use and Built Form Studies Working Paper No. 6, published in 1968. It was later republished in that form in the *Journal of Architectural Research and Teaching*. It was originally written while the author was supported by a grant from the Centre for Environmental Studies.

It is assumed that reality may be known through the processes of observation and abstraction. But these processes are subjective inasmuch as the observer, in making his observations, has certain intentions and, in his appraisal of reality, uses his own senses. This leads to the supposition that there exists a unique and total intrinsic reality and a plurality of partial and extrinsic realities which depend on each observer and his intentions. These assumptions help in the selection of relevant characteristics of reality because they are seen to be framed by the intentions of the model-maker. In other words, the questions the model is designed to answer determine the selection of these characteristics. The questions themselves depend on the training of the model-maker, the resources available, the institution in which he works, and so on.

Only by having a 'highly selective attitude to the information' (Haggett 1967) is it possible to collect facts that are useful. This selective attitude, which depends on the intention of the observer, makes 'finite' the infinite number of characteristics. The unity of each partial and extrinsic reality is exaggerated: 'The mind needs to see the system in opposition and distinction to all others, therefore the separation of the system from others is more complete than it is in reality' and 'the system is studied with a certain purpose in mind; everything that does not effect this purpose is eliminated' (Apostel 1961).

The means chosen to represent selected characteristics of reality may be physical or conceptual. Any such representation of reality is a model. Between reality and model we distinguish two kinds of analogy, the positive analogies (similarities) and the negative (differences). The selection of positive analogies again depends on the questions the model is designed to answer. In some cases, the material substance of the model may constitute a negative analogy with reality and yet make a positive analogy in terms of behaviour, or vice versa. For example, a hydraulic model of traffic flows may exhibit positive characteristics of flow behaviour, though the material substances involved are clearly very different.

It will be seen that 'only by being unfaithful in some respect can a model represent its original' (Black 1962). If it were not 'unfaithful', the model would be reality itself and not a representation (Fig. 7.1). Conditions for the process of model-making can now be specified. There will be an object or system to be investigated; an intention, clearly expressed, by which to make a selection; a process of observation and abstraction; a process of translation through the means of representation; and a process of testing and making conclusions.

Often, the word 'model' is used in an ambiguous way. It may mean 'a theory, a law, a hypothesis, a structural idea, a role, a relation, an equation, a synthesis of data' (Skilling 1964); or again, 'as a noun it means representation; as an adjective, degree of perfection; as a verb, to demonstrate' (Haggett 1967). Here, in these statements, the word 'model' is used as a substitute for the word 'theory', which may be defined as a scheme or system of ideas or as a statement held to explain or account for a group of facts or phenomena.

A,B properties of the real world
A_1,B_1 properties of the real world in the mind of the observer
a,b other properties in the mind of the observer
A_2,C_2 represented properties of the real world in the model (positive analogies)
α,β properties of the model (negative analogies)

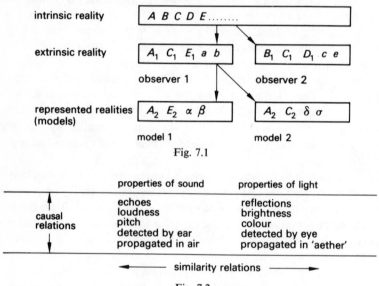

Fig. 7.1

Fig. 7.2

Hesse (1963) distinguishes three types of theories according to their predictive powers: formal theories, which are only weakly predictive, including the so-called mathematical model; conceptual models, which are strongly predictive but not justified by choice criteria; material analogue models, which are both strongly predictive and justified by choice criteria which appeal to the models as empirical data.

Taking these three categories in reverse order, material analogue models in science are based on the presumption that if things have some similar attributes, they will have other similar attributes. In these models, a theory that explains some of the phenomena of the real world is used as a model for predicting a new property in the 'explicandum' of other phenomena, based on the similarity of certain observable facts (Fig. 7.2). Here an example (from Hesse 1963) of theory is used as a model for the explicandum.

Material analogue models are now used in the urban design field. For example, the 'gravity model', for predicting traffic flow, uses a generalised version of the theory of gravity. There are similarity relations between mass, people and distance, and the causal relation of attraction is used in the prediction of traffic flows. In its simplest form, the traffic between two places is seen to be clearly proportional to the size of the two populations and inversely proportional to the distance separating them.

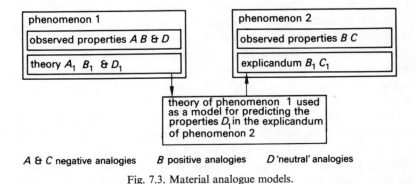

A & C negative analogies   B positive analogies   D 'neutral' analogies

Fig. 7.3. Material analogue models.

Other theories that can be used as models for the explicandum of an urban system include electrical network theory, hydraulic flows, etc. The conditions, then, for material analogy are:

The horizontal dyadic relations between terms are relations of similarity (between model and explicandum) where similarity can, at least for purposes of analysis, be reduced to identities and differences between sets of characters making up the terms.

The vertical relations in the model are causal relations in some acceptable scientific sense, where there are no compelling *a priori* reasons for denying that causal relations of the same kind may hold between terms of the explicandum.

The essential properties and causal relations of the model have not been shown to be part of the negative analogy between model and explicandum (Hesse 1963).

Another kind of model is called the conceptual model. It is one in which prediction of a new property of the explicandum is wholly imaginative and is not derived in any way from a causal theory. 'Such models would rather be regarded as imaginative devices to be modified and fitted *ad hoc* to the data' (Hesse 1963).

When a material analogue model cannot be found for the explicandum, the conceptual model plays a very important role, though it may be regarded as arbitrary in the early stages of development. For example, in an early stage of the development of atomic theory, conceptual models were used which were 'strongly predictive, since they give new interpretations of theoretical terms into observables which are non-arbitrary in the sense that they are determined by the model itself' (Hesse 1963). One of these conceptual models is the well-known representation of the atomic nucleus surrounded by variously populated shells of revolving electrons. Another conceptual model is the double helix used to represent the molecule of DNA, by which heredity is shown to have plausible mechanics. 'But the model itself must be regarded as arbitrary, since no further justification can be given for assuming that the world will be like the model' (Hesse 1963).

If neither material analogue nor conceptual models are used and phenomena are explained directly, the explanation becomes a formal theory, 'a mathematical hypothesis designed to fit experimental data' (Hesse 1963). Examples are familiar in the contingency plans for stacking airport traffic, or inventory control, in which commerce is rationalised by concepts ordering sufficient stock on hand without requiring excessive tying up of funds in unsold goods. Practically all operations research models can be classed as formal theories, weakly predictive in the sense that all the relationships are supposedly known so that new properties of the observable facts cannot be predicted. Such theories, commonly called mathematical models, are beginning to be used in the social sciences. They can be regarded as analogue devices that simulate the effects of different decisions within a system for the purposes of evaluation.

The main purpose of a model is to provide a simplified and intelligible picture of reality in order to understand it better. It should be possible to manipulate the model in order to propose improvements in the reality. Having stated the main purpose in general terms, functions can be specified in greater detail:

Psychological function: enabling some group of phenomena to be visualised and comprehended which could not otherwise because of its magnitude or complexity.

Acquisitive function: providing a framework where information may be defined, collected and ordered.

Logical function: explaining how a particular phenomenon comes about.
Normative function: comparing some phenomena with more familiar ones.
Cognitive function: communications of scientific ideas (Haggett 1967).

Three more functions may be added to these: systematic function – providing a framework where an idea of reality (or possible realities) can be tested; partitive function – providing a framework where partial studies can be defined, knowing their interaction with the rest of the system; and evaluative function – providing a framework where the effect of different decisions within a system can be simulated.

Chorafas (1965) suggests that 'a model should be simple enough for manipulation and understanding by those who use it, representative enough, in the total range of the implications it may have, and complex enough to accurately represent the system under study'.

Models may be classified into three categories depending on what the model is made for, what it is made of, and how the time factor is treated (Fig. 7.4).

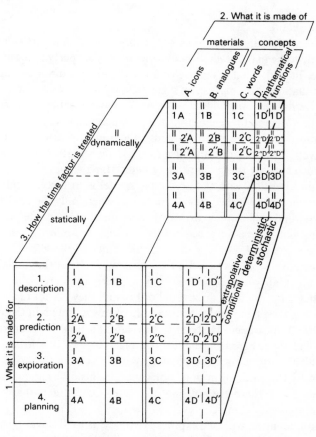

Fig. 7.4. Three-way classification system for models.

The first aspect, what the model is made for, takes into account the intentions of the model-maker and the questions the model is intended to answer. Four main types of models can be distinguished: descriptive model, predictive model, explorative model, and planning model.

The main intention with the descriptive model is the understanding of reality, usually in order to establish how a particular phenomenon comes about and to describe relationships between the relevant factors. In other words, the main intention is explanatory. This type of model is logically essential to any other type, because it is not possible to predict, explore or plan without a previous description of the reality under study. Here the question is often how accurate a descriptive model should be. Naturally, to obtain a good fit between model and reality is difficult, especially in the social sciences, because each fact or value presupposes a considerable amount of data which is either not available or requires very large resources to obtain.

On the other hand, the accuracy of the model itself in a particular situation is likely to be in contradiction to generality, a property that any theory must have. Indeed, what is the use of a theory which cannot be applied in different situations? In this respect it is necessary to 'compromise a model's accuracy by its generality' (Bunge 1966). Thus to establish a descriptive model with a degree of generality, it is not necessary or desirable to be very accurate. It is often possible to use theoretically determined values, existing available data or, in the case of a specific situation, to help match theory and reality by using empirically determined values.

The main intention with the predictive model is to forecast the future. We can distinguish two classes: extrapolative, where only the continuation of present trends that were already in the descriptive model is stated; and conditional, where the mechanisms of cause and effect governing the variables are specified, i.e. 'if x occurs, then y must follow'.

The predictive model is based on the assumption that the model represents the way reality is changing. However, alternatives are left out, either because they have not been discovered or because they do not fit the theory that describes the phenomena. An example of this is shown in the work of Morrill (1962) in Sweden. He tried to simulate the growth of central place patterns over time, based on the 'central place theory' of Christaller and Losch. This theory ignores the possibility of growth along radial routes, and naturally the simulation does not generate this alternative. As Berry (1962) points out, there are not only nucleated central activities but also linear developments along routes.

The main intention with the explorative model is to discover by speculation other realities that may be logically possible by systematically varying the basic parameters used in the descriptive model. This kind of model is associated mainly with conceptual theory. Its objective is not only to explore new possibilities but also to look back on reality to see whether the possibilities, theoretically determined, actually exist or not. An example in urban study is shown in March's investigation, presented on pages 47ff., of topological alternatives in the distribution of land uses. The paper illustrates methods of developing urban land by contrasting retiform with nucliform development, that is: development along lines intersecting at various intervals, as contrasted with development occurring as less structured and randomly spaced concretions. On the basis of these two theoretical alternatives, March then reappraises the existing situation. He finds examples of retiform development in the United States, and it can be seen that retiform development following existing routes, a natural tendency of urban growth, provides higher levels of accessibility (March 1967).

Another explorative model is that described by Jantsch (1967) in relation to morphological research in the field of jet engines. In this case, the characteristics of the jet engine are divided into eleven basic parameters such as: the source of energy, the type of thrust generation and augmentation, surrounding medium, fuel, etc., and for each one a specific range is defined. By combining these alternatives, displayed in a matrix, several types of jet engines, not hitherto considered, were shown to be feasible. If the locomotive medium were the oceans rather than the stratosphere, a theoretical submarine could be picked out from the parameters and ranges which would be fuelled by conversion of sea water and whose jet would be water. Or, if the medium were the vacuum of space, a ram jet would be described which derived its fuel by mopping up solar energy. An explorative model is promising if its 'implications are rich enough to suggest novel hypotheses and speculations in the primary field of investigations' (Black 1962).

With the planning model, 'a measure of optimisation is introduced in terms of chosen criteria in order to determine means of achieving stated planning goals' (Lowry 1965). There are many familiar examples of planning goals achieved by modelling: for instance, the location of factories in order to optimise the shipping costs involved in receiving raw materials and delivering finished products. Another illustration, where the goal was to place a man on the moon, chose between sending the rocket directly, or from a platform orbiting the earth, or from a platform orbiting the moon; a chief optimal condition was safety. These models are often used as analogue devices that, for purposes of evaluation, simulate the effect of different decisions within a system. In order to evaluate the outcome of the different decisions, the model requires a very precise description of the value to be optimised, such as minimising costs or maximising profits. For that reason, less quantitative descriptions, such as less destruction to the environment, are usually difficult to optimise. In some systems it is difficult to express the goals operationally; sometimes the goals conflict, such as in achieving higher urban amenities: is creating greater convenience by shortening the journey to work a higher goal than providing more generous home space standards which spread out houses and create longer journeys to work?

To achieve optimisation in the planning model, the following steps are required: 'specification of alternative programs or actions that might be chosen. Prediction of the consequences of choosing each alternative. Scoring these consequences according to a metric of goal-achievement. Choosing the alternative which yields the highest score.' (Lowry 1965.) Fig. 7.5 shows an ideal process of model-making in relation to reality.

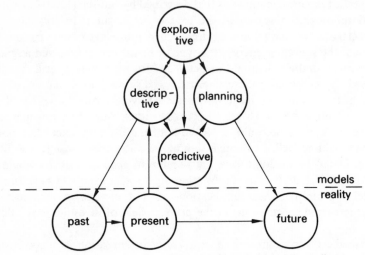

Fig. 7.5. Ideal process of model-making in relation to the reality.

The second aspect of classification, what the model is made of, relates to the means chosen to represent the reality. These can be classed as physical and conceptual. With the physical model, the physical characteristics of reality are represented by the same or analogous characteristics in the model. It can be divided into two categories:

The first is called 'iconic', in which 'the physical properties are represented only by a change of scale' (Ackoff, Gupta and Minas 1962). This class includes architectural models, photographs, etc. and is 'generally difficult to use to represent dynamic situations' (Churchman, Ackoff and Arnoff 1957).

The second is called 'analogue', and here 'the physical properties of the real world are represented by different properties' (Haggett 1967) 'according to some transformation rules' (Churchman, Ackoff and Arnoff 1957). This class includes maps, plans, graphs, etc. It is generally 'successful in representing dynamic situations, that is processes or systems' (*ibid.*).

With the conceptual model, the relevant characteristics are represented by concepts (language or symbols). Again the model can be divided into two, one verbal, and the other mathematical. For the first, the description of reality is in logical terms, using either spoken or written words. It does not 'assure explicitness as well as freedom from contradiction' (Bunge 1966). The second is mathematical, in which the description of reality is represented by the use of symbols and the relationships expressed in terms of operations. Among mathematical models a further sub-classification would make a distinction between deterministic and stochastic models. The classification is made according to the degree of probability involved.

When a model becomes complex and involves the interreaction of several separate mathematical expressions, techniques to determine the likely total result of all interreactions must be capable of increasing sophistication. Wilson (1967) distinguishes four kinds of techniques:

Statistical technique

Equation systems: the interrelationships of various parts of the model can sometimes be expressed as a simultaneous equation system, that implies that the relations between variables are known.

Simulation: not all the relations between variables are known; for these 'free' variables, a range is defined and there is one complete run of the model for each value of each variable in the range. In this case it is essential to use a computer.

Computer algorithms: rules for the computer not expressed as equation systems. A hypothesis like 'all the trips go by the route which has the shortest time' is of this kind.

Churchman, Ackoff and Arnoff (1957) distinguish three kinds of techniques in a mathematical model:

Analytic: 'Analytic procedures consist of the use of mathematical deduction.' They are always associated with equation systems.

Numerical: 'Inductive in character, trying various values of the variables in the model, and selecting that set of values of the variables which yields the best solution.' This is normally called iteration. 'An iterative procedure is one in which successive trials tend to approach an optimum solution.' One example of this technique is linear programming.

Stochastic: 'Some expressions in a model cannot be numerically evaluated with exactness because of either mathematical or practical consideration.' Such techniques as Monte Carlo or Markov Chain use a probabilistic approach. 'In essence the Monte Carlo technique consists of simulating an experiment to determine some probabilistic property of a population of objects or events by the use of random sampling applied to the components of the objects or events.'

Several mathematical models are available for certain types of problems in operations research like inventory, allocation, waiting-line, replacement, competitive and combined problems.

A third classification is possible, according to the treatment of time in the model: static model – concentrating on equilibrium of structural features (past, present or future), the position and possibilities at a single given time; dynamic model – concentrating on processes and functions through time.

This essay has attempted to define the word 'model' and it has stated the conditions necessary to build one. Also, the models' functions have been shown and the types of models that can be built, depending on the intentions, the means selected for representation and the treatment of the time factor. However, the words 'model' and 'theory' are generally used interchangeably and this can lead the modeller to confusion. Nevertheless, by attempting to distinguish the types of theories by the rank of their predictive power (Hesse 1963) it was hoped to avoid this difficulty. The confusion between 'model' and 'theory' arises because some theories are model-based (material analogue models and conceptual models) and the so-called mathematical model is, in fact, a formal theory.

For the modeller to avoid this confusion, it is necessary to establish that the construction of a model presupposes the use of a theory (either formal, conceptual or material analogue) which explains parts or the whole of the relationships established in the model. In certain cases, the lack of explicit theory in the construction process makes the model itself into a theory.

8. *Development of a model of urban spatial structure*†

DAVID CROWTHER & MARCIAL ECHENIQUE

Introduction

A city can be regarded as a complex system of interrelated elements such that a single change can lead to repercussions throughout the city. One of the principal aims of urban research is to discover which elements of the urban system are most significant and to determine the causal linkages between them. It will then be possible to explain the way in which an urban region responds to change and to predict the probable effect of different planning policies. Because of the number of elements and the complexity of their interrelationships, however, many researchers have come to the conclusion that it is only by using mathematical models to simulate the urban system that the intricate processes by which one element affects another can be analysed and understood. With the introduction of large computers, which can handle vast quantities of data and deal simultaneously with numerous variables, the construction of such models has become an important part of urban research.

In constructing the model presented in this paper, the particular aspect of the urban system that has been considered is its spatial structure, that is to say the location of different urban activities within a town and the spatial relationships between them. In terms of the classification put forward in the previous paper, 'Models: a discussion,' the model is type I3D′ (see Fig. 7.4). First of all it is a static model, in that it simulates the equilibrium of the spatial system at a given moment in time. Secondly it is an explorative model, in that by systematically varying the inputs it can reproduce not only urban spatial structures which exist but also all those which logically could exist if those elements of spatial structure represented

† This essay is based on Land Use and Built Form Studies Working Paper No. 26: Development of a model of a town, M. Echenique, D. Crowther, W. Lindsay, 1969. As with the other work of the Urban Systems Study, gratitude is acknowledged to the sponsorship of the Centre for Environmental Studies.

by the inputs were to be changed in corresponding manner. Thirdly it is a mathematical model, in that the elements of the spatial system are represented by mathematical symbols and the relationships between them by mathematical equations. Fourthly it is a deterministic model, in that for a particular set of inputs it produces a unique solution for the most likely state of the spatial system. Finally the model can also be called a simple model, in that relatively few elements of the spatial system are considered. It is worth emphasising that the model has been built for examining the spatial structure of individual towns and cities rather than of regions containing several urban settlements. Thus while subregional studies examine the distribution of population and employment within a region and the pattern of movement between towns, the concern of this study is with the detailed distribution of activity locations and traffic flows within the town itself and also with the ways in which the physical infrastructure of a town can be arranged to accommodate them. As will be shown, the intra-urban scale at which the model operates has an important bearing on the elements of the urban spatial system that need to be considered.

The paper takes the following form. In the first section, urban spatial structure is defined in terms of its component elements; this is the conceptual framework on which the model is based. In the next three sections the relationships between these elements are discussed and three submodels are presented: one for locating residential population, one for locating service employment and one for locating floorspace. For each submodel, different formulations are described and their merits assessed in terms of their ability to reproduce reality. Finally, in section five, the way in which the three submodels can be combined within a complete model of urban spatial structure is explained.

1. Components of urban spatial structure

It is possible to define urban spatial structure as the outcome of two interdependent processes by which first, artifacts and, second, activities are allocated to specific sites. The first locates the physical infrastructure (i.e. the stock of buildings, etc.) in response to the aggregate demand for space made by all activities; the second locates the activities within this physical stock according to their functional relationships with each other. This distinction between the spatial organisation óf activities and of the stock which accommodates them is well known (see Foley 1964). The overall process can be seen as symbiotic, with activities creating a demand for stock, which once built, constrains their location.

In general, activities are of two kinds: 'within place' and 'between place' (see Chapin 1965 and Webber 1964). The first relates to localised activities – industrial, commercial, recreational and residential – the second to flows of all types that occur between 'within place' activities – of information, money, people or goods. 'Between place' activities, or flows, can be seen as an expression of the functional relationships between 'within place' activities. One way of classifying the latter is to group together in one category all those which have common functional relationships to other categories. An elementary classification often adopted is to consider the three categories of employment, residents and services. The links between them are usually expressed in terms of the number and lengths of trips from one to the other. Thus the journey from home to work links residents to employment; the journey from home to services links residents to services; and finally, the journey from work to services links services to employment.

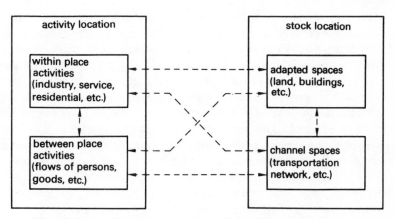

Fig. 8.1. Interaction of the components of the urban spatial structure.

'Within-place' activities can be further disaggregated into employment types, household types (subdivided into categories of socio-economic group, age and family structure) and service types (subdivided into categories of shopping at different hierarchical levels, schools, recreation, etc.). 'Between place' activities can be disaggregated into transportation modes (private vehicles, trade vehicles, etc.), information flows (telephone, post, etc.) and public utilities (water, gas, sewage, etc.).

The two corresponding kinds of physical structure which accommodate these activities are 'adapted spaces' and 'channel spaces' (see Lynch and Rodwin 1958). Adapted spaces refer to the buildings and land which contain 'within place' activities, while channel spaces refer to the transportation and communication networks which contain 'between place' activities. Adapted spaces can be distinguished by structural type, age and condition. Structural type is important since certain types may only be able to accommodate particular activities, while others may be more adaptable. For example, a large industrial building is not likely to be used for housing or for shops, whereas houses are generally more easily converted into shops or offices. Channel spaces can also be distinguished by type and capacity, etc. Figure 8.1 is a diagram of this conceptual framework, with activities ('within place' and 'between place') on the left and with the corresponding stock (adapted spaces and channel spaces) on the right.

A comprehensive urban model must take into account the interactions between all four components of the urban spatial structure if it is to be useful. Past models have tended to be concerned with only the left-hand side of the diagram, and have considered activity location to be independent of stock location.† That is they have concentrated on the functional relationships which exist between activities, and have assumed that these by themselves dictate their location. Even though the number and length of trips between activities, which represent these relationships, are recorded within a given distribution of stock, it is assumed that they can be used to predict the location of new activities without reference to a new distribution of stock. There is a tendency to regard empirically derived trip data as reflecting absolute laws of behaviour which will remain constant for any disposition of stock. This is surely a dangerous assumption. Trip data which show that certain percentages of the population locate at certain distances from employment cannot be taken as evidence that those people *wish* to locate at such distances, or do so simply to optimise their travel costs. These factors will certainly play a part in determining their location, but the availability of suitable accommodation cannot be ignored.

It would be valid to disregard the constraining effect of the stock if it was possible to demonstrate that a demand for space is automatically and instantaneously met by the supply. But as Foley (1964) has said: 'Physical facilities once developed tend to be either fixed or expensive to alter. The volumes, kinds and distribution of activities [on the other hand] may shift considerably over the years.' He concludes that 'the physical environmental pattern, once fixed, would seem to constitute a forceful determinant, having impacts or providing restraints on the spatial patterning of activities'. In most urban areas activities take place within a stock which has existed for a very long time. Activities change frequently at various rates of

† There are a few exceptions, but these are mainly partial models which do not attempt to describe the total urban system; for example, the San Francisco housing model (Robinson, Wolfe and Barringer 1965; and Wolfe 1967b), and transportation models in general, which tend to consider only the bottom half of figure 8.1.

growth, migration and decay, while the physical stock which contains them changes hardly at all. Parts of a typical town's road network have remained unaltered for centuries, and the average lifespan of a house in this country is over 60 years. Stone (1968) has shown that of today's housing (which constitutes by far the largest part of the total stock for all uses), more than 25% was built before 1881 and 75% before 1941. He estimates that the total future increase in housing stock will be less than 1% per annum for the next ten years, of which a sizeable proportion will be in the form of rehabilitation of old buildings. It is clear, therefore, that the stock of adapted and channel spaces can respond only very slowly to the shifting demands of activities, and that in consequence most activities can only locate at any one moment in time within an existing supply. In fact it is fair to say that the distribution of stock in a town does not merely constrain the location of activities, but in some ways dictates it.

Because the demand for stock cannot instantaneously be met by the supply, both activities and the stock itself have to adapt themselves in so far as they are able. Many activities have to locate in premises which were not specifically designed for their use, while others have to locate at less favourable positions within the town in order to find the particular type of accommodation that they require. Conversely, certain categories of stock are capable of being converted from one use to another. In many English towns today, a high proportion of the shops and offices are located in converted houses. The adaptation of activities to the available facilities, and the complementary process of 'stock use succession', together represent the natural compromise solution to the problem of accommodating changing activities within a more or less static supply of stock.

The importance of taking the supply of stock into account will vary to some extent according to the scale at which a model operates. At a sub-regional scale, it is probably safe to assume that, for example, straight line distances do not differ drastically from actual road distances. But even at this scale, it is difficult to achieve the correct distribution of activities without taking account of the varying capacity of different parts of a region to accommodate them. When a smaller, urban scale is adopted, as in this study, the supply of stock becomes crucial. The differences between straight line and actual road distances can be quite appreciable in certain cases, and the creation or deletion of a link between two points in a town can considerably alter the overall pattern of accessibility. Similarly, the particular distribution of buildings and land available within a town heavily constrains the possible location of activities. At this scale it is therefore imperative to consider both activities and stock together as the two major, interdependent components of the urban spatial structure.

2. Activity submodel: residential location

The discussion in the next two sections takes as a point of departure the Lowry model of Pittsburg (1964), which by virtue of its simplicity, elegance and versatility has had great impact. As Black (1962) has said, a promising model is one whose 'implications are rich enough to suggest novel hypotheses and speculations in the primary field of investigation'. The structure of the Lowry model is based on the functional relationships between three 'within place' activities: basic employment, service employment and residential population. Basic employment is that which sells its goods or services to customers coming from outside the town (e.g. manufacturing industry, large regional offices, universities, etc.), while service employment is that which sells its goods or services to customers from the town itself (e.g. shops, smaller offices, schools, etc.). Basic employment can also be thought of as that employment whose location cannot be attributed solely to accessibility to local markets (see Garner 1967 and Massey 1970). The Lowry model takes as given the location of basic employment and simulates the location of residents and service employees from this given input. The location of residential population is considered to be dependent on employment location (i.e. on the location of both types of employment) and the location of services is considered to be dependent on both residential and employment location. This is represented diagrammatically in Fig. 8.2.

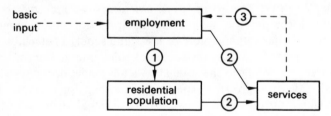

Fig. 8.2. The structure of Lowry's model.

In order to understand how the model works, one must imagine a town or urban region divided up into zones or cells. At the start all that is known is the number of basic employees in each cell. In the first iteration of the model, the residential population dependent on this basic employment (i.e. the basic employees and their families) is distributed to cells throughout the town (Step 1). Next the services dependent on these residents and on basic employment are distributed to cells throughout the town (Step 2). The service employment thus located becomes the input for the next iteration which determines the location of the housing and services for these additional workers (Step 3). Again, the residential population generated by the new employment input is distributed (Step 1) and this in turn leads to more services (Step 2) which become the input for the next iteration (Step 3). In this way the number of residents and service employees in each cell gradually builds up with successive iterations, the residents being located with respect to employment, and services with respect to residential population, basic employment and service employment located in previous iterations. Since the numbers of residents and service employees being located in an iteration is always smaller than in the previous iteration, the model tends to converge, that is to say, the stage is reached when so few residents and services are being located that they can be ignored. At this point the model is said to have reached equilibrium and the number of residents and service employees located in each iteration is added up to produce totals for the residential population and service employment in each cell.

Lowry defines the location of residents as a function of the location of employment, using the simple gravity formulation:

$$R_j = \Sigma_i E_i u \, d_{ij}^{-\theta},$$

where R_j = residents living in cell j,

E_i = employees working in cell i,

u = labour participation rate, or the ratio of the total residential population of a town to its total employment,

d_{ij} = distance between cell i and cell j,

θ = a parameter which can be interpreted as corresponding to the 'significance' of distance (see below). Note that $d_{ij}^{-\theta}$ is the same as $1/d_{ij}^{\theta}$.

Σ_i = summation sign indicating that the value for $E_i u \, d_{ij}^{-\theta}$ is calculated for each cell in turn and then summed.

Put into words, this formulation states that the residential population in a cell j is proportional to its aggregate accessibility to the town's employment. Thus if a cell j is close to several cells i containing large numbers of employees it will have more residents than a cell which is further away from employment centres. By putting this general statement into precise mathematical form, one can effectively predict the location of residential population in a town. The equation is not 'normalised', that is to say, it is possible for the total of all values for R_j ($\Sigma_j R_j$) to be different from the total of all values for $E_i u$ ($\Sigma_i E_i u$). Since, by definition, $\Sigma_j R_j$ should equal $\Sigma_i E_i u$, some normalisation procedure needs to be adopted to overcome this problem. The technique used by Lowry is to consider the R_j values produced by the model as representing the potential of each cell to attract residents. The total number of residents that need to be distributed ($\Sigma_i E_i u$) is then allocated in proportion to the potential of each cell, i.e.

Residential population in cell $j = \dfrac{R_j}{\Sigma_j R_j} \cdot \Sigma_i E_i u.$

A different method of normalisation is explained later.

If a town is divided up into cells or zones and if the number of employees in each cell is known, then the formulation above will predict the number of residents in each cell by distributing them from workplaces to surrounding cells according to the distance function (in this case $d_{ij}^{-\theta}$). If the value for θ is low (i.e. if distance is insignificant as a constraint on location), residents will be distributed more or less evenly throughout the town, while if the value for θ is high (i.e. if distance is a significant constraint), residents will be distributed close to employment centres. The distance between two cells, d_{ij}, can be measured either as the crow flies (as Lowry does) or via the transportation network, in which case the location of the nodes and links of the network need to be given as an additional input to the model. The latter is obviously preferable, especially at the town scale, since cells which are close geographically are not necessarily close in terms of accessibility. With reference to Fig. 8.1, the use of road distances relates the location of 'within place' activities with the location of channel spaces.

As pointed out by Garin (1966), the distribution of residents from work-places is in fact simulating the journeys made in the real world from work to home. In other words, the spatial relationship between employment and residential population can be expressed in terms of the numbers and lengths of work trips. For this reason it is often convenient in discussing residential models to refer to the workplace cell (cell i) as the cell of origin (i.e. where the 'trip' originates) and the residence cell (cell j) as the terminal cell or the cell of destination. By controlling the length of these 'trips', θ can be seen to represent (inversely) residents' willingness to spend money on the journey to and from work. As one would expect, experiments show that θ has a lower value for high socio-economic groups, who can afford to spend more money on travel and for whom distance is relatively insignificant as a constraint on location, than for low socio-economic groups. Referring to Fig. 8.1 again, one can see that Lowry's model can be used to relate the location of 'within place' activities with the location of channel spaces and with the 'between place' activities they contain.

Because of the relationship with journey to work behaviour, Lowry's model can be used to predict not only residential location but the traffic flows generated by work trips as well. Apart from being valuable in itself, this is useful for calibrating the model, that is to say for determining the value for θ. The simplest method of calibration is to find by trial and error the value for θ which produces the most accurate results for residential location in an existing town. But if journey to work data are available (see Fig. 8.3 for example), a second value for θ can be found which produces work trip lengths closest to reality. If these two independently derived values for θ are in fact the same then the internal consistency of the model has been verified and one can have confidence that the model is correctly calibrated. This process of calibration is common to all spatial models and applies not only to the residential submodel but also to the service and stock submodels (which are explained later), since they similarly use a function of distance with 'cost-impedance' parameters for which values have to be determined. Such parameters can be thought of as analogous to adjustment knobs on a piece of laboratory equipment which need to be set for a particular town before the model can be used. Although to begin with the parameters have to be determined in this way by testing the model results against reality for existing towns, continuing research is establishing norms for towns of different type for a range of different distance functions (such as the ones described later) and is also demonstrating the way in which they tend to change with time. In general all cost-impedance parameters, such as θ above, tend to decrease with time as increasing affluence enables more people to spend more on travel. The need to calibrate parameters of a model, therefore, does not prevent it from being used exploratively or for predictive purposes, especially as parameter values tend to vary only within fairly defined limits (even for towns of very different spatial structure) and the effect of assuming different values can in any case be tested.

In spite of its general applicability, several objections to Lowry's formulation have been raised;[†] two interrelated points can be discussed here. The first concerns Lowry's distance function which simply indicates that residential population decays in some form from workplace, producing a surface with peaks at employment centres, that can then be visualised as a tent with poles of different heights positioned at these centres with θ controlling the slope of the sides of the tent. This does not correspond to empirical evidence. Fig. 8.3 shows that the highest peaks of residential location do not occur at employment centres, but at some distance away from them; this is because in the central cells of a town residents tend to be displaced by employment activities. At a macro-urban, or subregional scale this peak may occur within the cell of origin because of the latter's

---

† A common criticism is against the 'premise that residential location is always oriented to the breadwinner's place of work' (Lowry 1964). Also a certain proportion of households consist entirely of retired or economically inactive persons who do not go to work. It has to be assumed that they are evenly distributed amongst all households.

size, in which case the simple decay function does have a certain validity. But at a smaller scale it cannot justifiably be used.†

The second point of criticism relates to the lack of terminal descriptors in the formulation. A terminal descriptor is a variable included within the mathematical equation to represent the inherent attractiveness or capacity of each cell (in this case) for residential location. Thus terminal descriptors modify the distribution of residential population from workplaces by

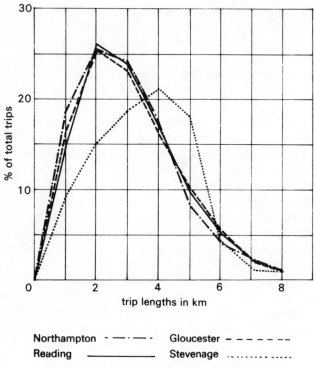

Northampton - — · — ·   Gloucester – – – – – –
Reading   ————   Stevenage ···············

Fig. 8.3. Journey to work by all modes of travel.

taking account of the varying capacity of each terminal cell to accommodate residents. As Lowry says: 'Our potential-formula distributes residents in a pattern which is radially-symmetrical with respect to workplaces: if the space available for residential use is radially asymmetrical, residential densities would vary without compensating variations in accessibility to the relevant workplace.' Empirical evidence shows that the space available for urban activities is indeed radially asymmetrical, due to the irregularity

† Even at subregional scale, it has proved necessary to resort to two separate functions, one for intra-urban distances, and another for inter-urban distances (see Batty 1969).

of the transportation network, topographical and planning constraints, and particularly to the unequal distribution of floorspace. Consequently, residential population does not distribute itself symmetrically around employment centres. Actual road distances distort the pattern by making some cells less accessible to an employment centre than others, even though they may be closer as the crow flies. Topographical and planning constraints restrict the amount of land for residential development, and prevent residents from locating in certain cells altogether. Also the varying quantities of floorspace in each cell impose limits to the number of residents that can be accommodated in a cell, however accessible it may be. The urban plane is thus 'non-Euclidean, heterogeneous and aelotropic' (March 1969).

In an attempt to solve these problems, Lowry resorts to maximum density constraints applied across the urban surface. This can be expressed as:

$$R_j \leqslant R(\text{max})$$

which states that the population in a cell j can never exceed a specified value R (max). Lowry argues that 'in order to prevent the model from generating excessive population densities in the vicinity of major employment centres, limiting values are determined outside the model, and imposed as constraints on the allocation process'. These constraints generate an overflow of residents which needs to be redistributed, and overflow is also produced when the services are allocated. Lowry proposes two alternatives for dealing with the redistribution. The first method is to allocate the overflow to cells in proportion to the population previously located. The second simply allocates the overflow to the eight neighbouring cells. In either case, the resultant distribution will be different from the originally proposed distribution that the model is supposed to be obeying. Fig. 8.4 demonstrates how the overflow, when treated in this way, converts a simple decay distribution into a 'gamma-type' distribution. Lowry thus deals with the first point – that a simple decay function does not reflect the distribution of residential population – but only by breaking his own rules. As he admits, 'it would seem more in keeping with our interpretation to send this surplus exclusively to tracts whose accessibility characteristics are similar to those of the tract from which the households were turned away'. But if he were to do so, he would not be able to cope with the overflow caused by the excessive peaking of the distribution function at the cell of origin, since there will not be any other cells with similar accessibility characteristics. One solution is to use a distribution function which takes account of the increased opportunities for finding accommodation that accrue with distance from employment centres, such as the one suggested by March (1969). It is shown in its most generalised form on page 189. A function of this kind will not by itself produce the right distribution of residents within an annulus, but at least the aggregate for the annulus as a whole will correspond to reality. The problem can only finally be overcome if, in conjunction with a March-type function, a measure of capacity is applied at the cell of destination. In this case, the overflow will eventually be redistributed to the right cells, though only after many iterations.

An alternative approach is to incorporate terminal descriptors within the formulation of the distribution. Recent applications of the Lowry model†

Fig. 8.4. Diagrammatic representation of residential location submodel (Lowry).

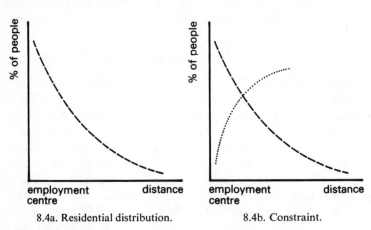

8.4a. Residential distribution.   8.4b. Constraint.

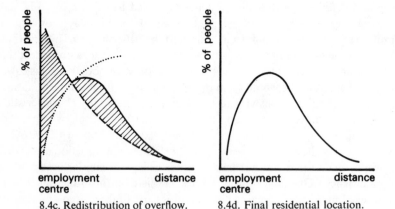

8.4c. Redistribution of overflow.   8.4d. Final residential location.

† See Batty (1969) and Cripps (1969).

at a subregional scale have used a modified formulation with a terminal descriptor, which attempts to take into account the different capacities of each cell.

i.e. $R_j = \Sigma_i A_i E_i u W_j f(d_{ij})$,

where R_j = residents living in cell j,
$\quad\quad E_i$ = employees working in cell i,
$\quad\quad u$ = labour participation rate,
$\quad\quad W_j$ = some measure of the capacity or attractiveness of cell j,
$\quad\quad f(d_{ij})$ = some function of the distance between cell i and cell j,
$\quad\quad A_i$ = a normalisation term equal to $1/\Sigma_j W_j f(d_{ij})$.
$\quad\quad\quad$ This ensures that $\Sigma_j R_j = \Sigma_i E_i u$ by computing the attractiveness and accessibility of cell j as a proportion of the total attractiveness and accessibility of all competing cells j.†

This formulation ensures that residential population is allocated not only as a function of distance from employment, but also with respect to the capacity W of the terminal cell j as a proportion of the competing capacities of all other cells. The use of terminal descriptors in this way has several advantages. Firstly, the residential population can be distributed asymmetrically around employment centres in response to the varying capacity of the surrounding cells. Secondly, the rather cumbersome method of imposing maximum density constraints on residential land can be dispensed with, since the model will distribute the population in each iteration without creating overflow. Thirdly, the overflow created by the distribution of service employment can be sent back to the relevant employment centres and redistributed to the cells with available floorspace in the next iteration. Finally, since terminal descriptors take account of the varying capacity of each cell, the model builder is free to use cells of different size and shape as convenient. Without terminal descriptors all cells should theoretically be of approximately the same capacity in order to equalise the probability of occupation, which is in practice difficult to achieve with any precision. Equal sized grid cells have many advantages – their boundaries do not change and their constant size facilitates direct comparison on a common areal basis of different towns, of different plans for the same town and of different areas within a town – but they are not an operational necessity: terminal descriptors enable any type of cell or zone to be used (e.g. traffic zones, enumeration districts, etc.).

† Normalisation is thus achieved in a different way from Lowry (see pages 181, 182) by including the normalisation term within the formulation rather than by normalising the R_j values after they have been calculated.

Once the principle of terminal descriptors has been accepted, the only problem is to decide on a suitable measure of capacity. One method which has been suggested is to put W_j equal to the existing residential population in cell j, R'_j, but this has serious objections. As the function of distance approaches unity, the population in cell j that the model outputs is set to the value of W_j, or the actual population in cell j which the model is supposed to be simulating, i.e.

if $\qquad\qquad W_j = R'_j$ and $\Sigma_j W_j = \Sigma_i E_i u$

when $\qquad\qquad\qquad\quad f(d_{ij}) \to 1,$

$$R_j = W_j = R'_j.$$

This means that the model is difficult to calibrate properly since the 'best fit' calibration will always tend to be such that $f(d_{ij}) \to 1$. Even if this were not so, the model cannot be used for predictive or explorative purposes. Since the future distribution of residential population is not known, there is nothing to use as a measure of the future attractiveness of each cell, and if the values of existing population are used instead as a rough approximation, the model will merely distribute the new population in proportion to the old. In any case, it is fair to question the validity of a formulation which requires as given inputs the very values which the model should be attempting to simulate.†

Instead of using the existing residential population as a measure of capacity, it is possible to consider the amount of residential land available in each cell as the terminal descriptor.‡ This would take account of the topographical and planning constraints which distort the distribution of residents, but not of the varying densities of development which occur on a unit of land according to its position in the town.

The proposed model uses as a measure of capacity the supply of available floorspace in each cell, the available floorspace being the total quantity of floorspace for all uses less the amount used by basic employment (which is given) and by service employment (which is determined by the service model). This variable accurately reflects the asymmetrical distribution of residential population around employment centres, the only differences being due to variations in residential space standard, and is also truly independent in that the existing residential population in each cell does not need to be assumed in order to determine it. There is thus nothing to prevent the model being used predictively, provided the future distribu-

---

† For an interesting discussion of this problem, and some possible solutions, see Batty (1969).

‡ An early model which uses the land available as a terminal descriptor is Hansen's (1959). Another measure, proposed by Lathrop and Hamburg (1965), is existing density.

tion of floorspace can be predicted (as it can – see section 4 below). A further important benefit of including floorspace within the formulation is that it brings together both the activity and stock components of urban spatial structure. The need to consider both components together was established earlier (see Fig. 8.1). The only drawback – if it can be called one – is that the residential model cannot now be considered independently from the service model, since both models need to be run concurrently in order to determine the proportion of the total available floorspace in each cell that is occupied by services. But this is no disadvantage either in operational terms, since the iterative structure of the Lowry model (Fig. 8.2) allows the residential and service models to be run concurrently, or in conceptual terms, since the interrelated nature of the urban system and the invalidity of considering subsystems separately are fundamental tenets of urban research. It should come as no surprise therefore that the most satisfactory solution for residential location (i.e. using available floorspace as a terminal descriptor) can only be achieved within the framework of a comprehensive model in which stock location, residential location and service location are considered together.

There remains the problem of choosing a suitable distance function. In practice a wide range of different functions have been used by different model builders, but March (1969) has shown they can all be considered to belong to the same family of functions, which, in its most general form, can be expressed as:

$$d_{ij}{}^{\alpha} \exp(-\beta d_{ij}{}^{\theta}),$$

where d_{ij} = distance between cell i and cell j. (The exponential term, exp, is frequently used in distance functions on account of its mathematical flexibility; the function $\exp(-\beta d_{ij})$ produces a simple decay very similar to $d_{ij}{}^{\theta}$ for the same values of d_{ij}.)

α, β, θ = parameters

March shows how this function can be reduced (by setting α, β or θ to either zero or unity as appropriate) to almost any of the distance functions that have been used and he also demonstrates the great variety of distributions that the complete function with all three parameters can describe. With suitable values, for example, it can accurately describe the distribution of residents around employment, while, as shown earlier, Lowry's simple decay function $(d_{ij}{}^{-\theta})$ cannot. On the other hand a function with three separate parameters, each one affecting the other, is obviously more difficult to calibrate than a function with only one.

Fortunately, this dilemma is resolved by the use of terminal descriptors;

this is where the two criticisms of Lowry's formulation made earlier come together. By taking account of the varying capacity of each cell to accommodate residents, the peaks of residential distribution produced by the model occur not at employment centres, even when a simple decay function is used, but at some distance away from them in a way which corresponds to reality. The increased opportunities for finding accommodation that accrue with distance from employment centres are represented by the terminal descriptors rather than in the function of distance itself. Thus apart from allowing for the asymmetrical distribution of residential population around employment centres according to the availability of stock, the use of terminal descriptors leaves the model builder free to choose between a simple decay function of distance with one parameter for ease of calibration (see Hyman 1969), or, if even greater accuracy is required, a more complicated function with, say, at most two parameters.

So far this discussion has been concerned with the operational problems of different formulations for residential location and their ability to produce accurate results in practice. Improvements to Lowry's original formulations, some of which have been suggested and used by other model builders, have been explained in terms of their relation to what actually happens in reality. It is therefore interesting at this point to compare the formulation put forward on page 187, which has been arrived at experimentally, with a formulation which has been derived from purely theoretical considerations by Wilson (1967 and 1971). Given an urban region divided up into cells and by considering the total number of possible permutations of the work trips that can occur between each pair of cells, Wilson has used the statistical theory of maximum entropy to show that the most likely value for the number of work trips occurring between one cell i and another cell j is:

$$T_{ij} = A_i B_j E_i P_j \exp(-\beta c_{ij}),$$

where T_{ij} = work trips generated between cell i and cell j,
      E_i = employees working in cell i,
      P_j = employees living in cell j,
      c_{ij} = cost of travel between cell i and cell j,
      β = a parameter,
      A_i = a normalisation term equal to $1/\Sigma_j B_j P_j \exp(-\beta c_{ij})$ which ensures that $\Sigma_j T_{ij} = E_i$,
      B_j = a normalisation term equal to $1/\Sigma_i A_i E_i \exp(-\beta c_{ij})$ which ensures that $\Sigma_i T_{ij} = P_j$.

Briefly, this theory shows that a system will tend towards that state which can be arrived at most easily, that is, by the maximum number of ways. It is an extremely powerful theory in that one can derive an equation describing the likely state of a system without having to know very much about the system at the start. Thus the equation above can be derived knowing only that: $\Sigma_j T_{ij} = E_i$ (i.e. that the sum of all individual work-to-home trips leaving cell i must equal the known number of employees working in cell i); that $\Sigma_i T_{ij} = P_j$ (i.e. that the sum of all individual work-to-home trips arriving in cell j must equal the known number of employees living in cell j) and that $\Sigma_i\Sigma_j T_{ij}c_{ij} = C$ (i.e. that the total money expended on all work trips must equal some finite sum – which does not need to be specified – at a particular moment in time). Given these constraints, the statistical theory of maximum entropy can be used to derive the equation shown. (For a full description of entropy-maximising principles, see Wilson 1967 and 1971.)

The above formulation, however, is concerned with the trips generated between cells, rather than the distribution of residents, and assumes that *both* the number of employees and the number of residents in each cell are known (hence the second normalisation term B_j). The formulation is thus doubly constrained in that both ends of the trip are fixed, whereas in a residential location model only the employment end of the trip is fixed at cell i, the object being to find the number of work-to-home trips ending in cell j. Wilson has therefore also derived a singly constrained formulation for residential location in which the second normalisation term B_j is dropped. i.e.

$$R_j = P_ju = \Sigma_i T_{ij}u = \Sigma_i A_i E_i u W_j \exp(-\beta c_{ij}) \, ,$$

where R_j = residents living in cell j,
   u = labour participation rate,
   W_j = attractiveness of cell j for residential location.

By comparing this formulation with the one on page 187, it can be seen that the two formulations, one derived experimentally, the other theoretically, show a heartening similarity, thereby inspiring confidence in the validity and applicability of both. The main difference between them is that while in practice different distance functions produce slightly better results according to particular circumstances, Wilson shows that the simple exponential function has the most general validity. His formulation also specifically requires the cost of travel as the measure of accessibility rather than any physical measures such as distance or time. The idea of using the cost of travel as a measure of accessibility is of course one which many model builders have suggested, but unfortunately it is a most difficult variable for which to collect data (as is time). For this reason, distance is the measure most commonly used, calculated either as the crow flies or, more properly, along the transportation network. Since distance will always be a major component of the cost of travel, it is in any case valid to use distance as a proxy for travel cost. If greater accuracy is desired, an extra parameter can be used to take account of the fact that travel costs rise non-linearly with distance, i.e.

$$c_{ij} \equiv d_{ij}{}^{\theta}.$$

Another difference is that Wilson leaves unspecified the variable to be used as the measure of the attractiveness of cell j for residential location. As has been shown, the physical capacity of a cell is a crucial determinant of activity location at the urban scale and certainly the inclusion of the available floorspace in cell j as the W_j term in the formulation has produced accurate results. At the level of aggregation of a simple model, in which residents are not differentiated by socio-economic group or by family size, no other additional variables to describe the attractiveness of a cell for residential location seem to be required. This can be seen as the major contribution of the work of the Urban Systems Study to the problem of residential location models.

The final version of the residential submodel is therefore:

$$R_j = \Sigma_i A_i E_i u F_j^r \exp(-\beta^r d_{ij}),$$

where R_j = residents living in cell j,

$\quad E_i$ = employees working in cell i,

$\quad u$ = labour participation rate,

$\quad F_j^r$ = floorspace available for residents in cell j,

$\quad d_{ij}$ = distance via the transportation network between cell i and cell j (used as a proxy for the cost of travel between cells i and j),

$\quad \beta^r$ = a parameter representing the significance of distance as a constraint on residential location, or residents' willingness to spend money on travel to work,

$\quad A_i$ = normalisation term equal to $1/\Sigma_j F_j^r \exp(-\beta^r d_{ij})$ which ensures that $\Sigma_j R_j = \Sigma_i E_i u$.

The model states that the number of residents living in a cell j is related to:

1. The number of employees working in cells i and their dependents $(E_i u)$.
2. The supply of available accommodation in cell j (F_j^r).
3. The accessibility of cell j to the cells i containing employment $(\exp(-\beta^r d_{ij}))$.
4. The supply of available floorspace in all competing cells j and their accessibility to employment $(\Sigma_j F_j^r \exp(-\beta^r d_{ij}))$.

Given a town or urban region divided up into cell or zones, the inputs required for the model are:

the number of employees (basic and service) in each cell;
the labour participation rate;
the amount of floorspace available for residents in each cell;
the distance via the transportation network of each cell to all others;
the parameter β^r.

From these inputs the model outputs the number of residents living in each cell and the number and length of journeys to work between each pair of cells. For any particular set of inputs there is a unique result for residential location, so that by changing the inputs one can explore the effects of different planning policies on residential location and journeys to work. Although on its own the residential model requires several inputs and provides few outputs, it should be appreciated that within the context of the complete model of urban spatial structure, the floorspace and service employment inputs are provided by the stock and service submodels, while the transportation network and basic employment inputs are common to the model as a whole. The only additional inputs required specifically for the residential submodel are thus the labour participation rate and the value for β^r (which is usually obtained by calibration – see pages 182–3). The output of residential location is used as an input to the service submodel.

The model can be further developed by distinguishing: firstly, different types of household according to socio-economic group, labour participation rate, age and family structure; secondly different types of floorspace (as terminal descriptors) according to structural type, age and condition; thirdly, different accessibility and cost impedances for each household type; and finally, by considering accessibility not only to employment but to other determinants of residential location, such as schools, recreation, etc.†

† An interesting proposal for extending simple residential models is one by Wilson (1969), which disaggregates employment into four types: 1. locationally unconstrained employees; 2. employees constrained to fixed residences; 3. employees constrained to fixed jobs; 4. employees constrained to both fixed residences and jobs. At this level of disaggregation, an apparent difficulty of Wilson's formulation is that since it is initially expressed in terms of trips from one cell to another, both the cell of origin and the cell of destination have to be specified. Problems thus occur in cases where there are more than one wage earner in a household, and when there is a need to consider accessibility not only to employment, but to other determinants of location, such as elementary schools, recreation, etc. Another interesting feature of his model is the way in which the cost of housing and the cost of travel are combined in the exponential term. Unfortunately it will be difficult to test this formulation until there is better

3. Activity submodel: service location

Given the location of residents, Lowry encounters several difficulties in distributing services. Using a simple gravity function, his model tends to disperse these services evenly amongst the residential population without achieving the clusterings that occur in reality. In his own words: 'Experiments demonstrated that the model was not clever enough to do this. Consequently we shifted to a different approach using the retail cluster

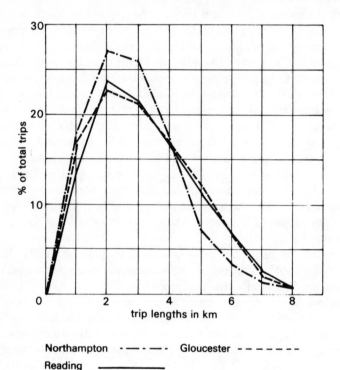

Northampton · — · — ·   Gloucester — — — — — —

Reading —————————

Fig. 8.5. Journey to services by all modes of travel.

itself as the unit to be located' (Lowry 1964). All services are then divided into three categories – neighbourhood, local and metropolitan – and a minimum size constraint is applied to each category to obtain the required clustering. If in a cell the number of service employees in any category does

data on rents and personal incomes related to location within the town. The findings of Chapin and Weiss (1962), relating to the factors influencing the location of private residential development, could also be incorporated in a future model. Some of the most important of these influences are: distance to nearest main road, availability of public utilities (i.e. water, sewage, etc.) and amenity of neighbourhood See also the work of Torres (1970), Anthony (1970b) and Apps (1971).

not reach the necessary size, these employees are redistributed to the clusters which have accumulated sufficient size. Lowry's service distribution takes into account the accessibility of services to both employees and residents, and he also varies the relative importance of residents and employees influencing the location of each type of cluster. This inclusion of the attraction of services to employment is an important feature at the urban scale, which tends to be ignored by subregional studies. The journeys between services and employment are considered to be short trips within the same cell (so that there is no need for a distance function in this part of the distribution), and the services are distributed from residents by what Lowry calls a differentiated product model,† calibrated from Pittsburg service trip data. The service distribution produced by this function conforms more closely to observed data than the distribution produced by a simple decay function (see Fig. 8.5). His formulation is:

$$S_j'^k = \alpha^k E_j + \Sigma_i \beta^k R_i f^k(d_{ij}),$$

where $S_j'^k$ = potential of cell j to attract services of type k,

E_j = employees working in cell j,

R_i = residents living in cell i,

$f^k(d_{ij})$ = a function of the distance between cell i and cell j for each service type k such that: $ds/dx = (a - bx + cx^2)^{-1}$ where s is the total number of potential services of type k generated at a radius x from a resident living in cell i and where a, b and c are parameters,

α^k, β^k = parameters controlling relative importance of employees and residents respectively in influencing location of service type k.

These potentials are then converted into service employees by calculating the total number of service employees of type k that need to be distributed and allocating them in proportion to the potential of each cell, i.e.

$$S_j^k = \frac{S_j'^k}{\Sigma_j S_j'^k} \cdot \Sigma_j S_j^k$$

where S_j^k = service employees of type k working in cell j,

$S_j'^k$ = potential of cell j to attract services of type j.

The total number of service employees of type k that the model needs to allocate ($\Sigma_j S_j^k$) is determined by multiplying the total residential population

---

† This function has been derived from Schneider's work (1959), and has similarities to the function proposed in this paper (see also March 1969).

of the town ($\Sigma_i R_i$) by the service employment to population ratio for each type k (v^k), i.e.

$$\Sigma_j S_j^k = \Sigma_i R_i v^k.$$

Within the context of the iterative structure of Lowry's complete model, $\Sigma_j S_j^k$ is determined within each iteration by multiplying the total number of residents to be located in that iteration (by the residential model) by v^k.

The minimum size constraint is expressed as:

$$S_j^k \geqslant S^k(\text{min});$$

otherwise

$$S_j^k = 0.$$

While it is reasonable to distinguish between different service categories, the eighteen parameters† which need to be calibrated make the model cumbersome to use as a simple explorative tool. Apart from this, there are several problems arising from the use of minimum size constraints. Firstly the minimum size constraints eliminate the small services dispersed amongst urban areas. Secondly, since they cause service employment to be shifted to other locations, the resultant distribution of service trip lengths does not obey the originally proposed distribution. Finally, there is no mechanism for distributing those services generated by residents who have been subsequently displaced by other uses, and as a result further distortions of the stated service trip distribution will occur.

Another approach to service distribution is a modification of the Lakshmanan and Hansen (1965) retail market potential model. Even though this model was originally intended to assess the retail sales of given service centres, it has been popular at subregional level for allocating service employment. The modified model can be expressed as:

$$S_j = \Sigma_i A_i R_i v W_j f(d_{ij}),$$

where S_j = service employees working in cell j,
         R_i = residents living in cell i,
         v = service employment to population ratio (i.e. the total number of service employees in a town divided by the total residential population),
         W_j = some measure of the attractiveness of cell j for service location,

---

† For each of the three types of cluster, there are values for a, b and c to be calibrated in the distribution function; one minimum size constraint; one service employment to population ratio; and one weighting factor to distinguish between the patronage of residents and employees. i.e. $3 \times 6 = 18$ parameters in all.

$f(d_{ij})$ = some function of the distance between cell i and cell j,

A_i = normalisation term equal to $1/\Sigma_j W_j f(d_{ij})$ which ensures that $\Sigma_j S_j = \Sigma_i R_i v$.

This equation can be seen to be of the same form as the one for residential location explained on page 187. Substituting $\exp(-\beta c_{ij})$ (where c_{ij} is the cost of travel between cells i and j) for $f(d_{ij})$, it is also identical to the equation for service location derived by Wilson from the statistical theory of maximum entropy (in exactly the same way as for residential location – see page 190). Since distance can be used as a proxy for travel cost, Wilson's work has once more provided the theoretical basis for a formulation derived independently from considerations of operational success.

As before, however, the problem is to choose a suitable variable to use as the terminal descriptor W_j. In some subregional models the variable used has been the existing service employment in each cell, but the same arguments as were levelled against the use of residential population as a terminal descriptor in the residential model can again be raised, especially with regard to the use of the model for explorative purposes. Lakshmanan and Hansen take as their measure of attractiveness the existing retail floorspace in each cell, which to some extent parallels the use of available floorspace as the terminal descriptor for the residential model. The problem here, however, is that in the context of the complete activity model the quantity of floorspace used by services in each cell is not known; if it was known one could simply multiply by an average service space standard to determine the number of service employees without resource to any model. In fact one of the objectives of the service model, on which the residential model relies, is to determine how much of the total quantity of floorspace in a cell is occupied by services. There is thus a 'chicken and egg' situation with each model requiring as an input the output of the other. The problem is most acute in the central cells of a town which contain a high proportion of floorspace but relatively few residents, since most of the floorspace is occupied by services. If the total available floorspace in a cell were used as the terminal descriptor for the residential model (rather than the total less that used by service employment), the results would therefore be wildly inaccurate for these central cells. Thus although the service model must be run after the residential model, in order for there to be residents to generate services, the residential model in its turn depends on the service model to determine the amount of floorspace in each cell that is truly available for residents. In practice this dilemma can be resolved by using Lowry's iterative procedure for the activity model and, in order to understand how, it is worth making a brief detour to explain the detailed mechanics of this procedure.

In the first iteration of the activity model, basic employees (whose location is given) generate residents who are distributed using the total available floorspace in each cell as the terminal descriptor (i.e. the total for all uses less that used by basic employment). These residents then generate services which can be distributed, using the total available floorspace again as the terminal descriptor and allowing services to displace residents if there is not enough room for both. The residents displaced in this way must be returned to the workplaces from which they were distributed and the services they have generated must be identified and discounted. In the next iteration, the successfully located services employees generate new residents and these, together with the old residents who were displaced in the first iteration, are distributed using a terminal descriptor which this time is equal to the total available floorspace less that used by both the service employees and the residents successfully located in the previous iteration. In this way the value of the terminal descriptor changes with each iteration. In the central cells, for example, the quantity of floorspace available for residents is pared down as more and more services are allocated there with successive iterations (attracted by the large quantities of available floorspace, which includes that used by residents since services take priority over residents), until, at equilibrium, the floorspace left over for residents is equal to the correct amount.

The problem with this procedure as it stands is that the use of available floorspace as the terminal descriptor does not by itself produce the right distribution of services and, since the two models are so closely interconnected, the wrong distribution of services will produce the wrong distribution of residents. If the floorspace available for services is considered to be the total quantity of floorspace in a cell less that used by both basic employment and by service employment successfully located in previous iterations, then as more and more services are located in successive iterations the floorspace available for services will tend to approximate the floorspace available for residents. At equilibrium, therefore, the resultant distribution of service employment will far too slavishly follow the distribution of residential population. The problem is compounded in that, even when the quantity of floorspace used by services in each cell is known as a given input to the service model, the results are not entirely satisfactory. As Lakshmanan and Hansen admit, when describing their model for the Baltimore region (which used retail floorspace in each cell as a given input): 'The sales comparison at the C.B.D. was inconclusive owing to the unaccountability of purchases made by workers and visitors.'

As the quotation above suggests, the problem can be resolved finally only by taking account of both the floorspace available *and* the patronage of services by employees. The importance of considering all three links between the boxes of Figure 2 (as Lowry himself does)† was discussed earlier. The proposed terminal descriptor for the service model is thus a combination of the employment located in each cell and the floorspace available in each cell. In order to reduce the two quantities to dimensionless units with the same scale of possible values, each one is expressed as a proportion of the total for all cells, i.e.:

$$W_j^s = \left(\frac{E_j}{\Sigma_j E_j} + \frac{F_j^s}{\Sigma_j F_j^s} \right)^\alpha$$

where W_j^s = terminal descriptor for the service model,

E_j = employees located in cell j; i.e., basic employment plus service employment successfully located in previous iterations,

F_j^s = floorspace available for services in cell j; i.e., total floorspace for all uses less that used by both basic employment and by service employment successfully located in previous iterations,

α = parameter representing the degree of service clustering.

With this function for the terminal descriptor the service model accurately simulates the location of services in a town.‡ The extra parameter α was found to be necessary in order to reproduce the degree of service clustering that occurs in reality. This clustering can be seen to be the result of two factors: the economies of scale (i.e. of selling more goods at cheaper prices) that tend to produce a concentrated pattern of large establishments at the most accessible point to the highest number of potential customers, and secondly the mutual advantages (i.e. of attracting each other's customers) gained by service establishments grouping together in one centre (see Cordey-Hayes 1968). It has to be remembered that while the residential model reproduces the dispersed pattern of residential location by distributing residents from concentrations of employment, the service model has the opposite task of reproducing a concentration of service employment from a dispersed pattern of residents. Lowry was only able to achieve the required degree of clustering with a cumbersome system of minimum size constraints and a formulation requiring eighteen parameters (although, to

† Lowry (1964) quotes some evidence to show that in Pittsburg's central business district in 1961, 'about 40% of the reported dollar value of department store purchases was attributed to persons whose primary reason for being downtown was work-connected.'

‡ When the simple static model was run for Santiago, Chile (Echenique and Domeyko, 1970), no floorspace data were available, so that E_j, the total employment in cell j, was used for the W_j term. This variable produced reasonable results in the case of Santiago, but in general it does not produce as accurate results as when the floorspace available for services is also taken into account.

be fair, he was able to simulate the location of three types of services). The inclusion of only one extra parameter therefore seems reasonable, especially as no minimum size constraints are required. Conceptually the extra parameter does not necessarily reduce the theoretical validity of the model with reference to Wilson's formulations derived from maximum entropy theory, since one is merely stating that the attractive power of floorspace and employment for services location is non-linear (i.e. twice as much floorspace and employment is more than twice as attractive). In practice α appears to be reasonably constant for different towns, the value typically being between 1 and 2.

The final version of the service submodel is therefore:

$$S_j = \Sigma_i A_i R_i v W^s_j \exp(-\beta^s d_{ij}),$$

where S_j = service employees working in cell j,
     R_i = residents living in cell i,
     v = service employment to population rate,
     W^s_j = the attractiveness of cell j for service location, equal to $[E_j/\Sigma_j E_j) + (F^s_j/\Sigma_j F^s_j)]^\alpha$
     E_j = total employment in cell j
     F^s_j = floorspace available for services in cell j
     α = parameter representing the degree to which services cluster in order to achieve economies of scale,
     β^s = parameter representing significance of distance as a constraint on service location, or residents' willingness to spend money on travelling to services.
     A_i = normalisation term equal to $1/\Sigma_j W^s_j \exp(-\beta^s d_{ij})$ which ensures that $\Sigma_j S_j = \Sigma_i R_i v$.

The model states that the number of service employees working in cell j is related to:

1. The number of service employees required by residents living in cell i ($R_i v$).
2. The accessibility of cell j to the cells i containing residents (exp $(-\beta^s d_{ij})$).
3. The attractiveness of cell j for service location as measured by the floorspace available for services and the employment located in cell j (W^s_j).
4. The attractiveness and accessibility of all competing cells j ($\Sigma_j W^s_j \exp$ $(-\beta^s d_{ij})$).

Given a town or urban region divided up into cells or zones, the inputs required for the model are:

the residential population in each cell;

the service employment to population ratio;

the total employment in each cell;

the floorspace available for services in each cell;

the distance via the transportation network between each cell and all others;

the parameters α and β^s.

From these inputs the model outputs the number of service employees in each cell and the number and length of journeys from home to services between each pair of cells For a particular set of inputs there is a unique result for service location, so that by changing the inputs one can explore the effects of different planning policies on service location and on journeys from home to services. Within the context of the complete model of urban spatial structure, the residential population and floorspace inputs are provided by the residential and stock submodels, while the total employment input is generated from basic employment within the iterative structure of the model as described above. The transportation network is a common input to the model as a whole. The only additional inputs required specifically for the service submodel are thus the service to population ratio and the values for α and β^s (which are usually obtained by calibration—see pages 182–3). The output of service employment location is used as an input to the residential and stock submodels.

The model can be extended by disaggregating the services into a hierarchy of scale (e.g. local, district and city serving) and by distinguishing at each level between different types of service (e.g. schools, shops, office, etc.). It is then possible to take account of the different functional relationships and space requirements of, say, schools as opposed to shops. In addition it would also be desirable to consider the accessibility potential of each type of service to different employment types and to different socio-economic groups, etc.

4. Stock submodel: floorspace location

In the preceding sections the importance of the supply of available stock as a determinant of the location of activities has been shown. It is clear that the stock is not located in response to the demands of activities at any one moment in time, for the vast majority of the stock has already been located in response to the demands of previous activities, aggregated over many years, and once built it cannot easily be changed. The problem in this study has been to simulate what is in reality a dynamic process in a static model. This has been possible owing to the enormous inertia of the physical structure of a town which develops only slowly from year to year (see Stone 1968), whilst maintaining its previous characteristics.

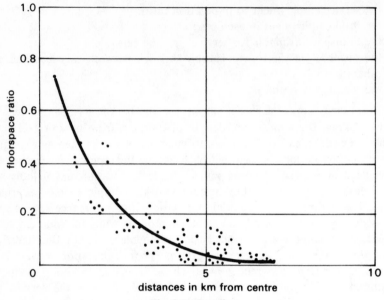

Fig. 8.6a. Reading

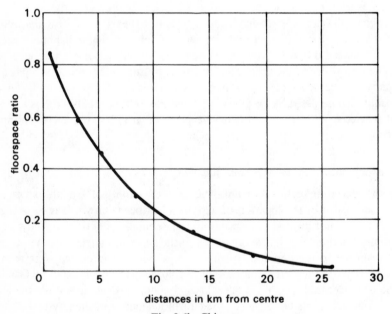

Fig. 8.6b. Chicago.

Fig. 8.6. Floorspace ratio decay from town centre.

There are two methods of approach. The first is to try to find empirical regularities in known data, following traditional population analysis, 'which asks not *why* births and deaths occur but simply observes that they do and seeks to determine if there are any statistical regularities to form a basis for prediction' (Bolan *et al.* 1963). The second is to seek cause-and-effect explanations of recorded phenomena in an attempt to formulate a theory.

Following the first approach, we have found that the floorspace ratio (i.e. the quantity of built floorspace divided by the land available for development) decays exponentially from town centres. This has been tested in Chicago (Echenique 1968b) and in Reading (Echenique *et al.* 1969a) (see Fig. 8.6). From purely empirical evidence, therefore a model can be formulated, such that

$$f_j = \phi \exp(-\beta d_j),$$

where f_j = floorspace ratio in cell j,
    d_j = distance of cell j from the town centre,
    ϕ = a constant of proportionality (i.e. for converting from units of distance to floorspace ratios),
    β = a parameter.

An attempt was made in an earlier paper (Echenique 1968b) to link together the findings of other studies in order to explain this phenomenon. The main arguments are briefly summarised. Wingo (1969), Alonso (1964) and Brigham (1964) have established the theoretical relationship between transportation costs and land values, by which a non-linear increase in transportation costs from employment centres defines a land value surface which decays from such centres. Kain (1961) has related the land value surface to population densities, and explains the decay of population densities from places of employment in terms of the existence of different socio-economic groups and transportation costs. Kain shows that, faced with different expenditures on both transportation and housing, low-income groups will tend to locate at high densities close to employment and high-income groups at low densities away from employment. The empirical observations of Clark (1967) show that residential density does decay exponentially after a certain distance from employment centres, but fails to account for the depression in densities that occurs in the immediate vicinity of these centres. As suggested earlier, these depressions are the result of employment activities acquiring residential floorspace and pushing the displaced residents further afield. Thus the curve of residential densities is not simply exponential, but reaches a peak from which it falls as it reaches employment centres. However, if Clark's exponential curve is extrapolated upwards towards the axis, it will then in fact describe the distribution of floorspace ratios around the centres, or in other words, the physical remains of the residential population which has been displaced. This no longer residential floor area must be counted, of course, together with the floorspace in the centre originally built for and permanently occupied by employment. Once outside the vicinity of the centre, the exponential curve describes the distribution of both floorspace ratios and residential densities equally well, as one would expect. The two curves will not be identical, owing to the different residential space standards that occur as one moves away from the centre, but of the two, the floorspace ratio curve will be the more stable. As the population of the town increases, the floorspace ratio curve will lengthen to accommodate the new residents, but the residential density curve will change more radically, as additional residents are forced out of the central cells by the influx of new employment and services. The total amount of stock in these central cells, meanwhile, will increase only slowly with time for historical and technological reasons. Fig. 8.7 illustrates how the residential density curve will change with time in relation to the more slowly changing floorspace ratio curve.

From these considerations, it is clear that a more generalised version of the empirically derived formulation stated above can be written, i.e.

$$f_j = \Sigma_i E_i \phi \exp(-\beta d_{ij}),$$

where f_j = floorspace ratio in cell j,
$\quad\quad E_i$ = employment in cell i,
$\quad\quad d_{ij}$ = distance between cell i and cell j,
$\quad\quad \phi$ = constant of proportionality,
$\quad\quad \beta$ = a parameter.

This model distributes floorspace ratios around all cells i containing employment. The floorspace in cell j, F_j, can then be found by multiplying f_j by the land available for development in cell j, L_j, i.e.

$$F_j = f_j L_j.$$

The land available for development is defined as the total amount of land in each cell less all large open spaces. Thus land subject to geophysical constraints (e.g. rivers, plains liable to flooding, quarries, etc.) and to planning constraints (e.g. public open spaces, areas of outstanding natural beauty, green belts, etc.) is excluded. Agricultural and forest land and large private open spaces, such as golf courses, large playing fields, etc., are also discounted. What remains is considered to be the land available for development. It includes, for example, all private gardens attached to housing and land contained within plots occupied by employment activi-

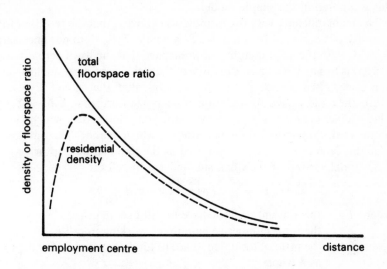

Fig. 8.7a. Relationship between residential density and total floorspace ratio.

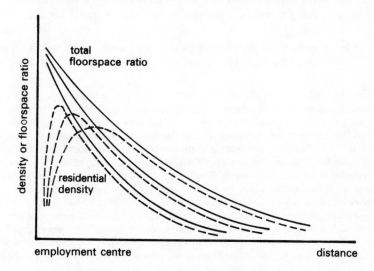

Fig. 8.7b. Population growth: density and floorspace ratio.

ties. Theoretically it should exclude the land occupied by channel spaces (i.e. roads and pavements, etc.) but for reasons of operational simplicity this is ignored in the simple model.

The main difficulty with the formulation above is that the resultant total quantity of floorspace for the town as a whole, $\Sigma_j F_j$, does not necessarily coincide with the total quantity of floorspace that the town actually uses, F. That is to say, if we know the value of the ratio, w, of the total floorspace in a town, F, to the towns's total employment, E (i.e. $w = F/E = \Sigma_j F_j / \Sigma_i E_i$), then the above formulation does not ensure that $\Sigma_j F_j = \Sigma_i E_i w$. This problem can be overcome by distributing floorspace, which can be normalised, rather than floorspace ratios, which cannot. The amount of available land in each cell is then used as the terminal descriptor.

The final version of the stock submodel is therefore:

$$F_j = \Sigma_i A_i E_i w L_j \exp(-\beta^f d_{ij}),$$

where F_j = the amount of floorspace for all uses in cell j,
      E_i = the total number of employees working in cell i,
      w = the ratio of total floorspace to total employment for the town as a whole,
      L_j = the amount of land available for development in cell j,
      d_{ij} = the distance via the transportation network between cell i and cell j (used as a proxy for the cost of travel between cells i and j),
      β^f = parameter representing the significance of distance as a constraint on activity location.†

† Since the stock of floorspace in a typical town has been built up slowly over many years of continuous development, this parameter will be influenced by the willingness of the people in the town to spend money on travel at some time *before* the date for which the model is run, reflecting the time-lag that occurs between the creation of a demand for additional floorspace and its construction. One would therefore expect the value for β^f to be slightly higher than for β^r (the cost-impedance parameter for residential location), as indeed it usually is. As with β^r, one would also expect the value for β^f to decrease with time as affluence and the amount of money available for travel increases. This trend is reinforced by the fact that as a town increases in size, the central cells gradually begin to reach their capacity (both economic and physical) to absorb additional floorspace. For this reason an increasing proportion of new floorspace (i.e. additional to what is already there or what is being replaced) tends to locate in surrounding cells where there is more room for it and where it can be built at less cost. In other words, the value for β^f will tend to be lower for a large city than for a small town. Thus if in Fig. 8.5 the two floorspace ratio curves are drawn to the same distance scale, the curve for Chicago starts only a little higher (in spite of being seventeen times the size) and is considerably shallower (indicating a lower value for β^f) than the curve for Reading. This reflects partly the greater affluence of the Chicago population and partly the economic and physical constraints on central development.

This formulation has also been derived theoretically, using the statistical theory of maximum entropy, by March (1970).

The model states that the amount of floorspace in a cell j is related to:

1. The demand for floorspace generated by employees in cells i ($E_i w$).
2. The accessibility of cell j to the cells i containing employment (exp $(-\beta^f d_{ij})$).
3. The attractiveness of cell j for development as measured by the amount of land available (L_j).
4. The attractiveness and accessibility of all competing cells $j(\Sigma_j L_j \exp(-\beta^f d_{ij}))$.

Given a town or urban region divided up into cells or zones, the inputs required for the model are:

the number of employees (basic and service) in each cell;
the floorspace to employment ratio;
the amount of land available for development in each cell;
the distance via the transportation network between each cell and all others;
the parameter β^f.

From these inputs the model outputs the amount of floorspace for all uses in each cell and gross floorspace ratios (F_j/L_j) for each cell. For a particular set of inputs there is a unique result for floorspace location, which can be used as an input to the activity model (i.e. as terminal descriptors for both the residential and service models). By changing the inputs one can thus explore the effects of different planning policies on floorspace location and on residential and service location as well. Within the context of the complete model of urban spatial structure, the service employment input is provided by the service submodel, and the basic employment and transportation network inputs are common to the model as a whole. The only inputs required specifically for the stock submodel are therefore the floorspace to employment ratio, the land available and the value for β^f (which is usually obtained by calibration).

It is worth pointing out that stock model assumes that the stock in a town has been built up over time under the influence of a more or less free market system. For most towns of any age, this assumption would seem to be valid. But in certain cases, especially in Britain, the location of stock has been controlled to some extent by planning authorities, either directly in that they have built a significant proportion of the stock themselves, or indirectly by the imposition of building bulk legislation, plot ratios, etc. In such cases, particularly when the stock has been completely controlled by the planning authorities as in most British New Towns, it will not be possible to use the results of the stock model as inputs for the activity model. But by incorporating the stock component of the urban spatial structure into the model, it is possible to assess the effect of those controls on the location of activities within the town, and also to compare the resultant locational pattern with the pattern that would probably have occurred had not these controls been applied (see Chapter 9 below).

The model can be developed further by considering the structural type of buildings and their age and condition. As mentioned earlier (page 178), some structural types tend to be able to accommodate only certain types of activity, while others are more adaptable. If residential population is divided into socio-economic groups, it is clear that the structural type, age and condition of housing will influence their location. Although structural type of buildings can be related (at least for housing) to floorspace ratio† and to the characteristics of the land on which they are built, it is likely that the age of buildings can only be simulated accurately within a dynamic context. In a static model the age of different parts of a town would therefore have to be considered as a given input. Since condition is related to age (see Wolfe 1967a) it would then be possible to simulate the condition of the stock.

The simple static model

Having described the formulation of each of the submodels in turn, it is now possible to describe the overall structure of the complete model. The framework is similar to Lowry's (see Fig. 8.2), but with an extra step, the stock model, at the front as shown diagrammatically below (Fig. 8.8). Given a town or urban region divided up into cells or zones, the principal inputs required for the model are:

the number of basic employees in each cell;
the amount of land available for development in each cell;
the distance via the transportation network between each cell and all others.

The model then operates as follows: First of all the stock model is run to determine the stock of floorspace in each cell. This requires a single iteration, the floorspace being distributed throughout the town from cells containing basic employment in response to the aggregate demand for floorspace for all uses and in proportion to the amount and accessibility of

---

† It is clear that a given floorspace ratio at least limits the range of probable structural types. A low ratio will tend to indicate detached housing with large private open spaces; a high ratio, high density housing (e.g. terrace houses, flats, etc.) with little or no private open space.

available land in each cell (Step 1). The floorspace used by basic employment in each cell is deducted from the total and the remainder is the total
available floorspace for residential population and service employment.
The activity model is then run iteratively to determine the location of
residents and service employees within this supply of floorspace. Residents
are distributed from workplaces to homes (representing journeys from
work to home) in proportion to the amount and accessibility of available
floorspace in each cell (Step 2). Service employees are distributed from their
patron's homes to workplaces (representing journeys from home to services) in proportion to the amount and accessibility of available floorspace
and employment in each cell (Step 3). In the first iteration the residential
distribution is from basic employment; that is to say the basic employees in
each cell are multiplied by the labour participation rate (the average

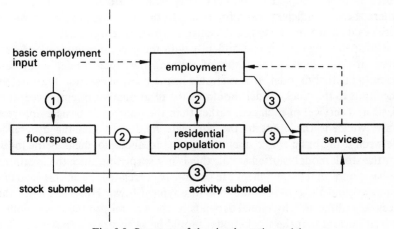

Fig. 8.8. Structure of the simple static model.

number of dependents per employee) and distributed to homes. The service
employees generated by these residents are then distributed to workplaces and, in the second iteration, they are also multiplied by the labour
participation rate and distributed to homes. The service employees that
they as residents generate are similarly distributed first to workplaces and
then in the next iteration to homes and so on, until the model reaches
equilibrium (see page 181). At this point the number of residents and service employees located in each iteration is added up to produce totals for
the residential population and service employment in each cell. In addition
the model can output for each cell gross residential and service employment densities, floorspace ratios and the amount of floorspace used by

residents and by service employees. The model can also output the number of work and service trips generated between each pair of cells, which can be allocated to particular routes along the transportation network by a subsidiary model if required.

Within this general framework a system of space checks is applied. At the end of every iteration the residents and service employees located in each cell are multiplied by a residential and service space standard respectively. In those cells where there is not sufficient room for both, services are allowed to displace residents, who are distributed back to their workplaces. The services that the displaced residents have generated are identified and discounted. The remaining successfully located service employees are then distributed to homes in the next iteration as described above, together with the displaced residents who need to be redistributed. Since the available floorspace in the cells to which they were previously distributed is now occupied by services, they will be attracted to other cells where there is sufficient room for them. In this way the process by which services displace residents in the centre of town is reproduced.

Unfortunately there is one difficulty with the general framework as outlined above, which is the result of running the stock model separately from the activity model. It was shown in the previous section that ideally the input to the stock model should be the total number of employees (i.e. basic and service) in each cell, rather than the number of basic employees only, which is the input to the complete model. In fact the difference between using basic employment as against total employment as the input for the stock model is often small; this is not surprising since the locations of basic and total employment are obviously correlated, basic employment being around 50%–60% of the total in a typical town. However, since the accuracy of the activity model depends on the accuracy of the stock model, it is important that the stock model should be as accurate as possible. One method of dealing with this problem is to reiterate the whole model, using basic employment as the input to the stock model at the start and then using the total employment output derived from the activity model as the input for the second run of the model. But, for the limited increase in accuracy gained, this method is too cumbersome operationally, requiring at least twice as much computer time. A more fruitful approach is to incorporate the stock model within the iterative structure of the activity model, so that the town's stock of floorspace is not distributed all at once but builds up, iteration by iteration, in a corresponding way to the build up of residents and service employees. The full integration of all three distribution procedures within the same overall framework can be seen as a logical development of the arguments put forward in the first section, that a town is a unified system of interrelated parts. Instead of a model split into two separately treated submodels, the revised model considers both submodels simultaneously, as shown below in Fig. 8.9.

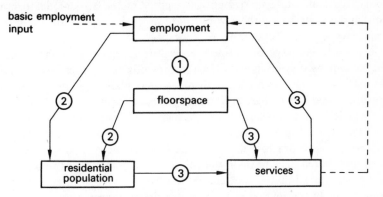

Fig. 8.9. Integrated structure of revised simple static model.

In the first iteration, the supply of floorspace required for basic employees and the residents and services they generate is distributed from basic employment (Step 1). The basic employees are then distributed to homes (Step 2) and the service employees that they as residents generate are distributed to workplaces as before within this supply of floorspace (Step 3). In the second iteration, these service employees are added to the basic employees and the total generates a new supply of floorspace (greater than and including the supply generated in the first iteration) within which employees (both basic and service) are distributed to homes from where further service employees are distributed. With successive iterations the total employees in a cell (and hence the floorspace generated) gradually builds up, each iteration producing a new and more complete distribution of floorspace, residential population and service employment.

In contrast to the previous model, which distributes increasingly small increments of residential population and service employment with successive iterations, the revised model distributes increasingly large quantities of each, although the *difference* between the quantities distributed in two consecutive iterations becomes smaller and smaller, so that the model tends to converge and reach equilibrium in exactly the same way. Thus the floorspace, residential population and service employment located within each iteration do not have to be stored to be added up at the end as before. At the beginning of an iteration, the service employees located in the previous iteration merely have to be added to the basic employees in each cell to form a revised input to the stock and activity submodels. Since each iteration produces more service employment than the last, the revised input of basic plus service employment becomes larger and larger, until, as the model approaches equilibrium, it increases only by insignificant amounts. At equilibrium the model is distributing the town's total stock of floorspace from total employment (as required by the stock model formulation) and is distributing the town's total residential population and service employment within this supply of floorspace.

A major advantage of the new procedure is that the system of space checks can be dispensed with. In the previous version, each new increment of service employment can displace residential population located in previous iterations if there is not enough space for both. This means that space checks have to be applied at the end of every iteration, causing some residents to be displaced by the new service employees, even though they may have passed previous space checks. The displaced residents then have to be distributed back to their workplaces to be redistributed to other cells in the next iteration and the services that they have generated have to be discounted. In the revised version of the model, the process is very much simpler, since residents and services (including those located in previous iterations) are generated and distributed afresh in each iteration. This means that the floorspace available for residents can be adjusted from iteration to iteration as the distribution of services builds up. Thus at the end of each iteration a record is kept of the floorspace required by service employment and this is deducted from the floorspace available for residents in the next iteration. In this way the floorspace available for residents is constantly adjusted as more and more service employment is distributed, until, in the last iteration, it corresponds to the total available floorspace left over when all services have been located (see formalised procedure below, page 215).

As well as integrating the stock and activity models within a common framework the procedure outlined above produces a simpler and shorter computer program, requiring less storage and computer time. It is also conceptually neater than the previous procedure in that, in the last iteration, the three submodel formulations are applied to the distribution of all floorspace, residential population and service employment: that is to say, all residents and service employees are treated in the same way. In the previous model residents and service employees are distributed piecemeal and since the value of the terminal descriptor for residential location, for example, varies with each iteration, they are thus treated differently according to the iteration in which they are located. It is in fact arguable whether this matters, since the results are the same in the end, but it is perhaps conceptually more satisfying that the formulations derived from theoretical and analytical studies of the locational behaviour of undifferentiated residents and service employees should be applied uniformly to all the residents and service employees being located in the model.

The complete model is summarised in the flow diagram (page 223) which shows the inputs on the left and the range of outputs on the right. The mathematical formulation of each submodel, the list of specific inputs and outputs and the formalised procedure of the model are presented below.

The simple static model
The stock submodel:

$$F_j = \Sigma_i A_i E_i w\, L_j \exp(-\beta^f d_{ij}) \quad (A_i = 1/\Sigma_j L_j \exp(-\beta^f d_{ij})).$$

The residential submodel:

$$R_j = \Sigma_i A_i E_i u\, F_j^r \exp(-\beta^r d_{ij}) \quad (A_i = 1/\Sigma_j F_j^r \exp(-\beta^r d_{ij})).$$

The service submodel:

$$S_j = \Sigma_i A_i R_i v W_j^s \exp(-\beta^s d_{ij}) \quad (A_i = 1/\Sigma_j W_j^s \exp(-\beta^s d_{ij})).$$
$$W_j^s = [(E_j/\Sigma_j E_j) + (F_j^s/\Sigma_j F_j^s)]^\alpha$$

where F_j = total floorspace for all uses in cell j,
R_j = number of residents living in cell j,
S_j = number of service employees working in cell j,
E_i = total number of employees working in cell i. In the first iteration $E_i = E_i^b$; thereafter $E_i = E_i^b + S_i$,
E_i^b = number of basic employees working in cell i,
L_j = amount of land available for development in cell j,
F_j^r = amount of floorspace available for residents in cell j, i.e. $F_j^r = F_j - E_j^b w^b - S_j w^s$,
F_j^s = amount of floorspace available for services in cell j, i.e. $F_j^s = F_j - E_j^b w^b$,
A_i = normalisation term for each submodel to ensure that $\Sigma_j F_j = \Sigma_i E_i w$, $\Sigma_j R_j = \Sigma_i E_i u$ and $\Sigma_j S_j = \Sigma_i R_i v$ respectively,
d_{ij} = distance between cell i and cell j via the transportation network (used as a proxy for cost of travel between cells i and j),†

† As explained earlier (page 192), d_{ij} can be replaced by $d_{ij}{}^\theta$ if a closer approximation to travel costs is required, the parameter θ taking account of the fact that travel costs rise non-linearly with distance. The value for θ can, for the sake of simplicity, be the same for all three submodels, but theoretically there should be a slight difference between θ for the stock submodel and θ for the activity submodels, reflecting the different cost/distance relationship current at the time that most of the stock was built. Alternatively θ can be used for the stock submodel only and omitted from the activity submodels for ease of calibration.

u = labour participation rate, i.e. $\Sigma_j R_j / \Sigma_j E_j$,

v = service to population ratio, i.e. $\Sigma_j S_j / \Sigma_j R_j$,

w = total floorspace per employee, i.e. $\Sigma_j F_j / \Sigma_j E_j$,

w^b, w^s = space standard per basic employee and service employee respectively,

α = parameter representing degree to which services cluster,

$\beta^f, \beta^r, \beta^s$ = parameters representing significance of distance as a constraint on activity location.

Inputs and outputs of the simple static model

Given a town or urban region divided up into n areal units or cells,† the model requires:

1. The number of basic employees working in each cell (E_i^b, n values).
2. The amount of land available for development in each cell (L_j, n values).
3. The distance from each cell to all others via the transportation network (half matrix of $\frac{1}{2}n \times n + \frac{1}{2}n$ values, one for each d_{ij}).‡
4. The values for the ratios u, v and w (one value each).
5. The values for the space standards w^b and w^s (one value each).
6. The values for the parameters α, β^f, β^r and β^s (one value each – usually determined by calibration).

The full list of the outputs of the model is:

1. The amount of floorspace for all uses in each cell (F_j, n values).
2. The gross floorspace ratio in each cell (F_j/L_j, n values).
3. The number of residents living in each cell (R_j, n values).
4. The amount of residential floorspace in each cell ($[F_j - E_j^b w^b - S_j w^s]$, n values).
5. The gross residential density in each cell (R_j/L_j, n values).
6. The number of service employees working in each cell (S_j, n values).
7. The amount of floorspace used by service employees in each cell ($S_j w^s$, n values).
8. The gross service employment density in each cell (S_j/L_j, n values).
9. The total number of employees working in each cell (E_j, n values).

† At least one cell should be considered to represent the region surrounding the study area (the environment of the system). This enables the model to cope with work and service trips originating in the study area but ending outside, and vice versa.

‡ This includes the n intra-zonal values for d_{ij}. The matrix can be generated automatically by digitising the nodes and links of the network and running a computer program to search for the shortest route from each cell to all others. A full matrix of $n \times n$ values is required if the distance between any two cells is not the same in both directions.

10. The amount of floorspace used by all employees in each cell ($E_j^b w^b + S_j w^s$, n values).
11. The gross employment density in each cell (E_j/L_j, n values).
12. The number of work trips between each pair of cells (T_{ij}^w, $n \times n$ values).
13. The distribution of work trip lengths and the mean work trip length.
14. The number of service trips between each pair of cells (T_{ij}^s, $n \times n$ values).
15. The distribution of service trip lengths and the mean service trip length.

Procedure of the simple static model

The model follows the sequence of operations described below; each step is carried out for all cells in turn. A system of asterisks is used to denote the number of the iteration. Thus F_j^* is the floorspace distributed to cell j in the first iteration, F_j^{**} the floorspace distributed to cell j in the second iteration, and so on.

Given: $E_i^b, L_j, d_{ij}, u, v, w, w^b, w^s, \alpha, \beta^f, \beta^r$ and β^s

First iteration

Step 1: employment input: $\quad E_i^* = E_i^b$.

Step 2: floorspace location: $\quad F_j^* = \Sigma_i A_i E_i^* w L_j \exp(-\beta^f d_{ij})$.

Step 3: residential location: $\quad R_j^* = \Sigma_i A_i E_i^* u F_j^{r*} \exp(-\beta^r d_{ij})$,

$\qquad$ where $F_j^{r*} = F_j^* - E_j^b w^b$.

Step 4: service location: $\quad S_j^* = \Sigma_i A_i R_i^* v W_j^{s*} \exp(-\beta^s d_{ij})$,

$\qquad$ where $W_j^{s*} = [(E_j^*/\Sigma_j E_j^*) + (F_j^{s*}/\Sigma_j F_j^{s*})]^\alpha$,

$\qquad$ and $F_j^{s*} = F_j^* - E_j^b w^b$.

Second iteration

Step 1: new employment input: $E_i^{**} = E_i^b + S_i^*$.

Step 2: floorspace location: $\quad F_j^{**} = \Sigma_i A_i E_i^{**} w L_j \exp(-\beta^f d_{ij})$.

Step 3: residential location: $\quad R_j^{**} = \Sigma_i A_i E_i^{**} u F_j^{r**} \exp(-\beta^r d_{ij})$,

$\qquad$ where $F_j^{r**} = F_j^{**} - E_j^b w^b - S_j^* w^s$.

Step 4: service location: $\quad S_j^{**} = \Sigma_i A_i R_i^{**} v W_j^{s**} \exp(-\beta^s d_{ij})$,

$\qquad$ where $W_j^{s**} = [(E_j^{**}/\Sigma_j E_j^{**}) + (F_j^{s**}/\Sigma_j F_j^{**})]^\alpha$

$\qquad$ and $F_j^{s**} = F_j^{**} - E_j^b w^b$.

Subsequent iterations

Steps 1 to 4 are repeated for all subsequent iterations. Thus for the third iteration, Step 1 is:

$$E_i^{***} = E_i^b + S^{**}$$

and in Step 3:

$$F_j^{r***} = F_j^{***} - E_j^b w^b - S_j^{**} w^s.$$

The model will continue to iterate until the number of service employees distributed in one iteration is insignificantly larger than the number distributed in the previous iteration. This can be determined either by inspection or by specifying the level of significance, in which case the model will stop iterating when:

$$\Sigma_j S_j^* \cdots ** - \Sigma_j S_j^* \cdots * \leqslant \text{specified value}.$$

At this point the model has reached equilibrium and will output the results listed above.

Conclusions

This paper has discussed the formulations contained in the simple static model and its procedural structure from the point of view of their operational success in reproducing reality. By examining several formulations in each case and by explaining the advantages of the formulations chosen step by step, it is hoped that the reader has gained some insight into the problems of model building and of combining several formulations within a common framework. Model building, however, is not merely a process of experimenting with different equations until one is found which happens to fit the data at hand. Any model, whether explicitly stated or not, is based on a body of theory and a set of assumptions, and it is on the validity of such theories and assumptions that the predictive power of a model depends. Thus an equation based on strong assumptions with little theoretical backing may be able to reproduce reality in one or two specific cases, but without a body of theory to explain why it should be those particular equations rather than any other, one cannot be confident of its ability to reproduce reality in all other cases or in future. In this context, the work of Wilson is of great importance, since he has provided a firm theoretical basis for the equations presented in this paper, that is to say he has shown how entropy-maximising principles can be used, given a set of specified assumptions, to explain why these particular equations should be applicable to all urban spatial structures for which these assumptions are valid, regardless of size, type or age. For a full description of these principles, of the models that can be derived using them and of the assumptions made in each case, see Wilson (1967 and 1971).

But if models depend on theory to prove their general applicability, it is also true that the ultimate test of a theory is still its ability to reproduce reality, and however valid a model is theoretically, it still needs to be tested for as many different types of town as possible. In this way the particular failings of a model can be analysed and the need for refinements of theory and procedure identified. In fact many of the problems of building models only emerge when they are made operational (e.g. the problem of what variable to use as terminal descriptor, the use of distance as a proxy for travel cost, etc.). The detailed examination of the operational success of different formulations, and the understanding of how each equation within the model framework affects the others, is thus a vital part of model building. It is with these aspects that this paper has been concerned. Another factor influencing the success of a model is the conceptual framework on which it is based, that is to say the elements of the urban system chosen to be represented in the model. In this connection the distinction between the activities within a town and the stock of floorspace that accommodates them has proved crucial to the simple static model and is partly responsible for its success.

To date the simple static model has been tested for four towns: Reading, Cambridge, Stevenage and Santiago (Chile), each one representing a different type of spatial structure. The results, which are fully reported elsewhere,† have been sufficiently encouraging to suggest that the model and the conceptual framework on which it is based do have a general validity. Since any model is a simplified abstraction there are inevitably some discrepancies between the model's predictions and reality, but these can be seen to be the result of the oversimplified nature of the model rather than of any fundamental flaw in the theory of the model itself. In spite of the good results so far obtained, however, it is clear that the model needs to be tested for many more towns and to be extended in scope and in the number of elements considered.

A more complex model, capable of relating together more elements of the urban spatial system, can be formulated by dividing each of the elements considered in the simple model into subelements (i.e. sectorial disaggregation). Thus residential households can be distinguished by socio-economic group, size, number of wage earners and age structure. Employment can be divided up into different types of basic and service employment (so that shops, schools and offices are considered separately for example) and distinguished by scale of patronage (local, district, town, regional, etc.), by space requirements and by employee characteristics (e.g. socio-economic group, full or part-time, male or female, etc.). The stock of buildings can be classified according to size, structural type, suitability for occupation by different activities, age, condition, length of street frontage, etc. The stock of channel spaces can be differentiated by the type and capacity of both nodes and links. Flows of traffic can be

† The results for Reading are described in Echenique *et al.* (1969a); the results for Cambridge are described in Booth *et al.* (1970); the results for Stevenage are described in Chapter 9, page 221; and the results for Santiago are described in Echenique and Domeyko (1970).

classified by mode (cars, bicycles, pedestrians, public transport, etc.) and these flows can be matched against the capacity of the transportation network so that the effects of congestion can be simulated. Accessibility between all these different elements can be measured in terms of both time and cost, taking account of congestion, parking facilities, waiting times for public transport, etc. The possibilities for sectorial disaggregation of this kind are obviously endless and it will be some time before a complete model considering even half of the elements listed above will be developed and tested. Analytical studies may well show that some of these elements are in any case insignificant in determining spatial relationships. Nonetheless, most of the data describing the elements above have already been collected for the town of Reading (see Perraton 1970 and Lenzi 1970) and work on a complex model is in progress.

Apart from sectorial disaggregation, there is also the possibility of areal disaggregation. The simple static model has so far been tested for towns divided up into 1 km × 1 km grid cells, but it is proposed that future models should be capable of operating at the level of 500 m × 500 m grid cells. Some of the problems of handling the larger number of cells that this involves have already been solved by the development of a 'cordon' model, which allows a mixture of cell sizes to be used (see Baxter 1970). Thus a particular part of a town can be considered in fine detail (e.g. at the 100 m × 100 m cell level) without ignoring its relationships with the rest of the town. It is certain, however, that there is a limit to the level of areal disaggregation at which a model (especially a complex model) can operate, owing to the small quantities of stock and activities contained in very small cells. No model of the overall spatial structure of a town can hope to simulate the behaviour of individuals.

Finally, the dynamic aspects of the urban system should be mentioned. Both the simple model presented in this paper and the more complex versions described above are static in that they simulate the distribution of stock and activities in space at a particular moment in time. That this has proved possible at all is partly the result of the inertia of a town's stock of floorspace and channel spaces, which change only very slowly with time. The urban system is nonetheless dynamic and the effect of a change in the system will not necessarily be apparent until some time has passed. The spatial structure of a town is clearly influenced by the particular ways in which the town has developed and evolved in the past and by the direction in which it is developing and evolving in the present. Although the need to study these dynamic processes is obvious, research is at present hampered by the general lack of time-series data, but it is hoped that preliminary work on a dynamic model will be begun in the near future.

9. *A structural comparison of three generations of New Towns*[†]

MARCIAL ECHENIQUE, DAVID CROWTHER &
WALTON LINDSAY

Introduction

The intention of this paper is to demonstrate how mathematical models can be used to simulate a town's spatial structure and to determine the likely consequences of different planning policies. For this purpose, the simple static model developed by the Urban Systems Study has been used to compare the physical structures of three New Towns with the older and more traditional town of Reading, for which the model was originally calibrated (see Echenique *et al.* 1969a). The three New Towns selected were Stevenage, Hook and Milton Keynes, representing the three generations of New Town built or proposed since 1945. This choice was governed partly by the availability of data and partly by the desire to compare three towns of

TABLE 9.1. *Population, employment and land totals for the four towns*

Town	Date	Population	Employment	Developed land (hect.)	No. of km² cells
Reading	1963	160,000	63,000	3100	130
Stevenage	1966	60,000	27,000	800	49
Hook	2000*	100,000	44,000	1300	35
Milton Keynes	2000*	250,000	120,000	5500	168

* proposed.

differing spatial characteristics. Table 9.1 lists the overall totals of population, employment and land for all four towns, and Figs. 9.1 and 9.2 illustrate their layouts in diagrammatic form, drawn to the same scale.

[†] This paper was originally published in a somewhat different form as Working Paper No. 25 of the centre for Land Use and Built Form Studies, prepared within the Urban Systems Study under the sponsorship of the Centre for Environmental Studies.

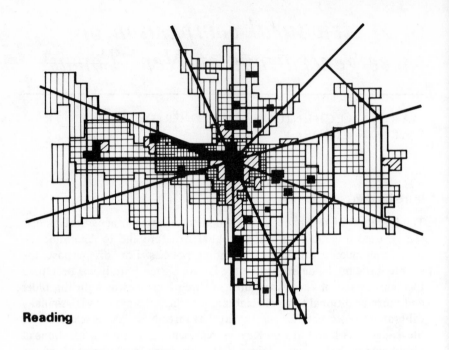

Reading

Stevenage

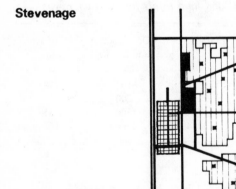

Fig. 9.1. Diagrammatic layouts of Reading and Stevenage.

Hook

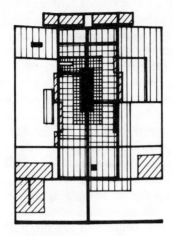

/////// basic employment

■■■■■ service employment

▦▦▦||||||| residential population

Milton Keynes

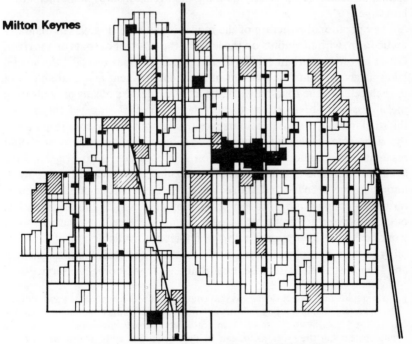

Fig. 9.2. Diagrammatic layout of Hook and Milton Keynes.

Although the simple static model is fully explained in Chapter 8, it is convenient to summarise briefly its operation and its conceptual framework. The model is based on a definition of urban spatial structure which distinguishes two fundamental components: the activities that occur in a town and the stock of physical infrastructure which accommodates them. These two components can be broken down into numerous categories, but the simple model considers only six for activities and six for stock. The activity component is divided into 'within place', or localised, activities and 'between place' activities, or flows. The localised activities considered are basic employment,† service employment and residential population; the flows considered are the journeys made from work to home, from home to services and from work to services. The stock component is divided into corresponding categories of 'adapted' spaces, which contain localised activities, and 'channel' spaces, which contain the flows of traffic between them. The adapted spaces considered are the land available for urban development, the total floorspace used for all purposes and the floorspace used by each of the three localised activities; the channel spaces considered are those of the transportation network. The formulation of the model consists of identifying these twelve components of urban spatial structure and precisely defining their relationships in mathematical language.

The operational structure of the model is shown in Fig. 9.3 in diagrammatic form, with the inputs on the left and the range of outputs on the right. Given a town or urban region divided up into zones or cells, the model takes as given inputs the amount of basic employment and available land in each cell and the road network, which provides the means of measuring the accessibility of each cell to all others. The first stage of the model, the stock model, distributes floorspace throughout the town in response to the aggregate demand for accommodation made by employment and residential population. The allocation of floorspace is governed by the availability of land and its accessibility to employment. Once the supply of floorspace has been located, the second stage, the activity model, distributes residential population and service employment within this supply. The basic employees are first distributed to homes (representing journeys from work to home) in proportion to the floorspace available and its accessibility to their workplaces. The services that they and their families generate are then distributed (representing journeys from home to services) in

† Basic employment can be defined as that employment which exports its goods outside the town (e.g. manufacturing industry) or which serves a larger community than the town itself (e.g. head offices of insurance offices, department stores, etc.). Service employment, on the other hand, can be defined as that employment which exists primarily to serve the resident population of a town (e.g. shops, schools, etc.).

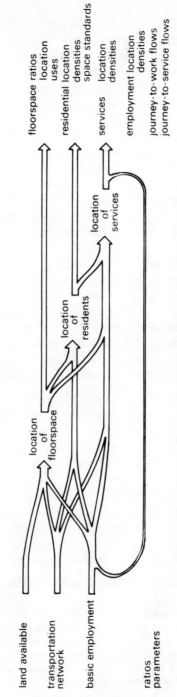

Fig. 9.3. Flow diagram of the simple static model, showing inputs and range of outputs.

proportion to the floorspace available and its accessibility to both residents and employment (representing journeys from work to services). This is the end of the first iteration of the activity model. In the next iteration the service employees are distributed to homes, where they as residents generate more services which are again distributed as before. In the third iteration the new service employees are distributed to homes where they generate yet more services and so on. With successive iterations the total number of located residents and service employees gradually builds up until so few extra residents and service employees are being located within an iteration that they can be ignored. At this point the model is said to have reached equilibrium. At the end of each iteration the number of residents and service employees in every cell is checked against the available floorspace and where there is an overflow of residents due to insufficient space this is redistributed in the next iteration to a cell where there is available space.†

From Fig. 9.3, it is clear that the outputs of the model listed on the right are dependent on the data inputs on the left and that a change in one of the inputs will result in changes to all the outputs (i.e. to the distributions of floorspace, residential population, employment and traffic flows). It is thus possible to use the model to test the likely effect of a planning decision which corresponds to a change in one of the data inputs. The following is a list of common planning proposals which could be experimentally studied by being run through the model:

(a) Land available for development: approval or prohibition of new land being made available for development; increase or decrease of public open space standards.

(b) Transportation network: any change in the geometry of the network creating a new link in the transportation map, or removing an old one.

(c) Location of basic employment: allocation of new basic industries to alternative sites and reallocations of old employment; policies of concentration or dispersal of employment.

(d) Stock of floorspace: creation or renewal of floorspace by direct public action (e.g. local authority housing estate).

The output of the model can also be controlled by various constraints

---

† With reference to Chapter 8 the model used in this study is the first of the two versions described, that is to say with the stock model run separately at the start rather than being integrated within the iterative framework of the activity model. The reason for this is that the location of stock had been controlled to such an extent in the case of Stevenage and Hook that it could not be simulated. It was therefore necessary to consider the stock and activity models separately.

which correspond to some of the actual controls exercised by planners, such as:

(*a*) Zoning controls: where certain sites are set aside for the exclusive use of a particular activity (e.g. industrial or residential estates).

(*b*) Plot ratio and density controls, which restrict the maximum amount of floorspace or population that can be accommodated on a site of a given size.

Finally, the performance of the model is regulated by a set of parameters and ratios. These are:

(*a*) Labour participation rate

(*b*) Service employment to population ratio

(*c*) Total floorspace to employment ratio

(*d*) Basic employment floorspace standard

(*e*) Residential floorspace standard

(*f*) Service floorspace standard

(*g*) Distribution parameters. There are four of these in all: one each for floorspace location (β^f), residential location (β^r) and service location (β^s), representing the cost impedance of distance as a constraint on activity location, plus an additional parameter for service location (α), representing the degree to which services cluster to achieve the economies of scale and pooling of customers. These parameters can be thought of as analogous to adjustment knobs on a piece of experimental apparatus and are the means by which the model is calibrated. Low values for the cost impedance parameters will produce a spread out town with long journeys to work and to services, while high values will produce a compact town with residents close to employment centres and services close to residents.

Although these parameters and ratios do not correspond directly to actual planning controls, they do represent factors which planners need to take into consideration. For example, a slight change in the labour participation rate, due to more women taking part-time work or to a high influx of school leavers, can significantly affect the distribution of jobs and homes, as can a change in the ratio of service employees to residents. Since these ratios are included in the formulation of the model, the planner can see what the overall effect will be of both upward and downward trends. Similarly the planner can test the consequences of raising the residential space standards (by rehabilitation or redevelopment) of the poorer and denser housing, or of improving the efficiency of service space standards. In addition the distribution parameters, in that they represent the cost of travel, can be altered deliberately so as to simulate the effect of increasing subsidies to public transport, or of building new urban motorways.

From the above list it can be seen that the simple static model is already an explorative tool of some power. Once it has been set up and calibrated for a town, a wide range of different types of planning decision can be tested in terms of their likely effects on the distributions of floorspace, residential population, service employment and traffic flows. A different problem then arises, however, in the assessment of whether these consequences are beneficial to the town as a whole or not. In other words, different courses of action will give rise to different distributions of stock and activities, but unless the merits of each result can be measured by means of some evaluative technique, it will be difficult to choose between them. In conjunction with a model, the use of evaluation procedures can thus help planners to determine the particular set of co-ordinated policies likely to have the most beneficial consequences.

Evaluative procedures

It is only meaningful to evaluate a town's spatial structure in terms of a well defined set of objectives which are themselves derived from a consideration of more general goals. The most widely used evaluative technique at present is cost-benefit analysis (see Lichfield 1969), which, as Hill (1968) puts it, draws up a balance sheet of development to compare 'all the "good" and all the "bad" consequences of a proposed course of action', and which judges the desirability of a consequence in relation to specified objectives. Intangible costs and benefits, although they cannot be measured directly, can be included and balanced against monetary costs and benefits. Hill, however, has suggested that even when they are omitted, it is not valid simply to add up total costs and benefits without first weighting and giving prominence to some items in preference to others.

The method of evaluation proposed here is not based on monetary costs but on a set of indicators which describe various physical characteristics of spatial structure. The social interaction indicator, for example, measures the distance within which residents have the opportunity of encountering a given number of other residents, and the employment opportunity indicator measures the distance within which residents can reach a given number of job opportunities. These indicators can be translated into costs at a later date, if suitable rates are defined, although there are some attributes of spatial structure which can more easily be measured than costed. It is also possible to weight each indicator (to say, for example, that more land per resident has a higher priority than shorter journeys to work) and by combining them to give a town an overall index which can be compared with the index of other towns. But because the weighting of indicators involves subjective judgement, this study has concentrated primarily on the development of appropriate indicators and on using each one individually to compare the four towns. Nonetheless, a crude method of weighting and combining them is described on pages 255ff.

Following Lichfield, costs and benefits have been considered from the standpoint of both producers, i.e. those who build, finance and maintain a town, and consumers, i.e. those who live, work and travel in it. The list below describes the 21 indicators that have been thought appropriate; indicators 1 to 3 represent costs borne by development agencies, local authorities and indirectly by tax payers (producers), while indicators 4 to 20 represent costs and benefits to residents, employers and employees (considered together), services and those involved in travel and communications (consumers). The last indicator, the size-compactness indicator, is included for interest only. Each indicator has been formulated in such a way that in every case the objective is to minimise its numerical value, all others being held constant. Thus for those indicators expressed in terms of distances a low value represents a high standard of accessibility and for those expressed in terms of densities a low value represents high space standards.

Producers

1. Cost of land indicator, representing the capital cost of acquiring all land required for development, excluding agricultural land, public open spaces, playing fields, etc.; measured in terms of hectares of total developed land per resident.
2. Cost of services indicator, representing the capital and running costs of installing and maintaining the road, water, power and sewerage systems. This indicator is measured in terms of the length of trunk road in metres per resident, the main road network serving as a proxy for all the other services.
3. Cost of construction indicator, representing the capital cost of constructing the town's stock of floorspace; measured in terms of the average gross residential density† of residents per hectare of developed land. (Higher densities are in general more expensive to build than lower densities – see Stone 1961.)

† The average gross residential density is calculated by weighting the average residential density of each kilometre cell by the number of people in that cell and then dividing the sum of all weighted densities by the total residential population, i.e.

$$d = \Sigma_i[d(i)\,p(i)]/\Sigma_i p(i)$$

where

d = weighted average density,
$d(i)$ = average density in cell i,
$p(i)$ = population in cell i.

Consumers – residents

4. Residential space indicator, representing the amount of private open space and usable floorspace available to residents; measured in terms of the average gross residential density of residents per hectare of developed land.

5. Social interaction indicator, representing the opportunities of making social contacts, visiting friends, etc; measured in terms of the distance in kilometres within which residents can reach a given number of other residents via the road network.

6. Employment opportunities indicator, representing the number, and hence choice, of jobs within easy reach of residents; measured in terms of the distance within which residents can reach a given number of job opportunities.

7. Service availability indicator; measured in terms of the distance within which residents can reach a given number of service employees.

8. Proximity to open space indicator, measured in terms of the distance within which residents can reach a given number of hectares of open space (i.e. public open space, agricultural land, playing fields, etc.)

9. Journey to work indicator, representing the distance that residents need to travel to work; measured in terms of the mean trip length in kilometres of all work trips.

10. Journey to services, representing the distance that residents need to travel to services; measured in terms of the mean trip length in kilometres of all service trips.

Consumers – employers and employees

11. Employment space indicator, representing the amount of land and usable floorspace available to employment; measured in terms of the average gross employment density of employees per hectare.

12. Labour market indicator, representing the accessibility of employment to the available labour force; measured in terms of the distance within which residents can reach a given number of job opportunities.

13. Employment clustering indicator, representing the degree to which employment clusters together; measured in terms of the distance within which employment can reach a given number of other employees.

14. Service availability to employment indicator; measured in terms of the distance within which employees can reach a given number of service employees.

Consumers – services

15. Service space indicator, representing the amount of land and usable floorspace available to services; measured in terms of the average gross service employment density of service employees per hectare.
16. Service market indicator, representing the accessibility of services to residents; measured in terms of the distance within which residents can reach a given number of service employees.
17. Service accessibility to employment indicator; measured in terms of the distance within which employees can reach a given number of service employees.
18. Service clustering indicator; measured in terms of the distance within which service employees can reach a given number of other service employees.

Consumers – travellers

19. Journey to work, representing the distance travelled by commuters; measured in terms of the mean trip length of all work trips.
20. Journey to services, representing the distance travelled by shoppers, etc.; measured in terms of the mean trip length of all service trips.

General

21. Size-compactness indicator; measured in terms of the average distance of all residents from the centre of the town.

Since several of the indicators in the above list are similar, a shorter list of fourteen was actually used for evaluating the four towns. These were:

A. Social interaction indicator (5).
B. Employment opportunities indicator (6 and 12).
C. Service availability indicator (7 and 16).
D. Proximity to open space indicator (8).
E. Employment clustering indicator (13).
F. Service availability to employment indicator (14 and 17).
G. Service clustering indicator (18).
H. Distance to town centre indicator (21).
I. Journey to work indicator (9 and 19).
J. Journey to services indicator (10 and 20).
K. Residential density indicator (4 and 3).
L. Employment density indicator (11 and 15).
M. Cost of land indicator (1).
N. Cost of services indicator (2).

Methodology

The structural comparison of the three New Towns with the older town of Reading provided the opportunity to demonstrate firstly the model's ability to reproduce urban spatial structures and the consequences of different planning policies, and secondly the use of evaluative techniques to assess the merits of these consequences in particular and of different types of urban structure in general.

Having collated the data for each town into 1 km × 1 km grid cells to provide a common areal basis for comparison, the study was carried out in two stages. The first stage was to use the model to reproduce reality, or the planners' intentions in the case of Hook and Milton Keynes which are as yet unbuilt, calibrating the model to produce the best results in each case. This proved particularly difficult in the case of Stevenage and Hook because of the way in which the location of floorspace had been (or was going to be) controlled by the planners. Since the model assumes that the stock of floorspace in a town is built up in response to the aggregate demands for space made by many different activities, it is not surprising that it could not cope with the situation where the location of floorspace had been decided by one body without regard to the likely pressures of demand (since, without a model, it would have been difficult to assess them). However, when the stock of floorspace was used as a given input to the activity model, good results for the location of residents, service employees and traffic flows were obtained.

In order to determine the consequences of this control of floorspace location, the model was run again for each New Town with the same data inputs as before (i.e. the location of basic employment and available land, the transportation network, the labour participation rate, etc.) but with the distribution parameters set to the same values as for Reading. In this way it was possible to determine the distributions of stock and activities that would probably have occurred if the location of floorspace had not been controlled, and thus, by comparing the two sets of model runs, the effects of such control on stock and activity location.†

† Reading was thus used as a proxy for a 'free market norm' against which to measure the performance of the three New Towns, so that the specific effect of the planning controls exercised in each case can be ascertained. It can be argued that a town like Reading has developed its particular spatial structure partly for historical reasons and cannot therefore be compared with any New Town. While admitting the strength of this argument, it can also be claimed that the structure of Reading has changed considerably over the last 50 years in response to various pressures and that compared with the three New Towns these changes have been relatively unaffected by 'exogenous' planning action. It therefore seemed fair to us to use Reading at least as a proxy for a town in which the locational behaviour of residents and services has been governed not by planning decisions but by the 'endogenous' forces of free market competition.

The next stage was to use the evaluation indicators firstly to assess whether the effects of controlling the distribution and use of floorspace were beneficial, and secondly to compare the merits of each of the spatial structures represented by the four towns. It should perhaps be emphasised that in making these evaluations the study was not concerned with the economic implications of the towns in their regional setting, or with the sociological implications of the different urban forms, but with those characteristics of spatial structure which can be measured in terms of densities and accessibilities.

TABLE 9.2. *Parameters and ratios for the four towns*

	Reading	Stevenage	Hook	Milton Keynes
Ratios				
Labour participation rate	2.5	2.1	2.3	2.1
Ratio of service employment to residents	0.19	0.13	0.18	0.19
Space Standards (sq. metres)				
Total demand for floor space per basic employee*	210.0	100.0	120.0	120.0
Basic space standard	23.0	18.0	18.0	18.0
Residential space standard	31.0	23.0	23.0	23.0
Service space standard	37.0	26.0	26.0	26.0
Parameters				
Stock β^t	0.7	—	—	0.6
Residents β^r	0.5	0·1	0.5	0.5
Services β^s	0.9	0.2	0.4	0.5
α	2.0	2.0	2.5	2.0

* These figures are not directly comparable since they are measured in terms of the total floorspace per basic employee and are thus dependent on the proportion of basic to total employment, which varies for each town as follows:

Reading 53%; Stevenage 74%; Hook 61%; Milton Keynes 60%.

In general, the percentage of basic employment is lower for large towns than for small towns (see Ullman and Dacey 1960). It is perhaps worth commenting, therefore, that considering its size, the planners of Milton Keynes are aiming at an unusually high proportion of basic employment.

The results of the first stage are presented in the next section for each town in turn, starting with Reading as the basis of comparison. For each New Town, the model runs using the Reading parameters are described first (Model 1), representing the 'natural', or uncontrolled, distribution of stock and activities one would expect to occur as a result of the particular disposition of the data inputs in each case. The model runs calibrated to produce results closest to reality or to the planners' intentions are presented second (Model 2). The difference between the two sets of results is then analysed in terms of the evaluation indicators with reference to Table 9.3 on p. 248. The results of comparing and evaluating the structure of all four towns (both Models 1 and 2) are contained in the following section.

The values for all the ratios and space standards used in the model, together with the 'best fit' parameter values, are shown for each town in Table 9.2. The ratios and space standards were determined from the data for each town, except for the residential and employment space standards in the case of Hook and Milton Keynes, which were taken to be the same as for Stevenage. The 'best fit' parameter values in the case of Reading were those which produced results closest to reality for both stock and activity location *and* for traffic flows of work and service trips. In Stevenage they were those producing the closest results for both activity location and work trips (service trip data being unavailable).† For Hook and Milton Keynes the 'best fit' parameter values were those producing results closest to the planners' intentions for stock (Milton Keynes only) and activity location, the model results for traffic flows having to be taken on trust.

Study results: model runs for each town

Reading

The spatial structure of Reading has evolved over several centuries of continuous development, and displays the characteristics of a typical traditional town. Basic and service employment are both highly concentrated in the central cell (cell 59) and, outside the centre, along the main routes. The road network is markedly radial, and residential densities vary considerably, being high in and around the centre and low towards the periphery. Development has been restricted by the flood plains, which

---

† Some difficulty was experienced in calibrating Model 2 for Stevenage, owing to the high proportion (12%) of work trips to outside the study area. The best fit that could be obtained for the mean work trip length was 3.04 km compared with the survey figure of 3.42 km. This problem could easily have been resolved by using a 'dummy' cell to represent all external destinations, but unfortunately the survey data did not identify the number or destinations of such trips so that their lengths and frequency could not be determined.

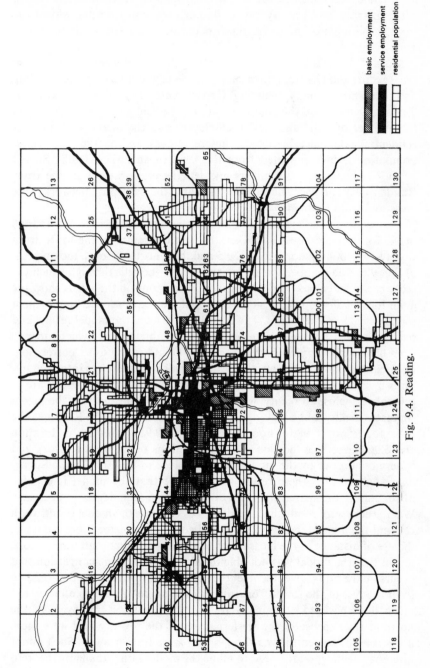

Fig. 9.4. Reading.

have tended to reinforce the radial cross-shaped structure of the town, while the river and railway cut off its northern arm from the rest of the town. Several parks and public open spaces are contained within the urban area.

Most of the data for running and testing the model were obtained from the Reading and District Traffic Survey carried out in 1962–3 by the Reading and Berkshire County Planning Departments, and from the work of Taylor (1968). From the land use and employment survey we determined the number of basic and service employees and the quantity of all non-residential floorspace in each kilometre cell, as well as 1962 residential population figures (updated from the 1961 census). The Traffic Survey provided details of the numbers and lengths of work and service trips. Residential floorspace, developed land and the transport network were measured from Ordnance Survey maps.

The results of the model are compared with reality in Figs. 9.5 and 9.6 in the form of cross-sections taken through the centre of the town, from west to east looking north in Fig. 9.5 and from north to south looking east in Fig. 9.6. The numbers on the x-axis refer to the cells through which the sections are taken (see Fig. 9.4), while the divisions on the y-axis show the quantities of floorspace, residential population and service employment found in each of these cells. The overall fit between the model results and reality was measured by the coefficient of determination, R^2, which can vary from 0.00, indicating no correlation, to 1.00, indicating exact correlation. In calculating this coefficient, the results for all cells are taken into account. Thus a score of 0.90, for example, indicates that the model results are in general very close to reality, while a score of 0.50 indicates that the model simulates reality only very approximately. In the case of Reading, the value for R^2 was 0.98 for floorspace location, 0.91 for residential location and 0.96 for service location. The distributions of journeys to work and to services output by the model were also close to the 10% Traffic Survey data ($R^2 = 0.97$). These results demonstrate that the model is capable of simulating the spatial structure of a town to a high degree of accuracy. Where there were residuals (i.e. differences between the model results for a cell and the data), these were small and could be explained. For example, the use of distance as the measure of accessibility, rather than time or cost, meant that the model was not able to take account of the congestion that occurs on the bridge over the river that divides the northern part of Reading from the rest of the town. Consequently the model tended to allocate too much floorspace and too many residents and service employees to the north at the expense of the western parts of the town, which were more accessible to the centre even though they were further away. Such minor discrepancies suggest the need to refine the model rather than any theoreti-

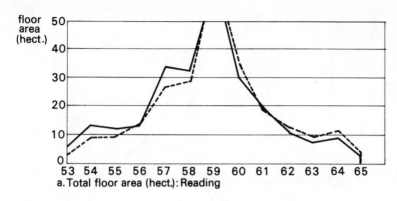

a. Total floor area (hect.): Reading

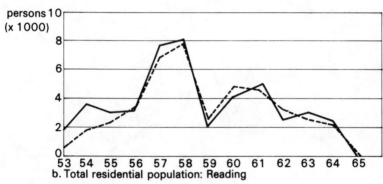

b. Total residential population: Reading

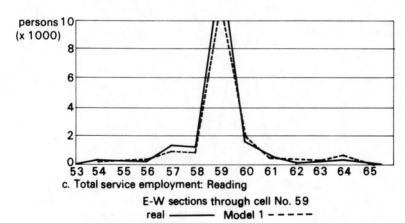

c. Total service employment: Reading

E-W sections through cell No. 59

real ————— Model 1 – – – – –

Fig. 9.5. E–W sections through the town comparing model results with data: Reading.

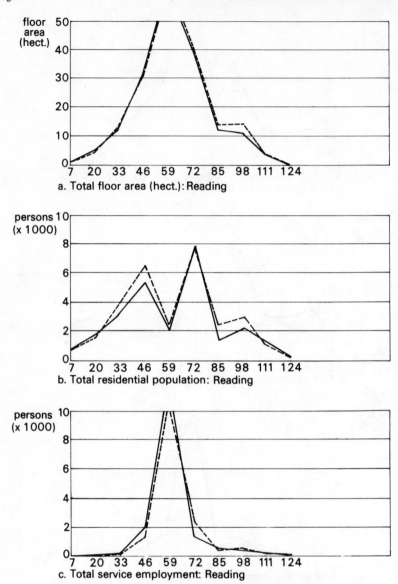

a. Total floor area (hect.): Reading

b. Total residential population: Reading

c. Total service employment: Reading

N–S sections through cell No. 59
real ——————— Model 1 - - - - - -

Fig. 9.6. N–S sections through the town comparing model results with data: Reading.

cal difficulties in the model itself. For a full discussion of the results of the model for Reading, see Echenique *et al.* (1969a).

Stevenage

The Master plan for Stevenage New Town was approved and building commenced in 1949; the town had grown to a population of 57,000 by 1966. Stevenage has been asymmetrically planned, with the basic employment concentrated in the zoned industrial estates between the motorway A1(M) and the railway line, isolated on the western edge of the town. The service employment is mainly concentrated in the town centre, which is located close to the industrial estates but on the other side of the railway, so that almost all the employment is grouped together on one side of the town. The road pattern is semi-radial and a large area of open space bisects the town. The residential areas, built with little variation in density, are organized into six neighbourhoods of 10,000 people, with a group of local services situated away from the main roads at the centre of each neighbourhood. From the beginning the planners have kept a tight control over the location of floorspace, and have recently developed sites to the east at slightly higher densities, so that the highest residential densities are furthest from employment. It was originally intended that most people should walk or cycle to work, but at present more than 80% of people travel by car or bus and over 12% commute to work places outside Stevenage.

The required data were obtained from the Traffic Survey of 1965–6, published by the Stevenage Development Corporation (1966), and from the Corporation itself, which supplied us with detailed maps and figures for each residential neighbourhood, the industrial estates and the town centre. From these we obtained employment and floorspace totals for each cell, while totals for residential population were obtained from the 1966 Census.

In the first run of the model (Model 1) the parameters of Reading were used in order to observe what would have happened if the allocation of floorspace had not been controlled (as in Model 2). Fig. 9.8a shows a much higher concentration of floorspace is produced in the central cells, especially cell 25, causing considerable changes in the distribution of residential population. Table 9.3 shows that this results in a lower mean residential density (76.82 pph) than for Model 2 and shorter journeys to work (1.94 km) and to services (1.73 km); all other measures of interaction (e.g. employment and social opportunities) are also improved.

In the second run of the model the floorspace was controlled to correspond with the Development Plans and the parameters of residential and

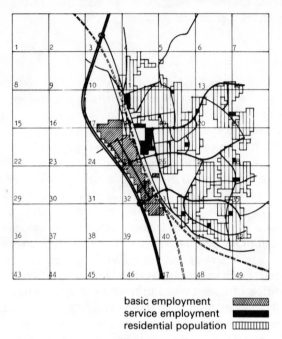

basic employment   ▨▨▨▨▨

service employment   ████

residential population   ⯑⯑⯑⯑⯑

Fig. 9.7. Stevenage.

services distribution were altered. A reasonable fit was obtained for residential location ($R^2 = 0.85$) and services location ($R^2 = 0.88$) by reducing
β^r to 0.1 and β^s to 0.2. These are unusually low parameter values and
suggest that the location of floorspace in Stevenage has forced inhabitants
to spend more on travel than is normal. With these parameters, the most
noticeable residuals occurred in cell 18 (Fig. 9.8b) where the model over-
estimated the residential population by more than 80% and underestimated
service employment by an equivalent amount. This cell corresponds to
Old Stevenage, which still maintains a high level of services, and the model
is unable to take into account the historical fact that Old Stevenage existed
before the arrival of competing service centres. It therefore distributes
services to other cells which are more accessible to the present location of
residents and employees. This suggests that equilibrium between old and
new development had not yet been achieved by 1966, and one would
expect, in the absence of any further changes, the services in Stevenage
to rearrange themselves with time in the manner suggested by the model
(provided they are not prevented from doing so by planning controls).

Compared with Model 1, Model 2 shows an increase in the length of

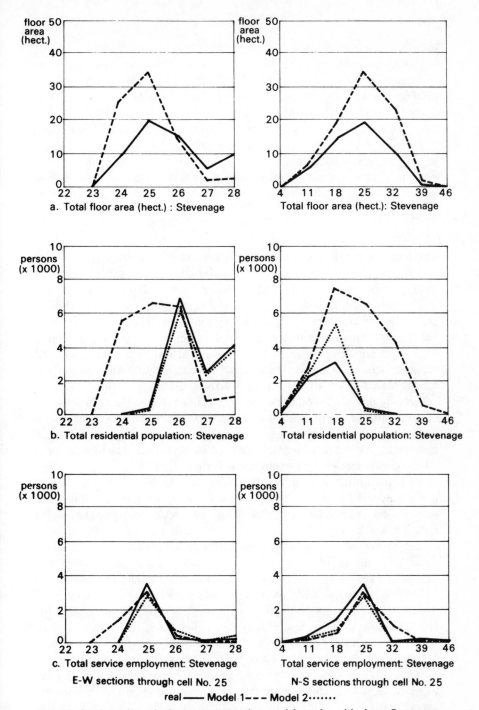

Fig. 9.8. Sections through the town comparing model results with data: Stevenage.

journeys to work to 3.04 km. This is lower than the survey figure of 3.42 km which includes some 12% commuting outside the study area (see note on page 232). The journey to services is increased to 2.52 km, the average density is now 83.87 (the highest of all four towns) and the mean distances to work opportunities, to other residents and to services are all increased. It would thus seem that the control of floorspace has not had beneficial conse-quences in the case of Stevenage. For exactly the same disposition of developed land, basic employment and transportation routes, closer proximity between activities and lower average densities would have been achieved by locating floorspace in the manner shown by Model 1.

Hook

The plan for Hook, designed for a population of 100,000, was published in a Report in 1961, but the town was never built. The main characteristic of the proposed town was its compact design. Almost all the service employ-ment was in a dominating semi-linear town centre built on a deck above a spinal motorway, from which secondary routes branched at regular inter-vals to form an axial grid. Residential densities were high in and around the centre, falling off towards the perimeter with little provision of local services. Basic employment was clearly separated into three industrial estates placed apart from the town. Recreational facilities and parks were generously provided around the perimeter, but there was very little public space within the town itself. In addition to an expensive system for motor traffic, the planners also made generous provision for segregated pedestrian movement. As in Stevenage, the location of floorspace was to have been tightly controlled by the Development Corporation.

All the required data were obtained from the very thorough Report published by the London County Council (1961), which provided detailed information on employment, floorspace and residential population for each section of the town. The developed land (excluding public open spaces, farm land, etc.) and the accessibility of each kilometre cell to every other were measured from the diagrammatic plan shown in Fig. 9.9. The estimates of traffic flows included in the Report were not used.

The first run of the model (Model 1), using the Reading parameters, pro-duced a distribution of floorspace which was less concentrated around the centre than the planners had proposed (see Fig. 9.10a), with large negative residuals in cells 8, 13, 18. This produced in turn less concentrated residen-tial and service allocations, with negative residuals again appearing in the centre. As a consequence, Table 9.3 shows the mean residential density to be 73.89 pph, which is lower than that obtained in Model 2, a similar average trip length for the journeys to work (1.84 km) and a shorter

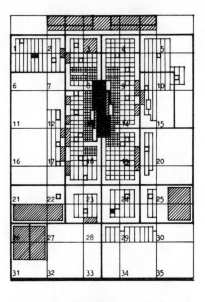

basic employment
service employment
residential population

Fig. 9.9. Hook.

average for journeys to services (1.36). However, the mean distances of all measures of interaction, with the exception of service availability from employment, are increased.

Model 2 was calibrated, as in the case of Stevenage, by controlling the floorspace in accordance with the planning proposals and by altering the parameters of service distribution. This provided a very close fit for residential location ($R^2 = 0.99$), with the parameter the same as for Reading. The service location was also close to the planned distribution ($R^2 = 0.99$), but was obtained only by reducing β^s to 0.4 and increasing the clustering parameter (α) to 2.5. This change in the calibration suggests that planners were relying on a greater concentration of services in the centre than might actually have been possible.

Compared with Model 1, the clustering of services in Model 2 resulted in an increase in the mean trip length to services from 1.36 to 1.86 km (Table 9.3). Model 2 also produced higher residential densities (81.37 pph) and as a result somewhat shorter average distances to employment, residential and town services opportunities, while mean distance to local services opportunities increased (Table 9.3).

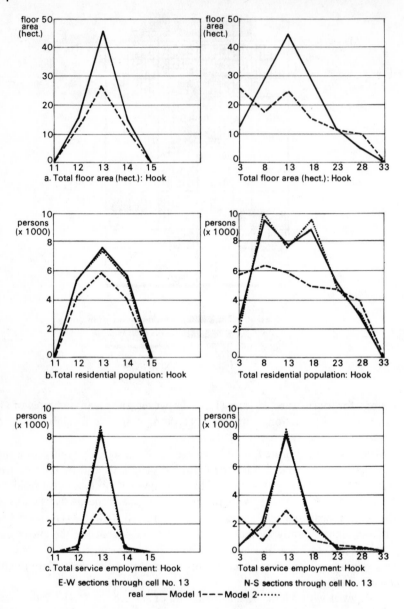

a. Total floor area (hect.): Hook

Total floor area (hect.): Hook

b. Total residential population: Hook

Total residential population: Hook

c. Total service employment: Hook

Total service employment: Hook

E-W sections through cell No. 13

N-S sections through cell No. 13

real ——— Model 1 — — — Model 2 ·······

Fig. 9.10. Sections through the town comparing model results with data: Hook.

Milton Keynes

Milton Keynes is the largest of the four towns, designed for a population of 250,000. The first Report by Llewelyn-Davies, Weeks, Forestier-Walker and Bor was published in 1968. In the proposed plan the basic employment is dispersed in several industrial estates about the town, on a loose grid of roads which roughly conforms to a neutral grid of 1 × 1 km cells. The service employment is mainly concentrated in a large town centre, although there is provision for district and local centres in residential areas along the main roads. In contrast to Hook and Stevenage the densities of development will not be tightly controlled but will vary according to the pressures of demand. Public open spaces are provided in thin bands within and between residential areas. The main forms of transport will be car and bus.

The required data were obtained from the plans and figures contained in the Report. The amounts of land for each type of use in each cell were measured from the map and these figures were aggregated and checked against the published land inventory. Employment was then allocated to the land according to the amounts specified in the Report, and the residential population was distributed at an average density. Floor area totals were derived from the residential and employment figures using average space standards.

It was difficult to calibrate the stock model since the planners had deliberately not specified the amounts of floorspace to be built, but the data described above were used as a basis for comparison. In general the model produced negative residuals in the south and positive in the north-east. The reason for this imbalance was that although the assumed floorspace was relatively evenly distributed, the employment which generated the floorspace in the model was more concentrated in north-east. Nevertheless, Model 1 produced good results for the stock model using Reading parameters ($R^2 = 0.93$). Since the residuals from the stock model were transferred to the activity model, the previous pattern of negatives was further accentuated in the residential distribution ($R^2 = 0.86$). Some of the residential densities planned for the southern area were at such a distance from employment that even with the planned input of floorspace the model still produced negatives. There were also negative residuals around existing villages, which had formerly been centres but within the context of the New Town no longer possessed such a large proportion of employment and were now situated in the outer areas where accessibility was lower. This suggests that the villages and their surroundings might contain a larger proportion of high socio-economic groups.† The service location in Model 1 ($R_2 = 0.82$) was less concentrated than the planners intended

† High socio-economic groups tend to travel further to work and to demand higher space standards (see Echenique 1968b).

and was distributed along the main routes rather than in one large centre. Thus the cells with a large planned service employment produced negative residuals (e.g. the town centre), while positive residuals appeared along the Bletchley to Stony Stratford route (the A5) and around the basic employment located by the intersection with the M1.

The results of Model 2 showed improved residuals although they still occurred in the same areas. The floorspace distribution gave a better fit ($R^2 = 0.96$), by reducing the parameter to 0.6, but still with negative

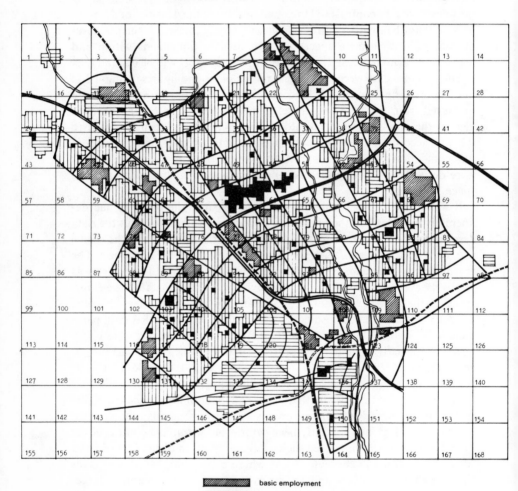

basic employment

service employment

residential population

Fig. 9.11. Milton Keynes.

residuals in the town centre. Residential location improved without any change in calibration ($R^2 = 0.93$) and services residuals were marginally improved ($R^2 = 0.84$) by reducing β^s to 0.5. This gave a better fit in the centre, despite the low allocation of floorspace, but the results still seemed to indicate that a very high concentration of services in this area might be difficult to achieve in reality. As compared with Model 1, the effect of these changes (Table 9.3) was to increase marginally the mean trip length to services, to decrease the mean distance from residents to their employment opportunities, and to increase the mean distance from residents to other residents. In general, these results suggest that apart from the distribution of services the planners' intentions are realistic and should be capable of being achieved without undue planning intervention.

Structural comparison of the four towns

The basis for the comparison of the four towns is the list of fourteen indicators explained earlier. Figs. 9.14 and 9.15 illustrate graphically how well each town performs for twelve of these indicators, and Table 9.3 lists the values of all fourteen for Reading and for both Model 1 (Reading parameters) and Model 2 (best fit parameters) of the three New Towns. The interaction indicators A to G are shown in Figs. 9.14 and 9.15 as cumulative percentage curves, indicating in graph (a), for example, the distances within which cumulative percentages of residents can reach a given number of other residents for each town. The indicator of social interaction is then taken to be the mean distance within which all residents of a town can reach that given number, or target figure, of other residents. In the course of the study, curves were plotted for several target figures for all seven types of interaction, and Table 9.3 shows the mean distances for four different target figures for each type. The asterisk indicates the highest target figure applicable to all four towns, for which the curves in Figs. 9.14 and 9.15 are plotted, and for which the mean distance was taken as the indicator. In all cases, the objective is to minimise the value of an indicator – that is, to reduce distances and densities.

It must be stressed that the comparisons discussed below do not take account of all possible facets of spatial structure. It has been assumed that such problems as congestion, safety and amenity can be solved equally well by all four types of structure, or in other words, that in each town the transportation network can be designed to accommodate the actual traffic loads and that the same standards of safety and amenity can be implemented. It is possible to argue that the problems of congestion are more difficult and expensive to solve for some types of transportation network than for others, but we have had to leave such considerations for future

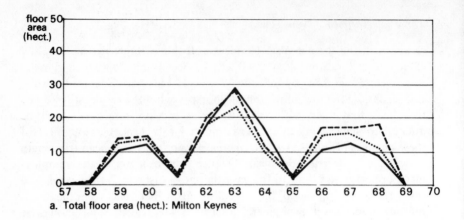

a. Total floor area (hect.): Milton Keynes

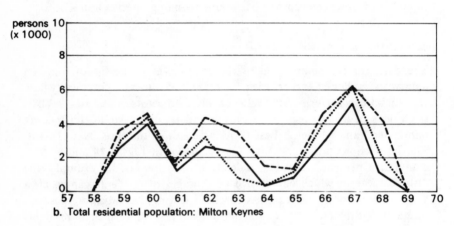

b. Total residential population: Milton Keynes

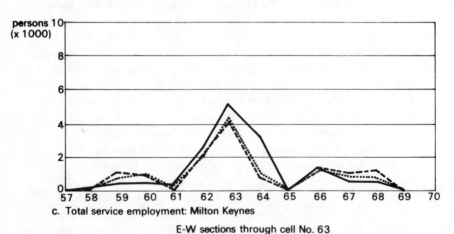

c. Total service employment: Milton Keynes

E–W sections through cell No. 63

data —— Model 1– – –Model 2········

Fig. 9.12. E–W sections through the town comparing model results with data: Milton Keynes.

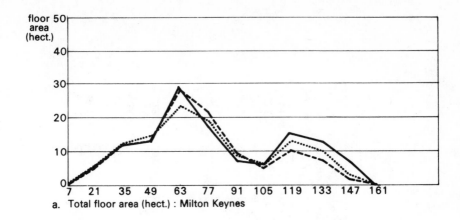

a. Total floor area (hect.) : Milton Keynes

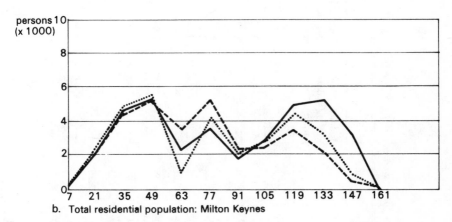

b. Total residential population: Milton Keynes

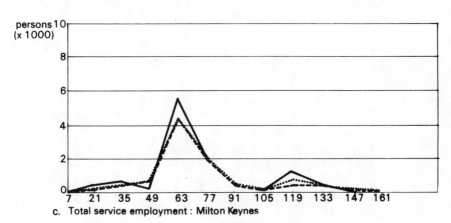

c. Total service employment : Milton Keynes

N-S sections through cell No. 63

data ——— Model 1 — — — Model 2 ·······

Fig. 9.13. N–S sections through the town comparing model results with data: Milton Keynes.

TABLE 9.3 *Values for indicators A to N for the four towns*

Indicators	Target figure x	Reading	Stevenage		Hook		Milton Keynes	
			Model 1 Reading param	Model 2 Best fit param	Model 1 Reading param	Model 2 Best fit param	Model 1 Reading param	Model 2 Best fit param
A. Social interaction	12,000	1.78	1.73	1.68	1.55	1.51	1.77	1.76
mean distance (km) within	24,000	2.34	2.15	2.67	1.99	1.82	2.48	2.42
which all residents can	48,000*	3.57	4.09	4.45	3.74	2.96	3.50	3.46
reach x other residents	96,000	5.25	—	—	7.04	6.03	4.98	5.13
B. Employment opportunities	6000	2.30	1.60	2.44	1.61	1.75	2.71	2.03
mean distance (km) within	12,000	2.72	2.25	2.93	2.14	2.13	3.69	2.75
which all residents can	24,000*	3.15	2.79	3.92	3.63	3.12	5.09	3.77
reach x jobs	48,000	5.01	—	—	—	—	8.16	5.08
C. Service availability to residents	3000	2.48	1.92	2.66	1.86	1.91	2.07	2.07
mean distance (km) within	6000*	2.91	2.79	3.81	2.32	2.30	2.88	2.92
which all residents can	12,000	3.08	—	—	4.30	2.71	3.96	3.99
reach x service employees	24,000	5.40	—	—	—	—	5.50	5.40
D. Proximity to open space	375	2.26	1.90	1.83	2.45	2.60	2.68	2.70
mean distance (km) within	750	3.26	2.94	3.16	3.81	3.77	3.57	3.57
which all residents can	1500*	4.47	4.47	4.47	6.77	6.51	5.13	5.15
reach x hectares	3000	6.20	—	—	—	—	7.68	7.69

E. Employment clustering mean distance (km) within which all employees can reach x other employees	6000	1.51	0.71	1.11	1.43	1.45	1.76	1.77
	12,000	1.78	1.61	1.77	2.19	2.19	2.64	2.61
	24,000*	2.38	1.71	2.77	4.07	3.18	3.64	3.70
	48,000	4.29	—	—	—	—	5.31	5.22
F. Service availability to employment mean distance (km) within which all employees can reach x service employees	3000	1.67	1.25	1.73	1.84	1.91	2.04	2.06
	6000*	1.92	1.71	3.89	2.37	2.58	2.91	2.88
	12,000	2.30	—	—	4.60	2.92	4.04	4.03
	24,000	4.49	—	—	—	—	5.62	5.49
G. Service clustering mean distance (km) within which all services can reach x other services	3000	1.55	1.18	2.10	1.70	1.15	1.88	1.85
	6000*	1.77	1.85	3.60	2.13	1.37	2.70	2.64
	12,000	2.22	—	—	4.29	1.97	3.80	3.71
	24,000	4.39	—	—	—	—	5.40	5.20
H. Size–compactness (km)		3.07	1.83	2.66	2.68	2.23	4.41	4.48
I. Mean work trip length (km)		2.77	1.94	3.04	1.84	1.83	3.14	3.21
J. Mean service trip length (km)		2.86	1.73	2.52	1.36	1.86	2.23	3.36
K. Mean residential density (pph)		62.43	76.82	83.87	73.89	81.37	44.84	46.41
L. Mean employment density (pph)		61.40	89.38	80.36	59.75	59.35	43.72	41.28
M. Developed land per resident (m²)		189	142		130		218	
N. Trunk road per resident (m)		1.04	0.98		0.59		0.88	

* Indicates highest target figure applicable to all four towns.

explorations. The present study concentrates instead on the performance of the four towns with regard to a few specified aspects of urban spatial structure, all others being considered as constant.

Comparisons (with reference to Figs. 9.14 and 9.15 and Table 9.3)

Indicator A: Social interaction. From the table it can be seen that Hook has the best score (2.96 km), mainly on account of its dense and compact form, and the graph bears this out. It is interesting, however, that Milton Keynes, which has the lowest mean residential density, also scores well (3.46 km). In fact if the indicators for Model 1 are compared, Milton Keynes does best of all (with Reading a close second), whilst still maintaining the lowest density; but if the target figure is lowered, the smaller towns score better. Stevenage, in spite of having the highest mean residential density, is consistently the worst of the four towns.

Indicator B: Employment opportunities. Again Hook has the best index (3.12 km), though the pattern is not so clear as for Indicator A. This is because the advantages of compactness and high densities are almost lost by having the employment placed at the edges of the town away from the high density areas. Reading's indicator is only marginally worse (3.15 km), although from the graph it can be seen that there is a marked disparity between some residents who are very close to job opportunities and others who are more distantly located. Stevenage, although it still has the worst indicator (3.92 km), does not fare as badly as for Indicator A. This is because the employment is highly concentrated in one area, so that once it is reached, a high number of opportunities is available. It is interesting that if the planners had allowed floorspace ratios, and hence residential densities, to decay from the town centre (Model 1) instead of increasing from it (Model 2), Stevenage would have had the best employment opportunity indicator of all.

Indicator C: Service availability. Although Hook has the best indicator (2.30 km), one can see from the graph that there is a certain disparity between the residents living at high densities around the town centre where all the services are concentrated and those living further out where there is little provision for local services. Readers will recall that in calibrating the model for Hook it was found necessary to use an unusually high value for the clustering parameter and a low value for β^s. Model 1, with Reading's parameters, scores better figures for the mean service trip length (Index J) and for the accessibility of residents to a target figure of 3000 service employees, but worse for the higher target figures. This indicates that the Hook planners' policy of service concentration (assuming that it could have achieved) results in excellent accessibility to a large range of services, but at the expense of longer service trips and few local services. The same can be said about Milton Keynes, although the difference between Model 1 and 2 are not so marked for this indicator as for the mean service trip length. Again, the planners have concentrated a large proportion of services in the town centre with some local services within residential areas. Model 1 distributes fewer to the town centre services and more local services, resulting in a 33% saving in the mean service trip length (Index J). The availability of services indicator in Model 1 is also marginally improved from 2.92 km to 2.88 km. There would thus seem to be no advantage in concentrating the services in the town centre to the extent proposed by the planners. The indicator for Reading is 2.91 km. This average figure is a reflection of the balance between the high concentration of service employment in the town centre and the accessibility of local services distributed near the residential areas along the main traffic routes. Stevenage again has the worst indicator (3.81 km), due to the concentration of services in the town centre and in Old Stevenage, which are surrounded by the lowest residential densities and cut off from the other residential areas by the large parkland. Local services are few and located away from the main roads, making them less accessible to other residents. It is noticeable how much the indicators improve in Model 1 (2.79 km) using Reading's parameters.

Indicator D: Proximity to open space. Reading and Stevenage have the best indicators (4.47 km each); the first because of its star shaped plan which results in most of the town being within easy reach of the perimeter, and the latter because of the large park in the centre of the town. Hook, being the most compact, has the worst indicator (6.51 km) in spite of its small size, while Milton Keynes has a relatively good score (5.15 km) because of the quantity of open space within the structure of the town.

Indicator E: Employment clustering. The best indicator is that of Reading (2.38 km), which has a high concentration of both basic and service employment in the centre and along the main traffic routes. Stevenage also has a good indicator (2.77 km) because of the proximity of the town centre to the industrial estates. Hook, and Milton Keynes, on the other hand, have less good scores (3.18 km and 3.70 km) because in both cases the industrial estates have been located mainly around the perimeter of the town.

Indicator F: Service availability to employment. Again Reading has a good indicator (1.92 km) because of the proximity of all types of employment in

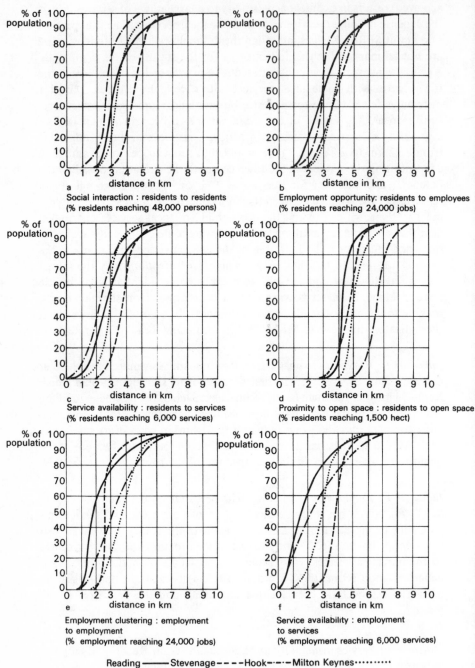

Reading ——— Stevenage – – – Hook –·–·– Milton Keynes ··········

Fig. 9.14. Spatial comparisons 1.

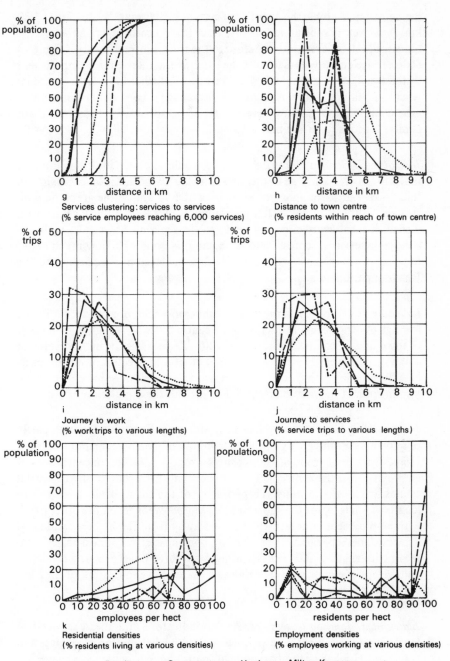

g
Services clustering: services to services
(% service employees reaching 6,000 services)

h
Distance to town centre
(% residents within reach of town centre)

i
Journey to work
(% work trips to various lengths)

j
Journey to services
(% service trips to various lengths)

k
Residential densities
(% residents living at various densities)

l
Employment densities
(% employees working at various densities)

Reading —— Stevenage ---- Hook --·- Milton Keynes ········

Fig. 9.15. Spatial comparisons 2.

the centre and along the main traffic routes. Stevenage's indicator (3.89 km), however, is substantially worse than for indicator E, for although the industrial estates are relatively close to the town centre, the target figure of 6000 service employees is almost the same as the total service employment of the town, so that employees need to travel further in order to reach it; when the target figure is lowered, Stevenage's performance improves. Hook and Milton Keynes have similar indicators as for Indicator E for similar reasons (2.58 km and 2.88 km).

Indicator G: Service clustering. As one would expect, Hook has the best indicator of 1.37 km, due to the unusually high concentration of services in the centre, but Reading is not far behind at 1.77 km, as the graph demonstrates. Milton Keynes, with a combination of a large service centre with dispersed local centres, comes next at 2.64 km, and Stevenage, with less accessible services, scores 3.60 km. Again it is noticeable how much better Stevenage would have scored if it had been developed according to the Reading parameters.

Indicator H: Size-compactness. This indicator, measured in terms of the average distance of all residents to the centre of town, is related to the size of town and its compactness. Thus Milton Keynes has the highest value of 4.48 km, followed by Reading at 3.07 km. Hook, because of its compactness, has the lowest value of 2.23 km, while the Stevenage indicator is 2.66 km, in spite of the fact that Stevenage has half the population of Hook.

Indicator I: Journey to work. The mean work trip length is a function partly of a town's size and partly of the distribution of employment and residents. Hook, with high residential densities around a large concentration of employment in the centre, is so compact that, even though the industrial estates are located around the periphery of the town, it has a mean trip length which is by far the shortest (1.83 km). Stevenage, on the other hand, with employment concentrated in areas away from the highest residential densities and separated from them by open space, has almost the longest mean trip length of 3.04 km. Reading, with three times as many residents, and Milton Keynes, with five times as many, have indicators of 2.77 km and 3.21 km respectively.

Indicator J: Journey to services. As for Indicator I, the mean service trip length is a function of the town's size and of the distribution of services and residents. Hook has the best indicator of 1.86 km, while Stevenage has 2.52 km, Reading 2.86 km and Milton Keynes 3.36 km. It is interesting that for each New Town substantial reductions in mean trip lengths can be achieved by using the Reading parameters.

Indicator K: Residential density. Table 9.3 and Fig. 9.15 show the wide differences in the (weighted) mean residential densities of the four towns and the way that these densities are distributed. Milton Keynes has by far the lowest gross residential density of 46.41 persons per hectare, fairly evenly distributed between 30 and 60 pph, while at the other extreme Stevenage has the highest mean density of 83.87 pph., with almost all residents living at between 80 and 100 pph. Between these two extremes, Reading exhibits a range of densities from 10 to 100 pph and a mean of 62.43 pph. Hook has almost as high a mean density as Stevenage (81.37 pph) but it is spread over a greater range. It is again interesting that the Reading parameters produce more residents living at lower residential densities, without using any more land, in each of the New Towns.

Indicator L: Employment density. In general, employment densities seem to follow residential densities, being lowest for Milton Keynes (41.28 eph) and highest for Stevenage (80.36 eph), with Reading and Hook in between at 61.40 eph and 59.35 eph respectively. The distributions, however, show rather a contrasting pattern, with peaks at either end of the spectrum at 10 eph and 100 eph, corresponding to the different densities within industrial estates and service centres.

Indicator M: Land per person. These indicators roughly follow residential density: 130 m^2pp for Hook, 142 m^2pp for Stevenage, 189 m^2pp for Reading and 218 m^2pp for Milton Keynes. Notice that Stevenage has more land per person than Hook even though it has more residents living at higher residential densities.

Indicator N: Length of road per person. The lowest length of trunk road per person is for Hook (0.59 m), but against this simple statistic, its road network is more expensive, with separated carriageways and interchanges. Milton Keynes and Stevenage come next with 0.88 m and 0.98 m respectively, which indicates that the neutral road grid does not necessarily use more road, while Reading has the worst indicator of 1.04 mpp. The Reading figure, however, includes more secondary roads than the other three towns.

General index

The general index used to compare the four towns is still at a rather early stage of development, but it serves to indicate a possible way of arriving at some conclusions about the indicators explained above. It can be said that urban spatial structure strikes a balance between two opposing forces; on the one hand there is a desire for space at home and at work, which is reflected in the overall densities in a town, while on the other hand there is a desire for ease of interaction between related activities, which is reflected in their proximity. With this basic assumption it is possible to develop two sub-indices.

Sub-index 1: Interaction. This sub-index refers to the proximity of different activities to each other. The interactions considered here are those measured by the employment opportunities indicator (B), the service availability to residents and to employment indicators (C and F), and the employment and service clustering indicators (E and G). These values are then weighted according to their relative importance, the weights in this case representing the frequency with which journeys are made.† Journeys to work have a weight of 0.40 (representing 40% of all trips), journeys to services of 0.30, residential journeys 0.10, service to service journeys 0.05, employment to services journeys 0.05, and journeys between employees 0.10. These weights can be altered if future predictions indicate any change in frequency. The sum of all these weighted means represents the sub-index 1 (SI 1) for each town.

Sub-index 2: Space. This sub-index refers to the amount of space both at home and at employment, expressed as the mean gross residential density and the mean gross employment density. Both figures are weighted, 0.66 for residential, and 0.33 for employment, according to the relative amount of time spent in one or the other. An initial objective would be to reduce densities as far as possible, because, apart from reflecting a desire for more space, low densities are less expensive to build and maintain, when all the costs of land, roads, services and construction have been taken into account (Stone 1961). The sum of the two weighted densities represents the sub-index 2 (SI 2) for each town.

The general index. Once obtained, the two sub-indices, which are expressed as densities (persons per hectare) and distances (kilometres), are transformed into similar numerical quantities. The method used here transforms them into standard measures,‡ by subtracting from the values of the sub-indices of each town the mean value for all towns, and then dividing each by the standard deviation.

† These values were obtained from the study by Taylor (1968), which included the frequency of different types of trip in Northampton, Gloucester and Reading.

‡ For a full statistical explanation of standard measures, see Davies (1961), pp. 17–18.

$$SM(i) = \sqrt{\frac{(x_i - \bar{x})}{\dfrac{\Sigma_i (x_i - \bar{x})^2}{n-1}}}$$

i.e.

where: $SM(i)$ = standard measure of sub-index for town i
    x_i = value of sub-index for town i
    $\bar{x}$ = the mean value of the sub-index for all towns
    n = number of towns

Once the sub-indices for each of the four towns have been transformed to standard measures it is possible to weight the relative importance of one index against the other and observe the rating of each town. That is to say by giving 90% weight to the 'space' index we favour towns with high space standards; if we invert the weights by giving 90% to the 'interaction' index, we favour the more compact towns. Fig. 9.16 shows the ranking of the four towns for a variety of weights.

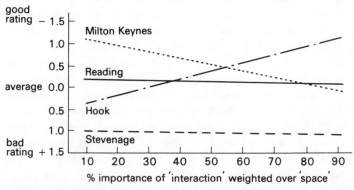

Fig. 9.16. Comparative ratings of all four towns.

It is clear from this graph that Hook and Milton Keynes represent extreme cases whose rating varies considerably according to the weights used. When less importance is given to interaction as opposed to space, Milton Keynes has the best rating; but as one changes the weights Hook improves its performance and Milton Keynes declines. The ratings of the other two towns, however, remain constant. Reading maintains second place for both extreme conditions and for this reason may satisfy more sections of the community than, for example, Hook, which sacrifices space for proximity. The town which scores badly is Stevenage, irrespective of the weights used, for as well as providing less residential and employment space than any of the other towns. Stevenage has also been planned in such a way that interrelated activities have relatively low proximity. However, if the results for Model 1 had been plotted, Stevenage's performance would be considerably improved.

Conclusions

Throughout this paper it has been shown how analytical models can be used to demonstrate the effects of different planning actions upon the urban structure. The effects of such different actions were apparent in all of the three New Towns. In Stevenage the planned distribution of floor-space resulted in long trips to work and services, in spite of uniformly high residential and employment densities. Milton Keynes, in contrast, provided a more dispersed pattern of employment and achieved reasonable distances to job opportunities without sacrificing low densities; but the high concentrations of services in the town centre created other problems, such as longer journeys to services from employment and from residences. Hook achieved very short travel distances for most interactions, but only at the expense of public and private space standards, while Reading fell between the two extremes of Milton Keynes and Hook, providing a wide range of densities and short distances to most opportunities.

Apart from the individual analyses, a system has been demonstrated for reaching some general conclusions about the performance of each town. It is possible, by using standard indices and systematically changing their weights, to explore the performance of each urban structure and to compare the resultant patterns of living and interaction. Similarly, alternative strategies for a town can be tested to find the one which has the optimum consequences according to whether importance is attached to high space standards or to high accessibilities between related activities. At present, no attempt has been made to establish preferred weightings for the general index, only to observe the degree to which the town's rating is affected as the weights are changed. Thus it is interesting to contrast Reading, which maintains a constant rating for all weights, with Milton Keynes or Hook, whose ratings vary considerably according to whether importance is given to the space index or the interaction index.

The explorations can be developed further by transforming these weights into relative cost terms and producing monetary costs and benefits for different towns. However, a more sophisticated system of evaluation will only come about as a result of a disaggregated model which analyses the performance of a town in relation to each section of the community. With such a model, it will be possible to explore the interactions between different socio-economic groups, working in a variety of jobs, requiring a wide range of public and private services and using several modes of transport, and to test the ability of spatial structures to meet their conflicting demands.

Afterword

The literature of urbanism is varied by widely conflicting viewpoints: it is also vast (Dyos 1968). It emanates on a considerable scale from many sources. The urban historians, the urban geographers, the urban sociologists and economists, the physical planners and the architects, the Utopians and the real estate men, the systems analysts and the traffic engineers, the administrators and the politicians, have all made their contributions.

Somewhere within all this there has been traditionally a basic argument. In one line of thought it is implicit that physical patterns of development can be foreseen: that the form of the environment can be laid down in advance and that it can be controlled by codes and regulations. In other words, there are certain goals that can be set and, since the objectives are often stated in terms of the interests of the community, it is assumed that there is or can be some general desire or some corporate will to achieve these goals. The opposite line of thought is that the way in which a population is grouped is determined by a free play of forces and a multitude of interests and choices and that this can never be effectively guided by any predetermined arrangement made by planners. In its extreme form of presentation, the city and the expanding metropolitan areas form some kind of final stage in the evolution of natural phenomena: cosmic gas, chemical stress, life...cities.†

The first of these attitudes can readily be criticised as Utopian. It can be associated with the fixed images and closed patterns that have appeared throughout the history of planning thought. More recently it is linked with the well meaning but vague talk about 'social balance', 'attractive environment', 'planned growth' and so on criticised by Alonso (1970). More directly, a plan, or a policy of land use control which it requires, or the zoning of building bulk or density in order to achieve its objectives, are all

† For a comment on this attitude see Stephen Zoll's review of *The Economy of Cities* by Jane Jacobs (Zoll 1970).

the constituent parts of a 'static concept' imposed on a process which by its nature is always changing. (Krasnowiecki 1970).

In contrast to this there is free choice. But the planners have argued with equal force that the choice and the freedom are not really so obvious. 'The vast majority (of people) are employees who must live where there are jobs and the location of jobs is not their choice' (Sundquist 1970). Nor are factory or other work locations the result of entirely free choices made by completely independent developers. Their choices may in turn be conditioned by a number of factors including transportation, markets or material supply (Sundquist 1970).

That is the fundamental argument: and behind it are deeply rooted convictions about population policy, high density concentration, low density dispersal and so on.

The essays presented in this volume have a different emphasis. They are part of a more general change in the direction of urban studies which has taken place in recent years. There is now a growing body of work in different fields of study which is increasingly concerned with the understanding of the process of urban development rather than the attempt to achieve some imagined or desirable end result. There is now, in sociology, geography and economics as well as in the studies of the physical and structural aspects of urban development a common assumption that the process itself can be described in rational terms and that it can become intelligible.

The volume of literature associated with this type of thought is at once more circumscribed and manageable. The main contributions even in its most developed areas can be contained within a period of less than fifty years and the bulk of the work has occurred within the last decade. Some aspects of the study, particularly the examination of the physical structure of the urban system, are of very recent origin.

The common background rests in the attempt to build up a substantial body of data from the real world and to illustrate all its complexities in some general representation or model so that the interaction and interrelationship can be understood. From this first general presentation the development of the theoretical explanation of the process is a natural step.

For the early geographers and economists the model itself was a kind of analogy.† Park, Burgess and McKenzie working in Chicago in 1916 (1925) saw the developing process of the relation of man to his surroundings in Darwinian terms; as a process of competition for a number of limited resources and a continuous adaptation to changing conditions of environment. In those terms an overall series of relationships was described and

† See Robson (1969) for a summary of the development of human ecology.

an effort was made to outline and clarify a process. Christaller's attempt in 1933 to produce some theoretical reason for the size, number and distributions of towns and Stewart's 'gravity model' of 1947 (1948) to demonstrate attraction and movement between centres, are steps towards the more sophisticated work of data collection and mathematical model building of more recent years.

Meanwhile urban geography has continued to provide a systematic investigation of the process of change within towns themselves (Conzen 1962). The study of town maps and urban morphology has illustrated the growth and developments of streets and street systems and of plot patterns and the building developments within these from which the process of change can be revealed as it moves through its transformative phases towards 'repletion' and 'climax': and ultimately to the point where a regenerative framework is necessary. From this we begin to grasp more clearly the capacity of a system to accept change and to see this in relation to a time element.

Professor Schnore (1968) has recently classified the work of the urban sociologists under four headings. The first, demographic, is concerned with the population size composition and distribution. But 'People are not randomly distributed nor are their activities. They tend to clump and cluster at certain points and to be spread out thinly at other points. The patterns assumed by these distributions are the second, or "ecological" investigation.' The way in which these clusters are organised can be described as a third or 'structural' aspect of sociological study and the relationship of individuals within these structural groupings makes a fourth category which Schnore describes as 'behavioural'.

Here then, as in the geographical studies, are a number of patterns of groupings and dispositions, all of which will change but all of which can be overlaid and studied at a particular moment of time. The attempt to study the physical structure of cities, the clustering of its buildings and the communication patterns within the system clearly forms a close parallel to these areas of work in other disciplines. The beginnings of a method and the concepts around which it is being formulated have been described in these essays. And once the complex series of relationships which form the urban structure can be described with a reasonable degree of accuracy then it becomes possible to know with greater certainty how a change in any single element will affect all the other constituent parts.

We have at least a valuable instrument. With its help comparative studies can be made of alternative propositions. The new towns of Stevenage, Hook and Milton Keynes are based on widely different assumptions about the land required, the density and distribution of facilities and so on, all of which, as theory, could now be tested in advance and assessed against a range of alternative propositions. All that is extremely important to the decision-making process in relation to major issues of policy.

But it is at a smaller scale that the multiplicity of the most pressing and urgent problems has to be faced: and it is these ultimately that shape the urban system. How can we test for example the alternative policies of growth in relation to the land available around a city or within a region? How can we know the effects of alternative locations for industry on residential requirements or roads? How can we be sure that road proposals are not isolated and dealt with separately from the physical structure of the town which they are supposed to serve?

At a more practical level how can we take decisions about interconnected buildings or institutions? Suppose there is a teaching institution, for example a polytechnic, dispersed on several central sites in which expansion must take place; how do we decide which are the best starting points to maintain a pattern of interrelationships both now and in the developing future? And what is the framework which will lend itself most effectively to future change?

These are questions that cannot be answered by development plans. In order to assess them we need to see the problem as part of a total pattern of relationships and to see this against a background of change.

It is this attempt to see the problem as part of a developing process which gives this particular approach its sharpest contrast with the traditional attitudes to planning. There is no mention here of visual impressions or goals to be achieved. The techniques that are used may seem to be much closer to the methods that are now being advanced in urban geography and sociology than to those common to established planning. There is indeed good reason for this.

What all those who are working on urban studies are facing is the extensive and complex nature of the problem. It is only in very recent years that relevant techniques have become available which allow the possibility of examining issues of this magnitude. In all areas of work the use of statistical methods and mathematical formulations of data that can be stored on a massive scale has made possible a new conceptual framework. Each discipline in turn has found it necessary to re-assess the possibilities of the new range of study within its own field. And what is interesting is that as a result of common techniques each discipline is now beginning to share with others a common language and a parallel method (Robson 1969).

The development of radically new techniques is then in the first place remarkable for the effect that it has had in establishing relationships between separate fields of investigation.† But there is second and more

† It is no accident that Joint Research Centres have been established at so many universities.

fundamental consequence. The fact that we can grasp the relatedness of complex things more completely has caused the boundaries of each separate discipline to be redefined. We adjust the position from which we view the subject. That change is not a matter of methodology: it is a question of an attitude of mind.

In subjects such as economics and geography this change has already been debated and new areas of work have been established. In the subjects which are normally called planning and architecture it seems possible that similar changes are now being developed. Once some means are formulated to grasp more closely the relatedness of activities and the physical structure of a city, and once the urban system is comprehensible as a set of interacting and changing elements it becomes impossible to isolate from that system the interdependent parts.

Within the totality of the changing urban system there are many restraints and there must be a range of choices. With the techniques that are now available we can extend the study of the urban process by our ability to set out and define more accurately the restraints and the consequences of these choices. That may be merely a more reliable guide to action than we as yet possess. But we shall know from the way we go about the problem that decisions about roads, for example, cannot be isolated from the locations and the quantities of buildings which they serve: that the alternative sites for new industry and new housing can be studied in relation to their effects on traffic and communications, and that the urban system itself is the total product of the way in which we accommodate developing nodal points and changing activities in buildings themselves. It is all interrelated. There are no divisions between the urban system and what we build.

In this sense the divisions that are set up by the normal use of the words 'planning' and 'architecture' are no longer tenable. The way in which we can look at and study an urban region is similar to the way in which we can study or examine the restraints and choices in one of its constituent parts, for instance the developing area around a university. Within this again is another study of the range of choices of areas and communications within buildings and the effect of these in turn on their external forms and the environment around them.

The essays in this volume, which start from different interests, seem to represent a way of thinking about a problem. We have called this a school of thought developing around an architectural approach. And that is all. They do not offer goals and solutions. The environment will have to be built by people. But we can learn about and extend our understanding of the total process and its constituent parts by the way we think.

Bibliography

Ackoff, R. L., Gupta, S. K. and Minas, J. S. (1962). *Scientific Method: Optimizing Research Decisions*, Wiley (New York).

Alexander, C. (1964). *Notes on the Synthesis of Form*, Harvard University Press.

Alexander, C. (Feb. 1966). A City is Not a Tree, *Design*.

Allen, P. J. and Miller, A. (July 1966). *Living Accommodation for Young People*, Bibliography No. 196, Building Research Station (London).

Allen, W. and Crompton, D. (Aug. 1947). A Form of Control of Building Development in Terms of Daylighting, *R.I.B.A. Journal*.

Alonso, W. (1964). *Location and Land Use: Toward a General Theory of Land Rents*, Harvard University Press.

Alonso, W. (Spring 1970). The Mirage of New Towns, *The Public Interest* (New York).

American Public Health Association. *Planning the Neighborhood*, Government Printing Office (Washington, D.C.).

Anthony, J. (1970a). *Urban Systems: Data on Household Income and Socio-Economic Group*, L.U.B.F.S. Working Paper No. 37.

Anthony, J. (1970b). *The Effect of Income and Socio-Economic Group on Housing Choice*, L.U.B.F.S. Working Paper No. 51.

Apostel, L. (1961). Towards the Formal Study of Models in the Non-formal Sciences, in Freudenthal, H., ed., *The Concept and the Role of the Model in Mathematics and Natural and Social Sciences* (Dortrecht, Holland).

Apps, P. (1971). *Theoretical Structure for a Residential Model*, L.U.B.F.S. Working Paper No. 52.

Archer, L. B. (June 1956). Intuition versus Mathematics, *Design*.

Batty, M. (1969). *Development of an Activity Allocation Model for the Nottinghamshire/Derbyshire Subregion*, University of Manchester, Department of Town and Country Planning.

Baxter, R. (1970). *Urban Systems: the Development of a Cordon Model*, L.U.B.F.S. Working Paper No. 47.

Baxter, R. (1971). *An Urban Atlas: Reading*, L.U.B.F.S. Working Paper No. 48.

Baxter, R. and Anthony, J. (1971) *The First Stage in Disaggregating the Residential Sub Model*, L.U.B.F.S. Working Paper No. 1.

Bazjanac, V. (1968). A Study of Movement in Educational Buildings, Paper for the Professional Education Conference, Washington University, Missouri (unpublished).

Beckett, H. E. (July 1942). Population Density and the Heights of Buildings, *Transactions of the Illuminating Engineering Society* (London).

Beresford, M. (1967). *New Towns of the Middle Ages*, Lutterworth Press (London).

Berry, B. and Mayer, M. (1962). Design and Preliminary Findings of the University of

Chicago's Studies of the Central Place Hierarchy, in *Proceedings of the L.G.U. Symposium in Urban Geography*, Royal University of Lund (Lund, Sweden).

Black, M. (1962). *Models and Metaphors*, Cornell University Press (Ithaca, N.Y.).

Bolan, R. S., Hansen, W. B., Irwin, N. A. and Dieter, K. H. (Oct. 1963). *Planning Applications of a Simulation Model*, Regional Science Association (Boston).

Booth, P. *et al.* (1970). Cambridge: *The Evaluation of Urban Structure Plans*, L.U.B.F.S. Working Paper No. 14.

Brigham, E. F. (1964). *A Model of Residential Land Values*, Rand Corporation (Santa Monica, California).

Bronowski, J. (1960). *The Common Sense of Science*, Heinemann (London).

Bullock, N., Dickens, P. and Steadman, P. (1968). *A Theoretical Basis for University Planning*, L.U.B.F.S. Report No. 1.

Bullock, N., Dickens, P. and Steadman, P. (April 1970). Activities, Space and Location, *Architectural Review*.

Bunge, W. (1966). *Theoretical Geography*, Lund Studies in Geography, Royal University of Lund (Lund, Sweden).

de Cerda, Ildefonso (1867). *Teoria General de la Urbanizacion* (Madrid).

Chapin, F. S. (1965). *Urban Land Use Planning*, University of Illinois (Urbana, Ill.).

Chapin, F. S. and Hightower, H. C. (1966). *Household Activity Systems: A Pilot Investigation*, Center for Urban and Regional Studies, University of North Carolina (Chapel Hill, N.C.).

Chapin, F. S. and Weiss, S. F. (1962). *Factors Influencing Land Development*, Center for Urban and Regional Studies, University of North Carolina (Chapel Hill, N.C.).

Choisy, Auguste (1899). *Histoire de l'Architecture* (Paris).

Chorafas, D. N. (1965). *Systems and Simulation*, Academic Press (New York).

Christaller, W. (1933). *Die zentralen Orte in Suddeutschland*, Jena; trans. Baskin, C. W. (1966). *Central Places in Southern Germany*, Prentice Hall (Englewood Cliffs, New Jersey).

Churchman, C. W., Ackoff, R. L. and Arnoff, E. L. (1957). *Introduction to Operations Research*, Wiley (New York).

Clark, C. (1967). *Population Growth and Land Use*, Macmillan (London).

Collins, G. R. and C. C. (1965). *Camillo Sitte and the Birth of City Planning*, Random House.

Committee on Education (1963). *Higher Education, The Report of the Committee under the Chairmanship of Lord Robbins* (The Robbins Report), Her Majesty's Stationery Office.

Conzen, M. R. G. (1962). The Plan Analysis of an English City Centre, in *Proceedings of the I.G.U. Symposium in Urban Geography*, Royal University of Lund (Lund, Sweden).

Coombs, C. H. (1964). *A Theory of Data*, Wiley (New York).

Cordey-Hayes, M. (1968). *Retail Location Models*, Centre for Environmental Studies, Working Paper No. 16 (London).

Cowan, P. (1962). Studies in the Growth, Change and Ageing of Buildings, in *Transactions of the Bartlett Society*, University College (London).

Cowan, P. (Nov. 1970). Some Recent Planning Reports, *R.I.B.A. Journal* (London).

Crease, D. P. (1967). *Building Study: Student House Conversion*, York University Design Unit.

Cripps, E. L. (May 1969). A Management System for Planning, *Journal of the Town Planning Institute*.

Cripps, E. L. and Foot, D. H. S. (Dec. 1969). A Land Use Model for Subregional Planning, *Regional Studies, Journal of Regional Studies Association*. Pergamon Press (Oxford).

Croghan, D. and Hawkes, D. (26 Feb. 1970). Spacing of Low Rise Terrace Housing, *Architects' Journal*.

Crompton, D. (Aug. 1947). A Form of Building Development in Terms of Daylighting, *RIBA Journal*.

Davidovich, V. G. (1968). *Town Planning in Industrial Districts* (from the Russian) Israel Program for Scientific Translations (Jerusalem).

Davies, O. (1961). *Statistical Methods in Research and Production*, Oliver and Boyd (London).

Dober, R. (1967). Universities in the United States of America, in Brawne, M., ed., *University Planning and Design*, Lund Humphries (London).

Donnelly, T., Chapin, F. and Weiss, S. (1964). *A Probabilistic Model for Residential Growth*, Center for Urban and Regional Studies, University of North Carolina (Chapel Hill, N.C.).

Dowson, P. (April 1967). Building for Science, *Architectural Design*.

Drewett, T., Hall, P. and Oram, J. (1967). The Location of a University, Battersea College of Technology Research (unpublished).

Dyos, H. J. (1968). Agenda for Urban Historians, in Dyos, H. J., ed., *The Study of Urban History*, Edward Arnold (London).

Echenique, M. (1968a). *Models: A Discussion*, L.U.B.F.S. Working Paper No. 6.

Echenique, M. (1968b). *Urban Systems: Towards an Explorative Model*, L.U.B.F.S. Working Paper No. 7.

Echenique, M., Crowther, D., Lindsay, W. and Stibbs, R. (1969a). *Model of a Town: Reading*, L.U.B.F.S. Working Paper No. 12.

Echenique, M., Crowther, D. and Lindsay, W. (1969b). *Development of a Model of a Town*, L.U.B.F.S. Working Paper No. 26.

Echenique, M., Crowther, D. and Lindsay, W. (1969c). *A Structural Comparison of Three Generations of New Towns*, L.U.B.F.S. Working Paper No. 25.

Echenique, M. and Domeyko, J. (1970). *A Model for Santiago Metropolitan Area*, L.U.B.F.S. Working Paper No. 11.

Echenique, M., Anthony, J., Baxter, R., Crowther, W., Lindsay, W. and Perraton, J. (1971). *Urban Systems Study: Report 1967–70*, L.U.B.F.S. Report No. 2.

Edwards, A. T. (1968). *Towards Tomorrow's Architecture: The Triple Approach*, Phoenix House (London).

Fairweather, L. and Sliwa, J. A. (1969). *A.J. Metric Handbook*, The Architectural Press (London).

Farley, J. U. and Ring, L. W. (July–Aug. 1966). A Stochastic Model of Supermarket Traffic Flow, *Operations Research* (Baltimore).

Fitch, J. M. (March 1965). The Rise of Technology 1929–39, *Journal of the Society of Historians*, Columbia University.

Foley, D. L. (1964). An Approach to Metropolitan Spatial Structure, in Webber, M. M., *et al. Exploration into Urban Structures*, University of Pennsylvania (Philadelphia, Pa.).

Ford, G. B. (1931). *Building Height, Bulk and Form, How Zoning Can be Used as a Protection Against Uneconomic Types of Buildings on High Cost Land*, Harvard University Press.

Frampton, K. (1968). Notes on Soviet Urbanism, in Lewis, D., *Urban Structure*, Elek (London).

Garin, R. A. (Nov. 1966). A Matrix Formulation of the Lowry Model for Intrametropolitan Activity, *Journal of the American Institute of Planners*.

Garner, B. (1967). Models of Urban Geography and Settlement Location, in Chorley, R. J. and Haggett, P., eds., *Models in Geography*, Methuen (London).

Goodman, P. and Goodman, P. (1960). *Communitas*, Vintage Books (New York).

Goodman, P. and Goodman, P. (Summer 1961). Banning Cars from Manhattan, *Dissent Magazine* (New York).

Gould, P. (1963). Man Against His Environment: A Game Theoretical Framework, *Annals of the Association of American Geographers*.

Gray, G. H. (1947). *Housing and Citizenship*, Reinhold (New York).

Gropius, W. (1931). *Rationelle Bebauungsweisen*, Julius Hoffmann Verlag (Stuttgart).

Gropius, W. (1956). *Scope of Total Architecture*, Allen and Unwin (London).

Hägerstrand, T. (1967). On Monte Carlo Simulation of Diffusion, in Garrison, W. L. and Marble, D., eds., *Quantitative Geography*, Northwestern University Department of Geography (Evanston, Ill.).

Haggett, P. and Chorley, R. (1967). Models, Paradigms and the New Geography, in Chorley, R. and Haggett, P., eds., *Models in Geography*, Methuen (London).

Hansen, W. G. (May 1959). How Accessibility Shapes Land Use, *Journal of the American Institute of Planners*.

Hardy, A. C. (Sept. 1966). Environmental Design of Buildings, *Science Journal*.

Hardy, A. C. and O'Sullivan, P. E. (1967). *Insulation and Fenestration*, Oriel Press (Newcastle-on-Tyne).

Harper, G. N. (1968). BOP—An Approach to Building Optimization, *Proceedings— 1968, Association of Computing Machinery National Conference*, Thompson Book Company (Washington, D.C.).

Harris, B. (May 1965). New Tools for Planning, *Journal of the American Institute of Planners*.

Hawkes, D. (1968). *Building Bulk Legislation: A Description and Analysis*, L.U.B.F.S. Working Paper No. 4.

Hawkes, D. (1970). *The Environmental Evaluation of Buildings, 5. Explorations*, L.U.B.F.S. Working Paper No. 30.

Hawkes, D. and Stibbs, R. (1969). *The Environmental Evaluation of Buildings, 1. A Mathematical Model*, L.U.B.F.S. Working Paper No. 15.

Hecht, S. (1912) Form and Growth in Fishes, *Journal of Morphology*.

Hemmens, G. (1966). *The Structure of Urban Activity Linkages*, Center for Urban and Regional Studies, University of North Carolina (Chapel Hill, N.C.).

Hesse, M. (1963). *Models and Analogues in Science*, Sheed and Ward (London).

Hill, M. (1968). A Local Achievement Matrix for Evaluating Alternative Plans, *Journal of the American Institute of Planners*.

Holister, F. D. (Oct. 1967). *A Report on the Problems of Windowless Environments*, Greater London Council, Research Paper No. 1.

Howard, Ebenezer (1898). *Tomorrow: A Peaceful Path to Real Reform*, republished 1945, as *Garden Cities of Tomorrow*, Faber.

Hutchinson, D. W. (Oct. 1970). Building Form, *Conrad* (Construction, Research and Development Journal), Department of the Environment (London).

Hyman, G. M. (1969). *The Calibration of Trip Distribution Models*, Centre for Environmental Studies, Working Paper No. 31 (London).

Isard, W. and Dacey, M. (1962). On the Projection of Individual Choice Behaviour in Regional Analysis, *Journal of the Regional Sciences* (London).

Jacobs, J. (1961). *The Death and Life of Great American Cities*, Random House.

Jantsch, E. (Oct. 1967). Forecasting the Future, *Science Journal*.

Kain, J. F. (1961). *The Journey to Work as a Determinant of Residential Location*, Rand Corporation (Santa Monica, California).

Kansky, K. T. (1963). *Structure of Transportation Networks*, University of Chicago Press.

Kasner, E. and Newman, J. (1949). *Mathematics and the Imagination*, Bell (London).
Krasnowiecki, J. Z. (1970). The Basic System of Land Use Control, in Marcus, N. and Groves, M., eds., *The New Zoning*, Praeger (New York).
Lakshmanan, T. and Hansen, W. (May 1965). A Retail Market Potential Model, *Journal of the American Institute of Planners*.
Lathrop, G. T. and Hamburg, J. R. (May 1965). An Opportunity-Accessibility Model for Allocating Regional Growth, *Journal of the American Institute of Planners*.
Le Corbusier (1927). *Towards a New Architecture*, Architectural Press (London).
Le Corbusier (1933). *La Ville Radieuse* (Paris).
Le Corbusier (1939). *Oeuvres Complètes 1934–1938*, Girsberger (Zurich).
Le Corbusier (1947). *When the Cathedrals Were White*, Routledge (London).
Lenzi, G. (1970). *Urban Systems: A Study of a Road Network 1. Data Base*, L.U.B.F.S. Working Paper No. 39.
Lichfield, N. (Sept. 1969). Cost Benefit Analysis in Urban Expansion. A Case Study: Peterborough, *Regional Studies, Journal of Regional Studies Association*, Pergamon Press, Oxford.
Llewellyn-Davies, R., Weeks, J., Forestier-Walker, G. and Bor, W. (1968). *Milton Keynes: Interim Report*, Milton Keynes Development Corporation (Wavendon).
London County Council (1961). *The Planning of a New Town*, Her Majesty's Stationery Office.
Lowry, I. S. (1964). *A Model of Metropolis*, Rand Corporation (Santa Monica, California).
Lowry, I. S. (May 1965). A Short Course in Model Design, *Journal of the American Institute of Planners*.
Lowry, I. S. (1967). *Seven Models of Urban Development: A Structural Comparison*, Rand Corporation (Santa Monica, California).
Lynch, K. and Rodwin, L. (Nov. 1958). A Theory of Urban Form, *Journal of the American Institute of Planners*.
Maldonado, T. and Bonsieppi, G.(1964). Science and Design, *Journal of the Hochschule für Gestaltung*, (Ulm).
Marble, D. (1964). A Simple Markovian Model of Trip Structures in a Metropolitan Region, in *The Regional Science Association Western Section Papers, Third Annual Meeting*, Arizona State University (Tempe, Ariz.).
Marble, D. (1967). A Theoretical Exploration of Individual Travel Behavior, in Garrison, W. C. and Marble, D., eds., *Quantitative Geography*, Northwestern University Department of Geography (Evanston, Ill.).
March, L. (April 1966). Heavens on Earth, *Cambridge Review*.
March, L. (Aug. 1967). Homes Beyond the Fringe, *R.I.B.A. Journal*.
March, L. (21 March 1968). Towards a Garden of Cities, *The Listener*.
March, L. (1969). *Urban Systems: A Generalized Distribution Function*, L.U.B.F.S. Working Paper No. 24.
March, L. (1970). *A Statistical Theory of Simple Spacial Distributions*, L.U.B.F.S. Working Paper No. 5.
March, L. and Steadman, P. (1971). *The Geometry of Environment*, R.I.B.A. Publications.
March, L. and Trace, M. (1968). *The Land Use Performances of Selected Arrays of Built Forms*, L.U.B.F.S. Working Paper No. 2.
Markus, T. A. *et al.* (7 Jan. 1970). Building Appraisal: St Michaels Academy, Kilwinning, *Architects' Journal*.
Martin, L. (May 1967). Architect's Approach to Architecture, *R.I.B.A. Journal*.

Martin, L. (Aug. 1968). Education Without Walls, *R.I.B.A. Journal.*

Martin, L. and March, L. (Dec. 1964). Study of a Building Type, *Architectural Design.*

Martin, L. and March, L. (April 1966). Land Use and Built Forms, *Cambridge Research.*

Martin, L. with March, L. and Taylor, J. B. (1965). *Whitehall: A Plan for a National and Government Centre,* Her Majesty's Stationery Office.

Massey, D. (1970). *The Basic Service Categorisation,* Centre for Environmental Studies, Working Paper No. 63 (London).

Ministry of Transport (1963). *Traffic in Towns* (The Buchanan Report), Her Majesty's Stationery Office.

Montgomery, R. M. N. and Jones, T. A. (1970). *Calculus and Elementary Functions,* Cambridge University Press.

Morrill, R. (1962). Simulation of Central Place Patterns Over Time, in *Proceedings of the I.G.U. Symposium in Urban Geography,* Royal University of Lund (Lund, Sweden).

Morrill, R. (1965). The Negro Ghetto: Problems and Alternatives, *Geographical Review.*

Moser, C. A. and Redfern, P. (1965). Education and Manpower: Some Current Research, in Lee, C. M. B., ed., *Models for Decision,* English Universities Press.

Nystuen, J. (1967). A Theory and Simulation of Intraurban Travel, in Garrison, W. C. and Marble, D., eds., *Quantitative Geography,* Northwestern University Department of Geography (Evanston, Ill.).

Olsen, D. J. (1964). *Town Planning in London,* Yale University Press.

OECD (1966). *Mathematical Models in Educational Planning,* (Paris).

OECD (1967). *Methods and Statistical Needs for Educational Planning,* (Paris).

Park, R. E., Burgess, E. W. and McKenzie, R. D. (1925). *The City,* University of Chicago Press.

de Parsons, H. (1888). Displacement and Area-Curves of Fish, *Transactions of the American Society of Mechanical Engineers.*

Perraton, J. (1970). *Urban Systems: Collection and Management of Data for a Complex Model,* L.U.B.F.S. Working Paper No. 46.

Reps, J. W. (1965). *The Making of Urban America,* Princeton University Press.

Richardson, B. D., Davies, E. M. and Dunsford, M. (1967). *Parking at the University of Birmingham,* Department of Transportation and Environmental Planning, University of Birmingham.

Robbins, Lord (1963). *Higher Education, The Report of the Committee under the Chairmanship of Lord Robbins* (The Robbins Report), Her Majesty's Stationery Office.

Robinson, C. M. (1916). *City Planning,* Putnam.

Robinson, I. M., Wolfe, H. B. and Barringer, R. L. (May 1965). A Model for Simulating Residential Development, *Journal of the American Institute of Planners.*

Robson, B. T. (1969). *Urban Analysis,* Cambridge University Press.

Rose, D. M. (1966). *Hatfield College of Technology, Traffic and Parking Survey 1966,* Traffic Research Unit, Hatfield College of Technology.

Rosen, R. (1967). *Optimality Principles in Biology,* Butterworths (London).

Schneider, M. (1959). Gravity Models and Trip Distribution Theory, *Papers and Proceedings of the Regional Science Association.*

Schnore, L. F. (1968). Problems of Quantitative Study of Urban History, in Dyos, H. J., ed., *The Study of Urban History,* Edward Arnold (London).

Schulze-Fielitz, E. (Feb. 1968). Dichte in Stadtban, *Bauen und Wohnen* (Zurich).

Schuyler, M. (July-Sept 1894). Modern Architecture, *Architectural Record,* in Jordy, W. H. and Coe, R., eds., (1964). *American Architecture and Other Writings,* Athenaeum (New York).

Segal, W. (March 1964). The Use of Land in Relation to Building Height, Coverage and Housing Density, *Arena* (Journal of the Architectural Association, London).

Shimbel, A. (1953). Structural Parameters of Communication Networks, *Bulletin of Mathematical Biophysics*.

Sitte, Camillo (1889). *City Planning According to Artistic Principles*, translated by Collins, G. R. and C. C. (1965). Phaidon Press.

Skilling, M. (1964). An Operational View, *American Scientist*.

Souder, J., Clark, W., Elkind, J. and Brown, M. (1964). *Planning for Hospitals: A Systems Approach Using Computer-Aided Techniques*, American Hospital Association (Chicago).

Stevenage Development Corporation (1966). *Stevenage Traffic Survey*, Part 2, 1965–6 (Stevenage).

Stewart, J. Q. (1948). Demographic Gravitation: Evidence and Application, *Sociometry*.

Stone, P. A. (1961). The Impact of Urban Development on the Use of Land and Other Resources, *Journal of the Town Planning Institute*.

Stone, P. A. (1967). *Building Design Evaluation: Costs in Use*, Spon (London).

Stone, P. A. (1968, Part 1 Oct., Part 2 Nov.). Housing Needs, Costs and Policies, *Architects' Journal*.

Stone, R. (1966). *Mathematics in the Social Sciences and Other Essays*, Chapman and Hall (London).

Sundquist, J. L. (Winter 1970). Where Shall They Live? *The Public Interest* (New York).

Tabor, P. (1970a). Traffic in Buildings, Unpublished doctoral dissertation, Cambridge University Library.

Tabor, P. (1970b). *Traffic in Buildings, 4. Evaluation of Routes*, L.U.B.F.S. Working Paper No. 20.

Tanner, J. C. (1961). *Factors Affecting the Amount of Travel*, Road Research Laboratory, Her Majesty's Stationery Office.

Taylor, J. (1967). *The Science Lecture Room, a Planning Study*, Cambridge University Press.

Taylor, M. A. (1968). *Studies of Travel in Gloucester, Northampton and Reading*, Road Research Laboratory (Crowthorne).

Thompson, D'Arcy (1917). *On Growth and Form*, Cambridge University Press (1942 edition).

Torres, H. (1970). *Accessibility and Residential Location*, L.U.B.F.S. Working Paper No. 38.

Toye, P. N. (1968). Appendix B, Timetabling Program, in Bullock, N. *et al. A Theoretical Basis for University Planning*, L.U.B.F.S. Report No. 1.

Ullman, E. and Dacey, M. (1960). The Minimum Requirements Approach to the Urban Economic Base, in *Proceedings of the I.G.U. Symposium in Urban Geography*, Royal University of Lund (Lund, Sweden).

University Grants Committee (1967a). *Non-Recurrent Grants*, Her Majesty's Stationery Office.

University Grants Committee (1967b). *Student Residence*, Her Majesty's Stationery Office.

Unwin, R. (1912). Nothing to be Gained by Overcrowding, in Creese, W. L., ed., 1967, *The Legacy of Raymond Unwin: A Human Pattern for Planning*, MIT Press (Cambridge, Massachusetts).

Vaizey, J. (Aug. 1968). Future Pattern of Resources for Education, *R.I.B.A. Journal*.

von Neumann, J. and Morgenstern, O. (1953). *The Theory of Games and Economic Behaviour*, Princeton University Press.

Watts, K. (23 Oct. 1963). Functional Controls and Town Design, *Architects' Journal.*

Webber, M. M. (1964). The Urban Place and the Non-Place Urban Realm, in Webber, M. M. *et al. Explorations into Urban Structure*, University of Pennsylvania Press.

Webber, M. M. *et al.* (1964). *Explorations into Urban Structure*, University of Pennsylvania Press.

Whitehead, A. N. (1929). *The Function of Reason*, Princeton University Press.

Willmot, P. and Young, M. (1957). *Family and Kinship in East London*, Routledge.

Wilson, A. G. (April 1967). Mathematical Models for Planning, *Arena* (Journal of the Architectural Association, London).

Wilson, A. G. (1967). *Disaggregating Elementary Residential Location Models*, Centre for Environmental Studies, Working Paper No. 37 (London).

Wilson, A. G. (1971). *Entropy in Urban and Regional Modelling*, Pion (London).

Wilson, C. St J. and Rowe, C. (March 1965), Contributions, *Journal of the Society of Historians* (Columbia University).

Wilson, H. and Womersley, L. (1967). *Manchester Education Precinct, Final Report of the Planning Consultants*, privately printed (Manchester).

Wingo, L. (1969). *Transportation and Urban Land*, Johns Hopkins Press (Baltimore).

Wolfe, H. B. (May 1967a). Models for Condition Ageing of Residential Structures, *Journal of the American Institute of Planners.*

Wolfe, H. B. (1967b). Model of San Francisco Housing Market, *Socio-Economic Planning Science*, vol. 1, Pergamon Press.

Wurster, C. B. (March 1965). The Social Front of Modern Architecture in the 1930's, *Journal of the Society of Architectural Historians.*

Yeomans, A. B. (1916). *City Residential Land Development*, University of Chicago Press.

Zipf, G. F. (1949). *Human Behaviour and the Principle of Least Effort*, Addison-Wesley (New York).

Zoll, S. (2 Feb. 1970). Cosmic Gas, Chemical Stress, Cities, *The Nation* (New York).